BREACH OF THE PEACE

*To Euan and Fraser, who breach my peace on a
daily basis – in the nicest of ways*

BREACH OF
THE PEACE

Pamela R Ferguson
Professor of Scots Law, University of Dundee

DUNDEE UNIVERSITY PRESS
2013

Published in Great Britain in 2013 by
Dundee University Press
University of Dundee
Dundee DD1 4HN

www.dundee.ac.uk/dup

ISBN 978 1 84586 149 0

No natural forests were destroyed to make this product; only farmed timber
was used and replanted

British Library Cataloguing-in-Publication data
A catalogue for this book is available on request from the British Library.

Typeset by Fakenham Prepress Solutions, Fakenham
Printed by Bell & Bain Ltd, Glasgow

CONTENTS

"*If there be one personal right belonging to every inhabitant of Scotland, to every citizen of Dundee, more than another, it is his right to spend his Sunday in peace, to say his prayers in public or in solitude, to meditate in silence upon the lights and shadows of existence, to think his own thoughts without distraction, whether they be profane or pious. But how could anyone not deaf, in the vicinity of High Street, Dundee, think his own thoughts and enjoy his Sabbath peace with one set of fanatics yelling about the miseries of the poor and the vices and oppression of the rich; another set singing hymns to various different tunes, some with sacred and many with secular associations; a few units in ecstasies of hope shouting 'Hallelujah'; and a greater number in paroxysms of despair practising the exercises of howling and groaning by way of preparation for a miserable hereafter? ... I am satisfied that you did commit a breach of the peace in collecting this crowd.*"

(Sheriff Campbell Smith, Summary Court, Dundee: Case against Hutchison and Connor, 1889 *Journal of Jurisprudence and Scottish Law Magazine*, vol 33, no 391, at p 388)

PREFACE

Writing in 1989, Michael Christie noted that "rather little" had been written about breach of the peace, despite it being a frequently prosecuted crime.[1] In the 24 years since then, more than two dozen articles and commentaries have been written on the subject, and there are now about 200 additional reported cases which involve breach of the peace charges. Some of these offer yet more examples of well-established ways of committing this crime, but others illustrate its incredible versatility – and unpredictable nature. The further effect given to the European Convention on Human Rights by the Scotland Act 1998 and the Human Rights Act 1998 have impacted on the crime's definition, with its ambit having been considerably reduced by such landmark decisions as *Smith* v *Donnelly*[2] and *Harris* v *HM Advocate*.[3] Following the re-establishment of the Scottish Parliament in 1999, several offences have been enacted which overlap, to varying degrees, with breach of the peace – raising the question of whether this common law crime would achieve greater clarity if it were to be redefined by statute.

My original aim was to provide an updated description. As even a superficial examination of the case law reveals, however, it is far from easy to be sure whether a particular set of circumstances now falls within the scope of breach of the peace. As well as attempting to delimit its ambit, this book therefore offers a critique.

---

[1] M G A Christie, *Breach of the Peace* (1990), Preface.
[2] 2002 JC 65; 2001 SLT 1007; 2001 SCCR 800.
[3] [2009] HCJAC 80; 2010 JC 245; 2009 SLT 1078; 2010 SCL 56, 2010 SCCR 15.

My thanks are due to Fiona Raitt, Robin White and Alan Page for insightful comments on drafts, and to Andrew Ashworth for commenting on a preliminary paper I gave on breach of the peace at a conference on criminalisation. I am also very grateful to Karen Howatson for editorial assistance.

I have endeavoured to state the law as at 11 January 2013.

Pamela R Ferguson
School of Law,
University of Dundee

TABLE OF CASES

SCOTTISH CASES

OTHER JURISDICTIONS

Canada

England and Wales

European Court of Human Rights

Ireland

United States of America

TABLE OF LEGISLATION

United Kingdom
Statutes

Bills

Draft Criminal Codes

Legislation of other jurisdictions
Canada

CHAPTER 1

THE IMPORTANCE OF BREACH OF THE PEACE

INTRODUCTION

This book aims to define and critique the common law crime of **1.1** breach of the peace. In 1949 Lord Mackay noted that Macdonald's *A Practical Treatise on the Criminal Law of Scotland* managed to describe "the whole doctrine of breach of the peace" in one and a half pages.[1] The first and second editions of Gerald Gordon's *The Criminal Law of Scotland,* in 1967 and 1978 respectively, each took less than six pages in which to define and describe the crime,[2] and in the third edition published in 2001 it merited little more than nine pages, within two volumes whose total length exceeded 1,200 pages.[3] Until Michael Christie's detailed account, published in 1990,[4] academic writers had not devoted much time to consideration of breach of the peace. This may be thought to reflect the fact that we are dealing with a crime of little significance. This chapter suggests that the crime is in fact of greater importance than one might imagine. Although the behaviour of the accused in most breach of the peace cases reflects relatively minor wrongdoing, this is not an invariable rule.[5] In the 1980s, breach of the peace was commonly referred to within the Crown Office and Procurator Fiscal Service as "the fiscal's flexible friend", an apt sobriquet for a very broadly defined crime with rather vague boundaries.[6] Thus its characteri-

---

[1] In *Raffaelli* v *Heatly* 1949 JC 101 at 104, referring to J H A Macdonald, *A Practical Treatise on the Criminal Law of Scotland* (5th edn by J Walker and D J Stevenson, 1948).
[2] G H Gordon, *The Criminal Law of Scotland.*
[3] *The Criminal Law of Scotland* (3rd edn by M G A Christie, 2000).
[4] M G A Christie, *Breach of the Peace* (1990).
[5] See section 1.3 below.
[6] Advertisements for the Access credit card in the 1980s highlighted the card's many uses with the slogan "your flexible friend".

1

sation as a trivial crime also belies the fact that it is highly useful for the prosecution.[7]

1.2   Chapter 2 considers the development of breach of the peace since the time of the institutional writer Baron David Hume, in the mid-19th century,[8] while Chapter 3 focuses on the modern law. The greatest impact on the crime in recent years has resulted from the further effect given to the European Convention on Human Rights (ECHR) by the Scotland Act 1998, and the Human Rights Act 1998. This requires all public authorities in Scotland, including the Lord Advocate as head of the Crown Office and Procurator Fiscal Service, to act in accordance with Convention rights, and allows individuals to claim the protection of these rights in domestic courts. As Chapter 3 explains, the definition of breach of the peace has undergone substantial revision since the ECHR became part of domestic law, and its ambit has been considerably reduced. The re-establishment of the Scottish Parliament in 1999 has resulted in the enactment of several offences which overlap, to varying degrees, with breach of the peace. Chapter 4 considers these legislative developments, and the extent to which the new offences have the potential to reduce the number and range of cases prosecuted for the common law crime. The critique is reserved for the final two chapters, allowing the reader whose main interest lies in understanding the history of the crime or the current law to focus on Chapter 2, or Chapters 3 and 4, respectively. Chapter 5 attempts to find a rationale for an offence such as breach of the peace, and explores whether criminalisation of the range of conduct which comes within the definition of this crime can be justified by the "harm" and/or "offence" principles, in particular. It also considers the public/private distinction favoured by liberalism and its implications for breach of the peace. The final chapter criticises the crime's definition, its use by the Crown in place of other, more apposite, offences, and the diverse range of wrongdoing which has been subsumed in this one crime. Despite the fact that the appeal court has redefined its *actus reus* in recent years, it is suggested that the uncertainty that surrounds its definition and application is such that breach of the peace should be reformed and restated by statute.

A MINOR CRIME?

1.3 Hume's *Commentaries* referred to "a mere breach of the peace",[9]

---

[7] See further at sections 1.5–1.6 below.

[8] D Hume, *Commentaries on the Law of Scotland Respecting Crimes* (4th edn, 1844).

[9] *Ibid*, ii, 77, and see *Macdonald's Criminal Law* (5th edn), which also refers to "mere breaches of the peace" (at p 197).

and 146 years later Christie concluded that it was still generally treated by the courts as "intrinsically a minor crime".[10] In *Kelly* v *Rowan*[11] in 1897, breach of the peace was described as "a paltry offence"; and in the leading modern case of *Smith* v *Donnelly*[12] in 2001, it was observed that "in many cases, it is a relatively minor crime".[13] It should, however, be noted that as a common law crime the maximum punishment which can be imposed is determined only by the general sentencing powers of the court which hears the case, and while those convicted of breach of the peace are often fined, offenders are not always dealt with by means of a monetary penalty. To cite but a few examples, in *MacGivern* v *Jessop*[14] (1988) a teenager was convicted for shouting, swearing and taunting rival football supporters who were leaving a football stadium. This was his second conviction for breach of the peace. Upholding a sentence of 3 months' detention, the appeal court stated that such conduct was "liable to lead to very serious consequences and must be severely discouraged".[15] In *McCrae* v *Henderson*[16] (1999) the appeal court affirmed a sentence of 3 months' imprisonment where the accused had caused a serious disturbance involving 190 people, and in *Halcrow* v *Shanks*[17] (2012) the appellant was sentenced to 12 months' imprisonment (with an additional 1 month for breach of bail) and made subject to the notification requirements of the Sexual Offences Act 2003 for 10 years,[18] for a breach of the peace involving public masturbation – despite the fact that no members of the public appear to have noticed his behaviour.[19] Such sentences suggest that the perception that this is a minor crime may not be entirely accurate. Christie was also of the view that breach of the peace "should not

---

[10] Christie, para 2.08; see also para 2.76.

[11] (1897) 2 Adam 357.

[12] 2002 JC 65; 2001 SLT 1007; 2001 SCCR 800. The case is discussed further at section 3.4 below.

[13] 2002 JC 65 at 71. See also H H Brown, "Breach of the Peace" (1895) 3 SLT 151 at 153: "trivial cases should be charged as breaches of the peace, and more serious cases as substantive offences".

[14] 1988 SCCR 511; (1988) 133 Sol Jo 211.

[15] 1988 SCCR 511 at 513, per Lord Brand. See also *Bell* v *HM Advocate* 2000 GWD 39-1451; and the case of the so-called "Naked Rambler", discussed further at sections 6.28–6.29 below. He was sentenced to more than 15 months' imprisonment for breach of the peace in November 2010, to 657 days' imprisonment in August 2011, and to a further 5 months in September 2012.

[16] 1999 GWD 33-1580.

[17] [2012] HCJAC 23; 2012 SLT 579; 2012 SCL 517; 2012 GWD 8-144.

[18] See s 80 of, and Sch 3, para 60 to, the Sexual Offences Act 2003, as amended by the Sexual Offences (Scotland) Act 2009, Sch 5, para 5(d). This is discussed further at section 3.31 below.

[19] It was, however, seen by police officers monitoring CCTV footage.

per se be taken on indictment".[20] That this is not an invariable rule is clear from a glance at this book's Table of Cases which reveals that many breach of the peace cases have been prosecuted under solemn procedure, and further examination reveals that it was often the main, or even the sole, crime.[21] Thus the teenage appellants in *Divin* v *HM Advocate*[22] (2012) were sentenced to more than 2 years' detention for breach of the peace following their guilty pleas. In *HM Advocate* v *McGovern*[23] (2007) 5 years' imprisonment was imposed for breach of the peace involving discharging a firearm. Christie had predicted that "increasing (as opposed to exceptional) use of solemn procedure [in prosecutions for breach of the peace] will inevitably entail reconsideration of its status"[24] and it is suggested that such a reassessment is now overdue.

PROVIDING CONTEXT

1.4   Breach of the peace may be prosecuted as evidence of motive for other offences, or to provide context for a more serious charge on the same complaint or indictment.[25] Thus the first charge may be a breach of the peace involving shouting and swearing at a particular person, or making threats, and the second charge is assault.[26] It has

---

[20] Christie, para 2.08. He cited *dicta* from the cases of *HM Advocate* v *Blair* (1868) 1 Coup 168; *McGuire* v *Fairbairn* (1881) 4 Coup 536 and *Kelly* v *Rowan* (1897) 2 Adam 357 in support of this (at para 2.09). He concluded that "breach of the peace is not a suitable appellation unless the accused's offence can be regarded as a minor one. It is, therefore, primarily an offence for the summary courts" (at para 2.12).

[21] See, eg: *HM Advocate* v *Greig* 2005 SCCR 465 (see sections 3.3 and 3.28 below); *HM Advocate* v *Murray* 2007 SCCR 271 (see sections 3.3 and 3.29 below); *Macdonald* v *HM Advocate* [2008] HCJAC 5; 2008 JC 262; 2008 SCCR 181 (see section 3.8 below); *LBM* v *HM Advocate* [2011] HCJAC 96; 2012 SLT 147; 2012 SCL 74; 2011 GWD 34-715 (see section 3.27 below); and *Gifford* v *HM Advocate* [2011] HCJAC 101; 2012 SCL 267; 2011 SCCR 751; 2011 GWD 36-741 (see section 3.22 below).

[22] [2012] HCJAC 81; 2012 SCL 837; 2012 GWD 19-395. The case is discussed further at section 3.32 below.

[23] [2007] HCJAC 21; 2007 JC 145; 2007 SLT 331; 2007 SCCR 173; 2007 GWD 10-180.

[24] Christie, para 2.12.

[25] For example, in *Beddie* v *HM Advocate* 1993 SCCR 970 four charges of breach of the peace formed the context for a charge of murder. The accused was convicted of culpable homicide and the breach of the peace charges were not insisted on by the Crown.

[26] See *Connorton* v *Annan* 1981 SCCR 307; *Carmichael* v *Boyle* 1985 SCCR 58; *Skilling* v *McLeod* 1987 SCCR 245; *MacDonald* v *Munro* 1996 SCCR 595 (assault and vandalism); and *Youngson* v *Higson* 2000 SLT 1441; 2000 GWD 29-1125. See also *Reid* v *Normand* 1994 SCCR 475, where the first charge was a breach of the peace which involved brandishing a baseball bat, and the second was vandalism using the bat.

also been used where the other charges were attempted abduction and indecent assault;[27] rape;[28] robbery;[29] murder;[30] and incitement to murder.[31] In *O'Neill* v *HM Advocate*[32] (2010) breach of the peace charges libelling (1) the accused's attempt to gain custody of a 6-year-old boy overnight, to the alarm of the child's grandmother, and (2) removing the child from the custody of his mother, formed part of the backdrop to more serious charges, including sexual grooming,[33] lewd, indecent and libidinous practices, and murder.[34] In *WM* v *HM Advocate*[35] (2010) the accused was convicted of sexual assaults and breaches of the peace, but the appeal court quashed the latter convictions which alleged that the accused had threatened further harm to his sons if they revealed that he had been sexually assaulting them. The court was not persuaded to substitute convictions for "criminal threats", noting that the breach of the peace charges "were present on this indictment for essentially evidential reasons only, and may be thought to have fulfilled their purpose".[36] In *Siddique* v *HM Advocate*[37] (2010) the breach of the peace charge libelled that the accused had shown his fellow students images of suicide bombers and terrorist murders, and threatened to become a suicide bomber. This helped establish his motive in

---

[27] *Thomson* v *HM Advocate* [2009] HCJAC 1; 2009 SLT 300; 2009 SCL 376; 2009 SCCR 415; 2009 GWD 2-34. The case is discussed further at section 4.11 below. See also *Gibson* v *Heywood* 1997 SLT 101: breach of the peace and sexual assault (see section 4.5 below).

[28] *Anoliefo* v *HM Advocate* [2012] HCJAC 110; 2012 GWD 31-628. See section 6.20 below.

[29] *Grugen* v *Jessop* 1988 SCCR 182.

[30] *HM Advocate* v *Ferrie* 1983 SCCR 1; *HM Advocate* v *Maitland* 1985 SLT 425; *Keane* v *HM Advocate* 1986 SCCR 491; *Boyle* v *HM Advocate* 1993 SLT 577; 1992 SCCR 824. See also *McDonald* v *HM Advocate* 1995 SCCR 252 involving the murder by the accused of his spouse. Uncorroborated evidence was led of an earlier assault and breach of the peace, and the Crown therafter withdrew these two charges.

[31] *Arshad* v *HM Advocate* [2006] HCJAR 57.

[32] [2010] HCJAC 90; 2010 SCCR 357.

[33] See the Protection of Children and Prevention of Sexual Offences (Scotland) Act 2005, s 1.

[34] In the event, the appeal court upheld the decision of the judge at a preliminary hearing to grant an application for some of the charges, including the murder charge, to be tried separately.

[35] [2010] HCJAC 75; 2011 JC 49; 2010 GWD 26-488.

[36] [2010] HCJAC 75 at para [18]. A similar use of breach of the peace is evident in *Beddie* v *HM Advocate* 1993 SCCR 970 and *McDonald* v *HM Advocate* 1995 SCCR 252 (see nn 25 and 30, respectively, above).

[37] [2010] HCJAC 7; 2010 JC 110; 2010 SLT 289; 2010 SCL 380; 2010 SCCR 236; 2010 GWD 5-80.

respect of several terrorism offences which were also included in the indictment.[38]

A USEFUL SUBSTITUTE

1.5 In *Horsburgh* v *Russell*[39] (1994) a breach of the peace conviction was substituted for the statutory offence of careless driving. In *Baxter* v *HM Advocate*[40] (1998) defence counsel submitted that there was insufficient evidence for a verdict of guilty on the charge libelled (incitement to murder) but accepted that the jury would have been entitled to convict for breach of the peace, and in *Harrison* v *Jessop*[41] (1991) a similar argument seems to have been made where the original charge was one of robbery.[42] The appeal court itself can substitute a conviction for breach of the peace where the accused has been prosecuted for a different offence,[43] but it seems that a trial judge may do so only if this is sought by the Crown.[44] If a charge for one crime is held to be irrelevant, the Crown may succeed in persuading a court that it may be amended to become a breach of the peace.[45]

---

[38] Terrorism Act 2000, s 57(1) (possession of articles for terrorist purposes) and s 54(1) (providing instruction or training in the making or use of firearms and explosives); and Terrorism Act 2006, s 2(1) (distributing or circulating terrorist publications). The sentence of 6 months' imprisonment for breach of the peace was ordered to run concurrently with the 6 years' imprisonment imposed for breach of s 57(1) of the Terrorism Act 2000. Motive is discussed further at sections 3.25–3.27 below.

[39] 1994 JC 117; 1994 SLT 942; 1994 SCCR 237.

[40] 1998 JC 219; 1998 SLT 414.

[41] 1992 SLT 465; 1991 SCCR 329.

[42] 1991 SCCR 329 at 329. Note that the SLT report of the case does not mention this.

[43] By virtue of the Criminal Procedure (Scotland) Act 1995, Sch 3, para 14(b). Examples include *Anderson* v *Griffiths* 2005 1 JC 169; 2005 SLT 86; 2005 SCCR 41; 2004 GWD 38-778 and *Martin* v *Howdle* (*sub nom Martin* v *Bott*) [2005] HCJAC 73; 2006 JC 35; 2005 SLT 730; 2005 SCCR 554; 2005 GWD 20-357. In each case the accused had been prosecuted for acting in a racially aggravated manner contrary to the Criminal Law (Consolidation) (Scotland) Act 1995, s 50A(1)(b), but was ultimately convicted of breach of the peace. This provision is considered further at section 4.2 below.

[44] See *Buchanan* v *Hamilton* 1990 SLT 244; 1989 SCCR 398, in which the sheriff convicted of breach of the peace on a charge of vandalism.

[45] See, eg: *Paterson* v *HM Advocate* [2008] HCJAC 18; 2008 JC 327; 2008 SLT 465; 2008 SCL 691; 2008 SCCR 605 in which two irrelevant charges of shameless indecency were amended in this way (the case is discussed further at sections 3.9 and 3.16, and critiqued at section 6.30 below) and *HM Advocate* v *Forbes* 1994 JC 71; 1994 SCCR 163 in which a breach of the peace was substituted for a charge of "housebreaking with intent to assault and rape", there being no such crime in Scots law. For further discussion and critique, see sections 2.9 and 6.33, respectively, below.

In some cases, the Crown has prosecuted breach of the peace where there is evidence that the accused intended to commit a different crime, often one involving a sexual offence such as indecent assault, but had not reached the stage at which a charge of attempting that other offence could be proved. Examples of this include *Biggins* v *Stott*[46] (1999); *HM Advocate* v *Greig*[47] (2005); *Kearney* v *Ramage*[48] (2007); *HM Advocate* v *Murray*[49] (2007); *Burns* v *HM Advocate*[50] (2009); *Thomson* v *HM Advocate*[51] (2009); *LBM* v *HM Advocate*[52] (2011); and *Jude* v *HM Advocate*[53] (2012).

Acceptance or substitution of this lesser charge has implications **1.6** for sentencing, however. In *HM Advocate* v *Campbell*[54] (1997) in which the indictment libelled sexual assault with breach of the peace as an alternative, the Crown appealed against the sentence (a fine of £250).[55] Lord Justice-General Hope in the appeal court emphasised that:

> "The Crown, having accepted the plea to the second alternative, and having assured the sheriff that so far as the Crown was concerned no element of assault was involved, cannot reasonably now complain about the sentence which the sheriff determined upon in the light of that conclusion."[56]

---

[46] 1999 JC 298; 1999 SLT 1037; 1999 SCCR 595; 1999 GWD 24-1136. Two charges of breach of the peace libelled that the accused had invited a 13-year-old girl to accompany him to his flat, and had offered her money to do so. This case is considered further at section 6.11 below.

[47] 2005 SCCR 465. See sections 3.3 and 3.28 below.

[48] 2007 SCCR 35. The charge libelled that the accused had approached the two complainers, seized one of their hands, uttered sexually explicit comments to them and invited them to go to a house with him.

[49] 2007 SCCR 271. See sections 3.3 and 3.29 below.

[50] [2009] 1 AC 720; [2009] 2 WLR 935; 2010 SC (PC) 26; 2009 SLT 2. The charge libelled that the accused used the internet to "encourage other people to commit indecent acts with children". See section 6.23 below.

[51] [2009] HCJAC 1; 2009 SLT 300; 2009 SCL 376; 2009 SCCR 415; 2009 GWD 2-34. The case is discussed further at section 4.11 below.

[52] [2011] HCJAC 96; 2012 SLT 147; 2012 SCL 74; 2011 GWD 34-715. The charge libelled that the accused had engaged two girls aged 10 and 11 in conversation, asked if he could tickle their legs, and tried to entice them into a car. See section 3.27 below.

[53] Also reported as *J* v *HM Advocate* [2012] HCJAC 65; 2012 GWD 20-411: the appellant was charged with having hidden a camera with a view to taking indecent photographs. See section 4.7 below. In *HM Advocate* v *Forbes* 1994 JC 71; 1994 SCCR 163 (see n 45 above) the appeal court substituted a charge of breach of the peace and reserved its opinion as to whether the facts libelled constituted attempted rape (1994 SCCR 163 at 167F–G). For a critique of such cases, see sections 6.35–6.37 below.

[54] 1997 SLT 354.

[55] Criminal Procedure (Scotland) Act 1995, s 108 allows the Lord Advocate to appeal against a sentence on the ground that it was unduly lenient.

[56] 1997 SLT 354 at 356.

He reminded the prosecution of "the care which must be taken in the framing of an indictment in a case of this kind where the charges are stated in the alternative" and "the consequences of accepting a plea such as the Crown decided to accept in this case".[57] More recently, the initial charge in *Heatherall* v *McGowan*[58] (2012) narrated that, while standing outside a public house, the accused had assaulted the complainer by exposing himself to her, seizing her and repeatedly thrusting his naked penis against her. The appeal court made clear that the acceptance by the Crown of a plea to breach of the peace involving only the exposure element of the original charge greatly reduced the seriousness of the case.[59]

IMPLICATIONS FOR CIVIL LIBERTIES

1.7   The very fact that breach of the peace is a useful and flexible crime from the point of view of the Crown underlines its potential to impact on civil liberties. As American author Robert Force has pointed out, criminalisation of any particular behaviour generally defines prohibited conduct by making clear what people may, and may not, lawfully do. It also allows the justice system to determine whom to prosecute and punish. This is equally true for breach of the peace, but that crime has the additional function of giving the police authority "to intervene and interrupt real or threatened public disorder".[60] While most offences involve "before-the-fact deterrence and after-the-fact adjudication of guilt", breach of the peace also provides "legal power for the police in during-the-fact situations".[61] Force believes that this aspect of breach of the peace is actually more important in terms of civil liberties than its other functions.[62] As we shall see, in Scots law, police powers to intervene in "during-the-fact situations" are considerable: an arrest for breach of the peace may be for actually causing public disorder, but may alternatively be based on the subjective assessment of a police officer that the behaviour in question was *likely to cause* disorder, or indeed that it had the potential to lead *other people* to cause a disturbance.[63]

1.8   The rule of law requires criminal prohibitions to be "intelligible,

---

[57] 1997 SLT 354 at 356.

[58] [2012] HCJAC 25; 2012 SLT 583; 2012 SCL 492; 2012 GWD 8-141.

[59] [2012] HCJAC 25 at para [12]. This also had the consequence that the notification requirements of the Sexual Offences Act 2003 were competent only if para 60 of Sch 3 was made out. See further at section 3.31 below.

[60] R Force, "Decriminalization of Breach of the Peace Statutes: A Nonpenal Approach to Order Maintenance" (1972) 46:3 *Tul L Rev* 367 at 373.

[61] *Ibid.*

[62] *Ibid.*

[63] See further at section 2.5 below. That a constable is entitled to arrest a person for

clear and predictable".[64] A criminal prohibition fails the requirement of certainty if its boundaries are ill defined: crimes must be specified with sufficient precision to enable citizens to know in advance whether their behaviour is liable to be subject to condemnation and punishment, so that they may fashion their behaviour accordingly.[65] Christie noted that the appeal court "has generally been wary of assigning precise definitions to common law crimes",[66] but such an approach is in danger of breaching the rule of law, and indeed the requirements of Art 7 of the ECHR relating to precision in offence definitions.[67] The concept of "fair labelling" is concerned to ensure that the distinction between different offences should be recognised by the criminal law, and that offences should be labelled in a way which accurately and fairly reflects different degrees of wrongdoing.[68] Thus if behaviour is inaccurately labelled as a "breach of the peace" this will lead to misunderstandings about how the person convicted must have behaved. The number of breaches of the peace recorded annually by the police in Scotland ranged from 72,734 in 2001–02, rising to a peak of 93,387 in 2006–07, before falling to 85,239 in 2009–10. The figure for 2010–11 was 56,519.[69] If the definition of breach of the peace is less than satisfactory, being insufficiently clear and covering too broad a range of conduct to correspond with rule of law and fair labelling requirements – as this book suggests – this has serious implications for the civil liberties of a great many people.

---

breach of the peace without a warrant was made clear in *Jackson v Stevenson* (1897) 24 R (J) 38; (1896) 4 SLT 277, and approved in *Adair v McGarry* 1933 JC 72.

[64] T Bingham, *The Rule of Law* (2010) at p 37.

[65] "The desideratum of clarity represents one of the most essential ingredients of legality." (L L Fuller, *The Morality of Law* (1969) at p 63).

[66] Christie, para 2.15.

[67] In *SW v United Kingdom* [1996] 1 FLR 434; (1996) 21 EHRR 363, the European Court of Human Rights stated that the guarantee enshrined in Art 7 "is an essential element of the rule of law" ((1996) 21 EHRR 363 at 398). See section 3.2 below.

[68] A Ashworth, *Principles of Criminal Law* (6th edn, 2009) at p 71. See also J Chalmers and F Leverick, "Fair Labelling in Criminal Law" (2008) 71 *MLR* 217.

[69] See *Statistical Bulletin: Recorded Crime in Scotland, 2010–11*, available at: http://www.scotland.gov.uk/Publications/2011/09/02120241/0, Table 2, p 18. The reduction in 2010–11 can be accounted for in large part due to the coming into force of the Criminal Justice and Licensing (Scotland) Act 2010, s 38. This provision is discussed further at section 4.8, and its impact on breaches of the peace considered at section 4.15 below.

CHAPTER 2

HISTORICAL DEVELOPMENTS

INTRODUCTION

As we shall see in Chapter 3, the definition of breach of the peace **2.1**
has been substantially revised in recent years. The current chapter
summarises the position prior to these developments. To what sort
of "peace" does breach of the peace refer? In respect of English law,[1]
it has been said that "the word 'peace'" is used in the expression
"breach of the peace" as "the opposite of 'war', rather than as in
the phrase 'peace and quiet'".[2] In contrast to this, Lord McLaren
stated in one of the leading Scottish cases in 1889 that "peace" was
not being used "as the antithesis of war".[3] In light of this, Michael
Christie considered dictionary definitions such as

> "freedom from civil commotion; public order or security; freedom from
> disturbance or perturbation; quiet; tranquillity; freedom from quarrel or
> dissension; freedom from mental or physical disturbance; and, absence of
> noise, movement or activity".[4]

He concluded that: "Most of these would be consistent with the
case decisions pertaining to the offence."[5] We are dealing then with
a public order offence – indeed, Gerald Gordon has described breach
of the peace as "the public order offence par excellence".[6]

---

[1] See further at section 6.25 below.
[2] R Stone, "Breach of the Peace: the Case for Abolition" (2001) 2 Web JCLI,
available at: http://webjcli.ncl.ac.uk/2001/issue2/stone2.html, quoting D Feldman,
Civil Liberties and Human Rights in England and Wales (1993) at p 787.
[3] *Ferguson* v *Carnochan* (1889) 2 White 278 at 281.
[4] See M G A Christie, *Breach of the Peace* (1990), para 2.105.
[5] *Ibid.*
[6] *Webster* v *Dominick* 2003 SCCR 525 at 544. J S More in his *Lectures on the Law
of Scotland: Volume II* (1864) discusses breach of the peace under the heading of
"Crimes Against the State".

DEFINITIONS

2.2   Christie's book provided a succinct history of the Scottish crime up to 1989, and the reader is referred to his excellent account. His analysis of Hume's *Commentaries on the Law of Scotland Respecting Crimes* (1844) led him to conclude that breach of the peace was originally a class of offences "connected in that the conduct involved effects a disturbance of the peace or tends to do so"[7] but had evolved since then to become a *nomen juris* in its own right.[8] Hume included in his list of "offences against the public peace": mobbing, making threats, challenging persons to a duel, and the bearing of mortal weapons.[9] He devoted a chapter to the first of these, describing "mobbing" as involving "a great host or multitude of people" assembled "to the fear of the lieges, and the disturbance of the public peace".[10] According to Hume, mobbing could be charged in Scotland in circumstances in which an English prosecutor would require to choose between "*Riot, Rout, and Unlawful Assembly*".[11] Mobbing had to be "accompanied with such circumstances of actual violence, or a plain tendency thereto, as beget a reasonable apprehension of what may ensue".[12] He continued his discussion of "offences against the public peace" by noting:

> "In familiar discourse, and sometimes, but rather improperly, in the proceedings of inferior courts ... the name of riot is also given to a mere brawl, or occasional quarrel and strife, among persons who were not assembled with any mischievous purpose. If, however, a contest of this sort happens in such a place, or is carried to such a length, as to disturb and alarm the neighbourhood, this seems to be cognisable at instance of the public prosecutor, as a breach of the public peace; to the effect at least of inflicting a fine and imprisonment, and exacting caution from the offenders, for their good behaviour for the future."[13]

---

[7] Christie, para 1.04. See also para 1.24: "Breach of the peace, therefore, was not a particular offence with a well-defined meaning in the early nineteenth century. It was more properly the name of a *genus* of innominate offences which caused, or could reasonably be expected to cause, public disturbance and alarm."

[8] *Ibid*, para 2.06.

[9] D Hume, *Commentaries on the Law of Scotland Respecting Crimes* (4th edn, 1844), i, Chaps XVI, and XVII, 439–445.

[10] *Ibid*, Chap XVI, 416. For modern breaches of the peace involving disorderly crowds, see *Stirling v Herron* 1976 SLT (Notes) 2 (discussed below at section 3.30); *Winnik v Allan* 1986 SCCR 35; *Boyle v HM Advocate* 1993 SLT 577; 1992 SCCR 824. Art and part liability for acting with others is discussed at section 3.30 below.

[11] Hume, i, 416.

[12] *Ibid*.

[13] *Ibid*, 439. "Caution" was a sum of money to be lodged with the court, as a means of ensuring future good behaviour.

Thus for Hume, a central element of breach of the peace was fighting or quarrelling in public – behaviour falling short of a riot or mob, but nonetheless with the potential to cause public disorder, in the sense of causing the general public to be alarmed by the prospect of further violence and unrest.[14] This suggests a relatively narrow focus for the crime. However, as we shall see below, the courts greatly expanded its ambit by stressing the need to quell behaviours which were "disorderly" in a broader sense.

Reflecting this, and having reviewed its historical development in some detail, Christie concluded that "a single definition of breach of the peace" was "impractical"[15] and offered the following summary: **2.3**

> "(1) breach of the peace consists of proven or admitted conduct on the part of the accused where there is also evidence that the conduct caused, or if allowed to continue would reasonably in all the circumstances have been likely to cause, by way of provocation of others or otherwise, real [meaning "significant"] disturbance of the standing peace of the immediate and surrounding area where the conduct occurred; and, (2) breach of the peace also consists of proven or admitted conduct on the part of the accused from which, in all the circumstances, a court can reasonably infer that any reasonable person might be alarmed, upset, annoyed or suffer any other similar mental trauma as a result."[16]

These definitions offered two different types of breaches of the peace: either the conduct did or could have caused a disturbance or, alternatively, it was conduct which caused or could cause alarm etc to reasonable people. It is noteworthy that the definitions provided by Christie describe the *actus reus*, but say nothing about *mens rea*. The latter is an aspect which, somewhat surprisingly, has been little discussed in the reported cases. For present purposes, it may suffice to note that the accused must have intended to engage in the conduct in question, but the Crown need not prove intention to cause a disturbance or to commit a breach of the peace. Although the *actus reus* of breach of the peace has been redefined since Christie's account, its *mens rea* remains underanalysed, hence a detailed discussion of this will be delayed until Chapter 3.[17]

---

[14] For a recent example of incitement to riot being charged as breach of the peace, see *Divin* v *HM Advocate* [2012] HCJAC 81; 2012 SCL 837; 2012 GWD 19–395 (see sections 1.3 above and 3.32 below).

[15] Christie, para 2.23.

[16] *Ibid* (parenthesis in original).

[17] At section 3.23 below. For a critique of the lack of a clear *mens rea* in breach of the peace, see section 6.2 below.

BEHAVIOUR

2.4 Returning to Christie's definition of the *actus reus*, in his second alternative a breach of the peace conviction could be based on a court making the inference that "any reasonable person" might have suffered alarm, upset, annoyance or "any other similar mental trauma"[18] as a result of the accused's conduct. As well as the commonly libelled "alarm"[19] or "fear and alarm",[20] other mental traumas averred to have been caused by the accused's behaviour include: "alarm and distress",[21] "distress and embarrassment";[22] or "fear and alarm and distress".[23] It has also been narrated that the accused did "harass, annoy, intimidate and frighten";[24] "annoy and

---

[18] Christie, para 2.23, cited at section 2.3 above.

[19] See *Palazzo* v *Copeland* 1976 JC 52; *Marshall* v *MacDougall* 1986 SCCR 376.

[20] Examples include: *Raffaelli* v *Heatly* 1949 JC 101; 1949 SLT 284 (the case is discussed at section 2.5 below); *M'Arthur* v *Grosset* 1952 JC 12 (see section 3.15 below); *Biggins* v *Stott* 1999 JC 298; 1999 SLT 1037; 1999 SCCR 595; 1999 GWD 24–1136 (see section 6.11 below); and *Elliott* v *Vannet* 1999 GWD 22–1033 (see section 4.10 below). Christie has suggested that since "fear" and "alarm" are synonymous, the use of both words in the same charge reflects the pleonasm commonly found in Scottish charges (at para 3.11). However, the Crown continues to use this phrase: see *Winter* v *HM Advocate* 2002 SCCR 720; 2002 GWD 19–621 (discussed at sections 3.3 and 6.23 below); *Webster* v *Dominick* 2003 SCCR 525 (see section 4.4 below); *HM Advocate* v *Greig* 2005 SCCR 465 (see section 3.28 below); *HM Advocate* v *Murray* 2007 SCCR 271 (see section 3.29 below); *Rooney* v *HM Advocate* [2007] HCJAC 1; 2007 SCCR 49; 2007 GWD 8–138 (see section 3.30 below); *Macdonald* v *HM Advocate* [2008] HCJAC 5; 2008 JC 262; 2008 SCCR 181 (see section 3.8 below); *HM Advocate* v *Harris* [2010] HCJAC 102; 2011 JC 125; 2010 SCCR 931 (see section 3.11 below); *O'Neill* v *HM Advocate* [2010] HCJAC 90; 2010 SCCR 357 (see section 1.4 above); *Hatcher* v *Harrower* [2010] HCJAC 92; 2011 JC 90; 2011 SCL 114; 2010 SCCR 903 (see section 3.15 below); *Johnstone* v *HM Advocate* 2012 JC 79; 2011 SLT 1257; 2011 SCL 825; 2011 SCCR 470; 2011 GWD 24–552 (see section 4.10 below); *Hay* v *HM Advocate* [2012] HCJAC 28; 2012 SLT 569; 2012 SCCR 281; 2012 SCL 492; 2012 GWD 8–142 (see section 4.11 below); *Anoliefo* v *HM Advocate* [2012] HCJAC 110; 2012 GWD 31–628 (see section 6.20 below).

[21] *Russell* v *Thomson* [2010] HCJAC 138; 2011 JC 164; 2011 SCL 295; 2011 SCCR 77. See section 3.14 below.

[22] *HM Advocate* v *Harris* [2010] HCJAC 102; 2011 JC 125; 2010 SCCR 931; *Borwick* v *Urquhart* 2003 SCCR 243 ("embarassment and distress": see section 3.21 below).

[23] *Russell* v *Thomson* [2010] HCJAC 138; 2011 JC 164; 2011 SCL 295; 2011 SCCR 77.

[24] *HM Advocate* v *Harris* [2010] HCJAC 102; 2011 JC 125; 2010 SCCR 931 (see section 3.11 below). For rare examples in which no "mental trauma" was narrated see *McIntyre* v *Nisbet* [2009] HCJAC 28; 2009 SCL 829; 2009 SCCR 506 (discussed further at section 3.10 below), in which the charge libelled simply: "you ... [did] conduct yourself in a disorderly manner shout and swear at the occupier ... and at paramedics who were then treating her and commit a breach of the peace", and *Miller* v *Thomson* [2009] HCJAC 4; 2008 SLT 59: "you ... did conduct yourself in

disturb";[25] or that the conduct was "to the terror and alarm" of the lieges.[26] At one point, the courts considered that indecent remarks which caused no annoyance or alarm but only "embarrassment" sufficed for a charge of breach of the peace.[27]

Christie's inclusion in his first alternative definition of distur- **2.5** bances which could have been caused "by way of provocation of others" was well illustrated by the case of *Raffaelli* v *Heatly*[28] (1949) in which the accused stood on a pavement and peered through a gap in curtains into a house, late at night. Lord Justice-Clerk Thomson stated that the crime was committed "where something is done in breach of public order or decorum which might reasonably be expected to lead to the lieges [ie the public] being alarmed or upset or tempted to make reprisals at their own hand".[29] The reference to "decorum"[30] allowed the court to hold that the accused's conduct constituted a breach of the peace. This "Peeping Tom" behaviour was far removed from the type of violent or noisy quarrelling or angry brawl described by Hume. In *Raffaelli* v *Heatly* the potential for public disorder came less from the accused's behaviour *per se*, but rather from the likely reactions of others to that behaviour. Thus where A behaved in a manner which was reasonably likely to cause B or C to retaliate or take the law into their own hands, A may be convicted of breach of the peace. In the words of Lord Justice-General Emslie in *Montgomery* v *McLeod*[31] (1977): "[I]t is perfectly clear that if there is established conduct such as to excite reasonable apprehension that mischief may ensue, a breach of the peace has been made out."[32]

---

a disorderly manner shout, swear, struggle with police officers and commit a breach of the peace". *Miller* v *Thomson* is discussed further at sections 3.6 and 3.7 below.

[25] *Hackston* v *Millar* (1906) 5 Adam 37; (1906) 8 F (J) 52; (1906) 13 SLT 826. In *Armour* v *Macrae* (1886) 13 R (J) 41; 1 White 58; 23 SLR 515 the court found that the accused had caused others to be "annoyed and alarmed".

[26] *HM Advocate* v *Ferrie* 1983 SCCR 1. See also *MacDougall* v *Maclullich* (1887) 1 White 328; (1887) 14 R (J) 17: "to the great terror, annoyance and alarm of the lieges".

[27] *Sinclair* v *Annan* 1980 SLT (Notes) 55.

[28] 1949 JC 101; 1949 SLT 284.

[29] 1949 JC 101 at 104; 1949 SLT 284 at 285.

[30] This was borrowed from the earlier case of *Ferguson* v *Carnochan* (1889) 2 White 278; 16 R (J) 93; 26 SLR 624.

[31] 1977 SLT (Notes) 77; (1977) SCCR Supp 164.

[32] 1977 SLT (Notes) 77 at 77; (1977) SCCR Supp 164 at 165. See also *Cameron* v *Normand* 1992 SCCR 866: "we are satisfied that the justice was entitled to conclude that what was being done by the appellant was something which might reasonably be expected to lead to members of the public being upset or tempted to take reprisals" (at 869 per LJ-C Ross). The accused had been kicking a ball in the street, hindering passing vehicles.

Similarly, in *Duffield* v *Skeen*[33] (1981) the appeal court noted that the trial judge had found the accused's conduct to be inflammatory and likely to occasion a breach of the peace *by other people* (the two accused had shouted pro-IRA slogans outside a football stadium). This has been the rationale behind many convictions and reflects the approach still taken today. If no actual disturbance has been caused, there has to have been a reasonable expectation that the behaviour in question *could have caused* a disturbance, and in *Grogan* v *Heywood*[34] (1999) it was stressed that a mere "possibility" of this was insufficient.[35] Those "likely to react" to an accused's behaviour must not be particularly sensitive or prone to anger, but may be entirely hypothetical; the test is how the "reasonable person" would have been likely to respond, rather than there being any actual response, or indeed anyone who was in fact in a position to respond.[36] Evidence that the conduct actually did cause alarm is of assistance in showing that such conduct was likely to alarm or disturb reasonable people, but is not determinative; the test is an objective one.[37] Thus in *Donaldson* v *Vannet*[38] (1998) the appeal court stated:

> "[If]... alarm or fear is actually caused, that may be strong evidence that the conduct meets the test, but it cannot be conclusive, since the subjective reactions of the alleged victims may vary according to their temperament and are thus merely indicators."[39]

 A rather notorious example of breach of the peace based on the hypothetical reactions of others is *Stewart* v *Lockhart*[40] (1990). The male accused was charged with dressing in women's clothing near the "red light" district of Aberdeen, "whereby a breach of the peace was likely to be occasioned, and did thereby commit a breach of the peace".[41] Upholding the conviction, the appeal court noted that:

---

[33] 1981 SCCR 66.

[34] 1999 SCCR 705; 1999 GWD 28–1317.

[35] 1999 SCCR 705 at 707, per Lord Coulsfield.

[36] See also the *dicta* in *Wilson* v *Brown* 1982 SLT 361; 1982 SCCR 49, discussed in Christie, para 2.20.

[37] In cases where there is evidence of actual alarm, this may allow a court to hold that the accused's behaviour was not merely "unusual and bizarre", but also a breach of the peace: see *McKenzie* v *Normand* 1992 SLT 130; 1992 SCCR 14, discussed at section 2.8 below.

[38] 1998 SLT 957; 1998 SCCR 421; 1998 GWD 20-1006.

[39] 1998 SCCR 421 at 424, per Lord Johnstone.

[40] 1991 SLT 835; 1990 SCCR 390.

[41] The justice found that the appellant "was dressed in a female trouser suit and high-heeled sandals. His hair was permed; he was wearing rouge, eye shadow

"The justice formed the view that in the circumstances there was a real possibility *that members of the public might cause a disturbance* having regard to the way in which the appellant was conducting himself at the material time."[42]

The implications of this approach from a civil liberties perspective are profound; that a particular type of behaviour had the potential to cause a (hypothetical) reasonable person to then cause a disturbance is an incredibly broad basis for criminalisation.

LOCUS

As Christie's definitions also made clear, there was no requirement **2.6** for the locus of the crime to be a public one – he referred to "disturbance of the standing peace of the immediate and surrounding area where the conduct occurred", and successful prosecutions had resulted where the locus was a private road,[43] office[44] or home.[45]

Initially, it seems that the behaviour had to have had at least the potential to impact on the wider public, but in later cases the fact that the accused's behaviour had caused alarm to a particular complainer or complainers, or even that it merely had the potential to do so, seems to have sufficed. Thus in *Young* v *Heatly*[46] (1959) the depute headmaster of a technical school was convicted of four charges of breach of the peace, each concerning indecent remarks (relating to masturbation) which he had made to some of his male students. Each conversation took place in the accused's private office, at a time when he and one of the students were the only people in the room. The decision was a controversial one which has been much criticised[47] – one commentator noted that "a breach of the peace in private where nothing is seen or heard by the public

---

and lipstick and was carrying a lady's umbrella and a handbag. He was wearing a brassiere padded out with cotton wool" (1990 SCCR 390 at 392).

[42] *Ibid* at 393 (emphasis added). The case is discussed further at sections 3.25 and 6.13 below. See also *McAvoy* v *Jessop* 1989 SCCR 301: "you ... did conduct yourself in a disorderly manner liable to provoke a breach of the peace and ... did commit a breach of the peace".

[43] *Saltman* v *Allan* 1989 SLT 262; 1988 SCCR 640.

[44] *Young* v *Heatly* 1959 JC 66; 1959 SLT 250; [1959] Crim LR 438.

[45] See *Ferguson* v *Carnochan* (1889) 2 White 278; 16 R (J) 93; 26 SLR 624; *Avery* v *Hilson* (1906) 5 Adam 56; (1906) 8 F (J) 60; (1906) 13 SLT 913; *Liszewski* v *Thomson* 1942 JC 55; 1942 SLT 147 (only the latter report refers to the locus); *Carmichael* v *Boyle* 1985 SCCR 58.

[46] 1959 JC 66; 1959 SLT 250; [1959] Crim LR 438.

[47] See G Gordon, "Breach of the Peace" 1959 SLT (News) 229 and Christie, paras 2.41–2.43. In 2003, Gordon called for a general review of breach of the peace, based on the potential impact of *Webster* v *Dominick* on cases such as *Young* v *Heatly*; see 2003 SCCR 525 at 544.

seems somewhat of an oxymoron"[48] – and the case has now been overruled.[49] Nevertheless, it does provide an illustration of the breadth of the crime before it was redefined by the appeal court in 2001:[50] it could be committed in private, there need be no evidence of a "public disorder" having been occassioned, nor evidence that the behaviour provoked any "disturbance" to others stronger than their embarrassment. [51]

SPECIFICATION OF CHARGES

2.7   Prior to the case of *Smith* v *Donnelly*[52] in 2001, it was not uncommon for charges to contain few details of the behaviour which was alleged to constitute a breach of the peace. An example of this is *Friend* v *Normand*[53] (1988) in which the second charge read simply: "date and place above libelled and within said house, you did conduct yourself in a disorderly manner and commit a breach of the peace". The Criminal Procedure (Scotland) Act 1995 states that complaints "shall be in the form ... set out in Schedule 5 to this Act; ... or as nearly as may be in such form", and provides model forms of certain charges, including breach of the peace.[54] Three styles are given for this, namely: "You did conduct yourself in a disorderly manner and commit a breach of the peace";[55] "You did threaten violence to the lieges and commit a breach of the peace"; and "You did fight and commit a breach of the peace". The courts had repeatedly held that a charge of breach of the peace libelled in

---

[48] *Jones* v *Carnegie* 2004 SCCR 361 at 383.

[49] By *Harris* v *HM Advocate* [2009] HCJAC 80; 2010 JC 245; 2009 SLT 1078; 2010 SCL 56; 2010 SCCR 15, discussed further at section 3.11 below.

[50] By *Smith* v *Donnelly* 2002 JC 65; 2001 SCCR 800, discussed further at section 3.4 below.

[51] The current position is discussed at section 3.11 below.

[52] 2002 JC 65; 2001 SLT 1007; 2001 SCCR 800, discussed further at section 3.4 below.

[53] 1988 SCCR 232.

[54] Criminal Procedure (Scotland) Act 1995, s 138. The previous law was similarly expressed in the Criminal Procedure (Scotland) Act 1975, s 312 and the Summary Jurisdiction (Scotland) Act 1954, Sch 2.

[55] This is the form used in: *Wilson* v *Brown* 1982 SLT 361; 1982 SCCR 49; *Steele* v *MacKinnon* 1982 SCCR 19; *Addison* v *MacKinnon* 1983 SCCR 52; *Alexander* v *Smith* 1984 SLT 176; *Campbell* v *HM Advocate* 1986 SCCR 516; *McGuigan* v *Wilson* 1988 SCCR 474; *Scott* v *McGlennan* 1990 SCCR 537; *McKenzie* v *Normand* 1992 SLT 130; 1992 SCCR 14; *Carr* v *Lees* 1993 SCCR 316; *Normand* v *McIntosh* 1994 SCCR 895; *Cavanagh* v *Wilson* 1995 SCCR 693; *Ely* v *Donnelly* 1996 SCCR 537; *Stephen* v *McKay* 1997 SCCR 444; *McGlennan* v *McKinnon* 1998 SLT 494; 1998 SCCR 285; 1998 GWD 13-660. In *Dyce* v *Aitchison* 1985 SCCR 184 the complaint libelled that the accused had conducted himself in an "improper and disorderly" manner.

one of these ways could not be held to be irrelevant on the basis of a lack of specification.[56]

In some older cases very little advance warning was given of the Crown's allegations. In *Craig* v *Herron*[57] (1976), for example, the charge libelled that the accused did "conduct [himself] in a disorderly manner, bawl, shout, curse and swear and commit a breach of the peace". The accused was convicted on the basis that he had driven his taxi in front of a car, forcing it to stop to avoid a collision, and had then lectured its driver, calling him an idiot. The charge was amended to read "conduct yourself in a disorderly manner and commit a breach of the peace".[58] In *Butcher* v *Jessop*[59] (1989) four accused were charged that "... within Ibrox Stadium ... while participating in a football match, you did conduct yourselves in a disorderly manner and commit a breach of the peace". In the appeals against their convictions it was argued that since there was no reference to "fighting" in the complaint, the sheriff ought not to have considered evidence to that effect. However, these submissions were described by Lord Justice-Clerk Ross as "misconceived":[60]

2.8

> "It is well recognised that a charge of breach of the peace may be libelled in the form of the present complaint, and that no further specification is required ... a charge in this form is expressly provided for by Parliament ... There are many forms of conduct which are capable of constituting disorderly conduct, and whenever a charge is framed in this form, evidence of disorderly conduct will require to be led. Acts of violence are just one type of conduct which may constitute disorderly conduct, and as to which the prosecutor will require to lead evidence."[61]

In *McKenzie* v *Normand*[62] (1992) the accused had entered a shop in the evening while wearing reflective sunglasses, moved around the shop, left the premises and stared through its window, then

---

[56] See *HM Advocate* v *James Swan* (1888) 2 White 137; *Anderson* v *Allan* 1985 SCCR 399. See *Horsburgh* v *Russell* 1994 JC 117; 1994 SLT 942; 1994 SCCR 237: "So far as fair notice in charges of breach of the peace is concerned, it is well established that a charge of breach of the peace need say no more than 'You did conduct yourself in a disorderly manner and commit a breach of the peace.' Thus a person may be convicted of such a charge when all that is contained in the complaint is these words" (1994 SCCR 237 at 241, per LJ-C Ross).

[57] 1976 SCCR Supp 152.

[58] The appeal court upheld the conviction but found this to be a breach of the peace "of a somewhat technical character and of trivial significance" (*ibid* at 153) and reduced the fine from £15 to £5.

[59] 1989 JC 55; 1989 SLT 593; 1989 SCCR 119.

[60] 1989 JC 55 at 63; 1989 SCCR 119 at 128.

[61] 1989 JC 55 at 63; 1989 SCCR 119 at 128–9.

[62] 1992 SLT 130; 1992 SCCR 14.

crossed the road but continued to watch the shop. He re-entered, moved towards the counter and joined a queue, but then moved to the end of the queue. He did this twice, before leaving and staring through the shop window for another period of time. The specification given to the accused in the charge was merely that "in the premises of Haddow's Off Sales ... you did conduct yourself in a disorderly manner and commit a breach of the peace". The lack of detailed information in such charges had been criticised,[63] since it was impossible for the accused in cases such as *Butcher* v *Jessop* and *McKenzie* v *Normand* to determine from the wording of the charges what it was that they were alleged to have done. As we shall see in Chapter 3, the incorporation of the European Convention on Human Rights into Scottish domestic law has led to much greater specification being provided in breach of the peace charges.[64]

2.9   Finally as regards specification, it should be noted that the appeal court had made clear that it was not competent for a breach of the peace charge to include details of acts which the accused had not committed, but which it was alleged that he or she was intending to commit. Thus in *HM Advocate* v *Forbes*[65] (1994) the indictment libelled that the accused

> "... did climb a drainpipe and break into the first-floor flat there occupied by *inter alia* [the complainer], aged fourteen years, ... and did remove [his] clothing with the exception of a pair of boxer shorts, prowl around said flat, remove articles from a chest of drawers in a bedroom, cut holes in a sweatshirt and fashion it in the manner of a hood, all with intent to assault and rape [the complainer]".

The appeal court supported the sheriff's decision to uphold a plea to the relevancy of a charge in this form, on the grounds that there was no crime in Scots law of housebreaking with intent to rape, and the Crown then offered to amend the charge to a breach of the peace. The court stressed that the effect of the accused's conduct had to be judged by what he did or by what he said, not by reference to his state of mind or his intention, or to things that he had not yet done. It followed that the reference to his behaviour being "with intent to assault and rape" required to be deleted. In the words of the court: "[A]cts not yet committed cannot be held to form part of the disorderly conduct or be expected to alarm or upset the lieges. In our opinion these words have no place in a charge of breach of

---

[63] Christie refers to the perceived unfairness of this, at para 2.03.
[64] See sections 3.2 and 3.3 below.
[65] 1994 JC 71; 1994 SCCR 163.

the peace."[66] As we shall see below, this too seems to have changed in recent years.[67]

DOUBLE CHARGING — *could be alternative only.*

It is not competent for the Crown to charge a breach of the peace **2.10** and a different offence if the same *species facti* are being used to establish both charges. Thus in *Farquhar* v *Heatly*[68] (1964) the appeal court quashed the conviction for breach of the peace, the Lord Justice-Clerk noting that:

> "the facts alleged to constitute the breach of the peace were nothing more and nothing less than the facts constituting the assaults which were committed. In effect the appellant was charged twice over on precisely the same facts. This is an undesirable practice and can indeed lead to injustice".[69]

The other two judges concurred, Lord Wheatley adding:

> "[I]f a practice has developed of libelling breach of the peace and assault when the only *species facti* justifying the charge of breach of the peace is the assault otherwise libelled then the sooner this practice is discontinued the better because it is quite improper."[70]

CONCLUSION

By the end of the 1980s when Christie was writing, an enormous **2.11** variety of behaviours had been prosecuted as breach of the peace. This raises the question as to why the Crown relied so heavily on this one crime. In large measure, this was due to the fact that Scotland had (and continues to have) a predominantly common law system. Being dependent on the UK Parliament in Westminster, Scots law lacked a comprehensive criminal code and indeed there was a dearth of criminal legislation generally. In such circumstances, breach of the peace was frequently charged for want of any alternative.[71] As previously noted,[72] the re-establishment of the Scottish Parliament

---

[66] 1994 SCCR 163 at 168. For a critique of this case see section 6.33 below.

[67] See *LBM* v *HM Advocate* [2011] HCJAC 96; 2012 SLT 147; 2012 SCL 74; 2011 GWD 34–715, discussed at section 3.27 below.

[68] (1964) SCCR Supp 7.

[69] *Ibid* at 7, per LJ-C Grant.

[70] *Ibid*.

[71] See Gordon's commentary to *Paterson* v *HM Advocate* where he asks whether the case is "an example of the bad old Crown maxim that if conduct is objectionable but you can't find any known offence to cover it, charge it as breach of the peace" (2008 SCCR 605 at 617).

[72] See section 1.2 above.

has resulted in the enactment of several offences which may reduce the number of cases and the range of behaviours prosecuted as breach of the peace, and these legislative reforms are considered in Chapter 4. However, the development of breach of the peace in the 21st century has been in large part due to the further effect given to the European Convention on Human Rights,[73] and the impact of the ECHR is assessed in the following chapter.

---

[73] See section 1.2 above.

CHAPTER 3

THE MODERN LAW

INTRODUCTION

As Chapter 2 has made clear, by the end of the 20th century breach **3.1** of the peace was a crime which lacked a precise definition. This raised issues as to its compatibility with the principle of legality,[1] and the further effect given to the European Convention on Human Rights (ECHR) in domestic law led to a series of challenges.[2] The Convention upholds *inter alia* the right to life,[3] liberty,[4] a fair trial,[5] respect for private and family life,[6] and freedom of thought, conscience and religion.[7] The Convention rights which have had the greatest potential to impact on the crime of breach of the peace are Art 7 (which prohibits retrospective criminalisation and requires clarity in offence definitions), and Arts 10 and 11 (which protect freedom of expression, and freedom of assembly/association,

---

[1] In his commentary to *Donaldson* v *Vannet* in 1998 SCCR 421, Gerald Gordon analysed some of the previous case law and concluded that some of the fine distinctions the courts had drawn "may all become academic, if and when some European-trained lawyers apply the Convention on Human Rights to breach of the peace" (*ibid* at 425). See also P R Ferguson, "Breach of the peace and the European Convention on Human Rights" (2001) 5 *Edin LR* 145; C Gane, "The Substantive Criminal Law", Chapter 2 in R Reed (ed), *A Practical Guide to Human Rights Law in Scotland* (2001) at para 2.17; B Napier, "Human Rights in Employment Law", Chapter 8 in Reed, *ibid*, at para 8.09: "It is suggested that the wide discretion which the present law [of breach of the peace] gives to the police may have to be reviewed in light of Article 11 [freedom of association]."

[2] See in particular *Smith* v *Donnelly* 2002 JC 65; 2001 SLT 1007; 2001 SCCR 800; *Jones* v *Carnegie* 2004 JC 136; 2004 SLT 609; 2004 SCCR 361; *Quinan* v *Carnegie* [2005] HCJAC 24; 2005 1 JC 279; 2005 SLT 707; 2005 SCCR 267; 2005 GWD 22-394, discussed in this chapter.

[3] Art 2.

[4] Art 5.

[5] Art 6.

[6] Art 8.

[7] Art 9.

respectively). These are considered further below. States may limit some of these Convention rights, but only if this is "prescribed by law", "necessary in a democratic society" and "proportionate". The Convention therefore recognises that interference in one person's rights may be necessary in order to safeguard the rights or interests of another, or others.

THE IMPACT OF THE ECHR: SPECIFICATION OF CHARGES

3.2   As noted in Chapter 2,[8] prior to the "domestication" of the Convention, it was not uncommon for charges to contain few details of the behaviour which was alleged to constitute a breach of the peace, with little advance warning given of the Crown's allegations. Thus we noted that in *Butcher* v *Jessop*[9] (1989) there was a submission by the defence that the lack of any reference in the complaint to "fighting" ought to make inadmissible any evidence of such fighting. It will be recalled that the appeal court found such arguments to be "misconceived"[10] since no further specification of the conduct was required. However, Art 7(1) of the ECHR provides:

> "No one shall be held guilty of any criminal offence on account of any act or omission which did not constitute a criminal offence under national or international law at the time when it was committed"

and this has been interpreted to require criminal laws to be both accessible and foreseeable. As the European Court of Human Rights (ECtHR) has put it, Art 7 embodies the principle

> "that the criminal law must not be extensively construed to an accused's detriment, for instance by analogy; it follows from this that an offence must be clearly defined in law".[11]

In 2001, in the leading case of *Smith* v *Donnelly*[12] the appeal court noted:

> "[N]otwithstanding the decision in *Butcher* v *Jessop,* that a charge of breach of the peace in statutory form is sufficient to meet the requirements of notice,

---

[8] At sections 2.7 and 2.8 above.
[9] 1989 JC 55; 1989 SLT 593; 1989 SCCR 119. See section 2.8 above.
[10] 1989 JC 55 at 63; 1989 SCCR 119 at 128.
[11] *Kokkinakis v Greece* (1994) 17 EHRR 397 at para [52]. See also *Kafkaris* v Cyprus (2008) 49 EHRR 35 at para [141]: "An individual must know from the wording of the relevant provision and, if need be, with the assistance of the courts' interpretation of it, what acts and omissions will make him criminally liable ...".
[12] 2002 JC 65; 2001 SLT 1007; 2001 SCCR 800, discussed further at section 3.4 below.

it will normally be proper, now that regard must be had to the [European] Convention, to specify the conduct said to form the breach of the peace in a charge ...".[13]

In the five conjoined appeals in *Jones* v *Carnegie*[14] (2004) the appeal court noted that in relation to one of the appellants, Frank Carberry, the only allegation in the charge was that he had conducted himself in a disorderly manner.[15] His counsel argued that further specification was a prerequisite for a fair trial, however, the appeal court held that there was no merit in this claim since the appellant had been provided with a list of Crown witnesses who could have been precognosced by the defence, he could have challenged the specification of the charge at the trial diet.[16] Nevertheless, the Solicitor General, who represented the Crown at this appeal, conceded that it would generally be proper for the prosecutor "to specify the conduct which was said to form a breach of the peace rather than to rely on the statutory form of charge".[17]

We now see a wealth of details being included in breach of **3.3** the peace charges. Some notable examples include *Winter* v *HM Advocate*[18] (2002) in which the charge libelled:

"... you did ... conduct yourself in a disorderly manner, pretend to [the complainer] ... that you had assaulted a person by repeatedly punching and striking that person on the face with a knife, smear your hands and said knife with red liquid, cause said [complainer] to believe that said red liquid was blood, clean said red liquid and fingerprints from said knife in [his] presence and place [him] in a state of fear and alarm and this you did in order to induce him to participate in crimes of violence and did thus commit a breach of the peace".[19]

In *HM Advocate* v *Greig*[20] (2005) the charge libelled:

"... [you] did conduct yourself in a disorderly manner and knowing that there was likely to be a large number of children at a fireworks display there, dress yourself in such a manner as to be easily mistaken for a steward or first aid officer, position yourself adjacent to all the public facilities there, place a police

---

[13] 2002 JC 65 at 72, para [20], per Lord Coulsfield.
[14] *Jones* v *Carnegie*; *Tallents* v *Gallacher*; *Barrett* v *Carnegie*; *Carberry* v *Currie*; *Park* v *Frame* 2004 JC 136; 2004 SLT 609; 2004 SCCR 361. See section 3.5 below.
[15] *Carberry* v *Currie* 2004 JC 136 at 150, para [37].
[16] Criminal Procedure (Scotland) Act 1995, s 192 provides that: "No conviction ... shall be ... set aside in respect of any objections to ... the want of specification [in the complaint] ... unless such objections were timeously stated."
[17] 2004 JC 136 at 151, para [45].
[18] 2002 SCCR 720; 2002 GWD 19-621.
[19] The case is discussed further at section 6.23 below.
[20] 2005 SCCR 465.

officer who was in attendance at said event, to whom you are known and who was aware of the conviction aforesaid, in a state of fear and alarm for the safety of children and the public and did commit a breach of the peace."

And the charge in *HM Advocate* v *Murray*[21] (2007) narrated:

"... [you did] ... conduct yourself in a disorderly manner, state to [a social worker] ... that you had been recently in possession of a hammer while behaving in a manner which may lead police officers to search you and with the intention of assaulting said police officers with said hammer, display a hammer to him and thereafter threaten to sexually assault and murder a child, further state that while in an area in Falkirk to the prosecutor unknown, you had seen a boy of 11–12 years whom you considered to be a possible victim and that said crime would be committed at a distance from your home, that you would dig the grave deep and in doing this you would avoid detection and prosecution for said crime and you did place said [social worker] in a state of fear and alarm for the safety of the lieges and you did commit a breach of the peace".[22]

These cases raised issues relating to the inclusion in a charge of references to previous convictions, and are discussed further below.[23]

ACTUS REUS

Smith v Donnelly and *Jones* v *Carnegie*

3.4 As noted above, the leading modern case and the first to be decided with explicit reference to the ECHR is *Smith* v *Donnelly*[24] (2001). The appellant, Pamela Smith, was charged with breach of the peace by lying on a roadway, disrupting the traffic. This was part of a public protest against nuclear weapons at a naval base. She argued that the definition of the crime was in violation of Art 7 of the ECHR, and that her prosecution was a breach of Art 10 (which safeguards freedom of expression).[25] In respect of the former, Smith contended that individuals could not know with reasonable certainty which of their actions would infringe the law: "breach of the peace is an all-encompassing charge which has been used to cover any type of behaviour deemed inappropriate in various circumstances and is

---

[21] 2007 SCCR 271.

[22] See also the charges libelled in *Johnstone* v *HM Advocate* 2012 JC 79; 2011 SLT 1257; 2011 SCL 825; 2011 SCCR 470; 2011 GWD 24-552; and *HM Advocate* v *Harris* [2010] HCJAC 102; 2011 JC 125; 2010 SCCR 931, noted below at section 6.9.

[23] At sections 3.28 and 3.29 respectively.

[24] 2002 JC 65; 2001 SLT 1007; 2001 SCCR 800. See F Leverick, "Breach of the Peace after *Smith* v *Donnelly*" 2011 34 SLT 257.

[25] See section 3.17 below.

therefore too vague to be aligned with the [Convention]."[26] This was rejected by the appeal court, but it nonetheless accepted that in some cases breach of the peace had been held to be established "on grounds which might charitably be described as tenuous".[27] Lord Coulsfield offered a narrower definition to that which had been employed hitherto: breach of the peace requires conduct on the part of the accused which was "*severe* enough to cause alarm to ordinary people *and* threaten *serious* disturbance to the community".[28] Whether this is an appropriate definition will be discussed in Chapter 6.

The appeal court in *Smith* v *Donnelly* was not able to overrule   3.5 any previous breach of the peace cases since it comprised the usual number of three judges. As noted earlier,[29] a court comprising five judges was, however, convened to consider several conjoined appeals in *Jones* v *Carnegie*[30] (2004). Three of the accused had been convicted of breach of the peace while engaging in various forms of civil disobedience: Jones and Barrett had, in separate incidents, sat on a roadway approach to a naval base, and Tallents had engaged in a protest in the Scottish Parliament. The first appellant argued that there required to be evidence that persons were in fact alarmed by her behaviour, and that *Smith* v *Donnelly*, *Raffaelli* v *Heatly*[31] (1949) and *Young* v *Heatly*[32] (1959) had each been wrongly decided. However, the appeal court endorsed Lord Coulsfield's definition, and reiterated that although the accused's acts must have been severe enough to be able to cause alarm to others, it was not essential for a successful prosecution that the Crown establish that the accused's conduct actually produced such alarm:

> "[I]f the crime of breach of the peace were to be limited to cases in which there was evidence of actual alarm or annoyance, whether given by the persons who were alarmed or annoyed or by others, this would represent an unfortunate and unjustifiable narrowing of the common law. The safeguard against any undue expansion of the law is provided by the need, which was emphasised by the court in *Smith (P)* v *Donnelly*, for the conduct to be genuinely alarming and disturbing to any reasonable person."[33]

Returning to *Smith* v *Donnelly*, Lord Coulsfield was critical of some

---

[26] 2002 JC 65 at 66.
[27] *Ibid* at 72, para [19].
[28] *Ibid* at 71, para [17] (emphases added).
[29] See section 3.2 above.
[30] *Jones* v *Carnegie*; *Tallents* v *Gallacher*; *Barrett* v *Carnegie*; *Carberry* v *Currie*; *Park* v *Frame* 2004 JC 136; 2004 SLT 609; 2004 SCCR 361.
[31] 1949 JC 101; 1949 SLT 284, discussed at section 2.5 above.
[32] 1959 JC 66; 1959 SLT 250; [1959] Crim LR 438, discussed at section 2.6 above.
[33] 2004 JC 136 at [13].

"recurrent themes" which emerged from a consideration of the case law. These included prosecutions based on: (i) swearing, (ii) refusal of co-operation with the police or other officials, and (iii) private words and actions.

Swearing

3.6   Lord Coulsfield noted that the mere use of bad language does not justify a conviction for breach of the peace.[34] That point had been established by the appeal court many years earlier in the case of *Logan* v *Jessop*[35] (1987). However, some defence agents had interpreted that case as giving individuals carte blanche to swear at the police with impunity, and in a series of subsequent cases the appeal court clarified the position, stressing that:

> "It is not the law that if upon the evidence it appears that the only persons present at the immediate scene were police officers there can be no breach of the peace, nor is it the law that a police officer is not to be regarded as a person liable to be affected by disorderly conduct. *Logan v Jessop is* to be understood only as a decision upon its own special facts."[36]

In *Miller* v *Thomson*[37] (2009) the charge consisted of shouting, swearing, and struggling with police officers. When informed by the police that they wanted the names and addresses of the youths who were present, the appellant had shouted "I've done fuck all – you're not talking to me". The appeal court held that the use of a swear word in response to the police was not, in itself, a breach of the peace.

Refusal of co-operation

3.7   Lord Coulsfield had also noted that

> "... there have been repeated instances in which refusal to co-operate with police or other officials has led to a charge of breach of the peace: but such a refusal, even if forcefully or even truculently stated, is not likely to be sufficient in itself to justify a conviction".[38]

---

[34] 2002 JC 65 at 72, para [20].

[35] 1987 SCCR 604. See also *Grogan* v *Heywood* 1999 SCCR 705; 1999 GWD 28-1317.

[36] *Saltman* v *Allan* 1989 SLT 262 at 264; 1988 SCCR 640 at 644, per LJ-G Emslie. See also *Stewart* v *Jessop* 1988 SCCR 492; *McMillan* v *Normand* 1989 JC 95; 1989 SCCR 269; *Norris* v *McLeod* 1988 SCCR 572; *Boyle* v *Wilson* 1988 SCCR 485; and compare *Cavanagh* v *Wilson* 1995 SCCR 693; *Kinnaird* v *Higson* 2001 SCCR 427. For a useful discussion, see D Field, "Once more unto the breach: the retreat from *Logan* v *Jessop*" 1989 13 SLT 145.

[37] [2009] HCJAC 4; 2009 SLT 59.

[38] 2002 JC 65 at 72, para [20].

In *Montgomery* v *McLeod*[39] (1977) the police ordered a group of youths to leave a car park, following a disturbance there. The appellant refused to leave and was arrested for breach of the peace. In light of Lord Coulsfield's statement, it is doubtful that a conviction of this nature would be upheld in future cases. Indeed, *McMillan* v *Higson*[40] (2003) may be an illustration of this. The charge libelled that the accused had blocked a roadway with his car and refused to allow people to pass. This seems like a classic example of the type of breach of the peace commonly found pre-*Smith* v *Donnelly*, particularly given the narration in the charge that he had "fail[ed] to desist in said action when required to do so by police officers". The appellant was one of three people charged on the same complaint, and the appeal of a second accused is reported separately as *Hamilton* v *Higson*[41] (2003). Hamilton had lined up several wheelie bins at the intersection of a public and private road in order to stop the complainer driving a lorry into the private road. The convictions were quashed in both cases, Lord Hamilton stating in the latter case:

> "There appears to have been nothing in the particular circumstances of the appellant's conduct which made it ... likely to be a catalyst for any serious disturbance ... such as to constitute a breach of the peace. No doubt, it might on one view be thought to be indecorous to refuse to co-operate with a police officer. But, as is made plain in *Smith* v *Donnelly* ..., such refusal is not likely, as the law is presently understood, to be sufficient in itself to justify a conviction for breach of the peace. ... ."[42]

In *Dyer* v *Brady*[43] (2006) the breach of the peace charge narrated:

> "you ... did conduct yourselves in a disorderly manner, chain yourselves together, and obstruct the roadway and the lawful passage of persons there, [and] *refuse to desist from carrying out said acts when requested to do so* ...".[44]

The sheriff upheld a submission of no case to answer, and the appeal court refused the Crown's appeal. The court did not place any significance on the accused's failure to desist when instructed to do so by the police. Lord Coulsfield's reminder that refusal to co-operate was insufficient for breach of the peace was also reiterated in *Miller* v *Thomson* (above). The judgment is worth quoting, for its civil liberties flavour:

---

[39] 1977 SLT (Notes) 77; (1977) SCCR Supp 164.
[40] 2003 SLT 573; 2003 SCCR 125.
[41] 2002 Scot (D) 39/12.
[42] *Ibid* at para [15]. Lord Cameron of Lochbroom dissented in both cases.
[43] [2006] HCJAC 72; 2006 SLT 965; 2006 SCCR 629; 2006 GWD 31-664. The case is discussed further at section 3.20 below.
[44] Emphasis added.

"... it appears that the police officers did not give the appellant and his companions any reason for requiring their 'details'. ... [A]ny reasonable person in the position of the appellant at the time might well have taken umbrage when two police officers, in the absence of any explanation, suddenly started to demand particulars from him and his companions. The appellant's immediate response was no doubt expressed somewhat coarsely, but the words which were used cannot have been of a kind which the police officers had never heard before; and, simply as a matter of common sense, they cannot, in the circumstances be regarded as amounting to a breach of the peace. On the contrary, they can properly be regarded as a mild, albeit rudely expressed, protest at what appeared to be wholly unjustified harassment on the part of the police officers. That being so, it follows that the purported arrest of the appellant was unlawful; and, from that, it follows that the struggle which then ensued cannot be regarded as an integral part of a continuing breach of the peace".[45]

Crucially, there was no basis for the police requiring the group of youths to provide their names and addresses.[46] As one commentator put it:

"It is extraordinary that no one in authority put a red pen through this case before the Appeal Court required to rule on it. ... It clearly fails the objective test for breach of the peace set down in *Smith v Donnelly*".[47]

Private words and actions

3.8 *Smith v Donnelly* also cast doubt on the future of breach of the peace charges involving what might be regarded as "private" conduct. As Lord Coulsfield put it:

"there have been cases in which actions done or words spoken in private have been held to amount to breach of the peace, or conduct likely to provoke such a breach, more because of some perceived unpleasant or disgusting character than because of any real risk of disturbance. In such cases, it is perhaps particularly necessary to bear in mind what the essential character of the crime is".[48] *Smith*

Similarly, in *Jones v Carnegie* the court stated "we would caution that where conduct complained of took place in private there requires to be evidence that there was a realistic risk of the conduct being discovered".[49] The court did not, however, elaborate on what it meant by conduct being discovered.[50] The incongruity of holding

Miller v Thomson

---

[45] [2009] HCJAC 4 at paras [13]–[14].
[46] The court also noted that the allegation of a struggle with the police could have formed a separate charge under the Police (Scotland) Act 1967. The appeal court referred to the proffering of the statutory charge as "normal practice".
[47] (2009) *Scottish Criminal Law* (April) 385 at 392.
[48] 2002 JC 65 at 72, para [20].
[49] 2004 JC 136; 2004 SLT 609; 2004 SCCR 361 at [12].
[50] As was noted by the court in *WM v HM Advocate* [2010] HCJAC 75 at para [13], per LJ-G Hamilton. That case is discussed further at section 6.10 below.

that behaviour committed in a private place could form the basis of a public order crime such as breach of the peace had been identified several years previously. In *Boyle* v *Wilson*[51] (1988) the accused was convicted of a breach of the peace based on his behaviour in a town centre, a police car and a police station. One commentator wondered "how a challenge [to fight] in a police vehicle containing only police officers, or an assault in a police station where members of the public cannot be presumed to be present, can constitute part of a breach of the peace".[52] It was not, however, until 20 years later that the case of *Macdonald* v *HM Advocate*[53] (2008) addressed the private nature of an act alleged to constitute a breach of the peace. Here, the accused had been convicted of sexually assaulting a child and was coming towards the end of the custodial part of an extended sentence. He faced two charges of breach of the peace which libelled that he had caused fear and alarm to two psychologists by telling them that he was a dangerous predator who had not been rehabilitated during his custody, and that he intended to commit a sexually violent crime. This was alleged to have been said during interviews with the psychologists as part of a risk assessment process designed to determine whether the accused was suitable for release into the community. The appeal court held that these charges were not competent. In a very short opinion, Lord Johnston concluded that "the context of the interview does not lend itself to the definitions of breach of the peace".[54] Lord Marnoch dissented, on the ground that it was for the jury to determine whether the context was one in which a breach of the peace could be committed, but he also suggested that "there are real questions arising from the fact that this offence was allegedly committed in private" and opined, albeit *obiter*, that *Young* v *Heatly*[55] (1959) would "one day have to be formally reviewed by a larger court".[56] This proved to be prophetic, as we shall see further below.[57]

The public/private issue arose again 6 months later in *Paterson* **3.9** v *HM Advocate*[58] (2008) in which the accused was convicted, *inter alia*, of charges which libelled:

---

[51] 1988 SCCR 485.

[52] *Ibid* at 487.

[53] [2008] HCJAC 5; 2008 JC 262; 2008 SCCR 181.

[54] 2008 JC 262 at 263.

[55] 1959 JC 66; 1959 SLT 250; [1959] Crim LR 438. See section 2.6 above.

[56] *Macdonald* v *HM Advocate* 2008 SCCR 181 at 191.

[57] See section 3.11 below. For a critique of the case, see M Plaxton, "*Macdonald v H M Advocate*: Privately Breaching the Peace" (2008) 12 *Edin LR* 476. Plaxton notes that the case "raised important issues concerning the extent to which private conduct can amount to a breach of the peace" but that the court "failed to provide any such guidance" (*ibid* at 476).

[58] [2008] HCJAC 18; 2008 JC 327; 2008 SLT 465; 2008 SCL 691; 2008 SCCR 605.

> "you ... did induce [the 17-year-old complainer] ... to sit on your knee causing your private member to become erect and did conduct yourself in a disorderly manner and did commit a breach of the peace"

and

> "you ... did place your hands around [the same complainer's] ... waist, did squeeze her tightly, pull her towards you and did conduct yourself in a disorderly manner and did commit a breach of the peace".

The locus in the first charge was the accused's car, and in the second was the home of the complainer's parents. Lord Justice-General Hamilton was mindful of the need to show that the conduct had the potential to cause a "public" disturbance:

> "[I]t is important to notice that the conduct alleged in [the first breach of the peace charge] occurred in a public place and that that in [the second charge], although on private property, occurred in relatively close proximity to where [the complainer's] parents were sitting in an adjacent room. The conduct does not require to cause serious disturbance to the community. It is sufficient that it threatens such disturbance. Such conduct by a mature man towards an adolescent girl was such that, if discovered, was likely to cause a serious reaction among other adults. In these circumstances the nature of the conduct was such that, if proved, it constituted ... breach of the peace."[59]

Thus the public/private nature of the locus is not determinative, but the potential for discoverability is crucial. In respect of the first charge, the accused had been giving the complainer a driving lesson at the time, and his car was on a public road. In the second charge, since the conduct was liable to be discovered by the complainer's parents, it had the potential to alarm others, thereby leading to public disorder. While this approach confirms that taken in *Jones* v *Carnegie*, it sheds little light on what "discoverability" might mean, in general.[60]

3.10   In *McIntyre v Nisbet*[61] (2009) the appellant was convicted of a breach of the peace whose locus was a flat. Two paramedics, employed by the Scottish Ambulance Service, had attended the flat in response to an emergency call. They found a woman suffering from a panic attack and in a state of some distress. While they were there, the appellant arrived, shouted and swore at the woman, and acted in an aggressive manner towards, her. He also made derogatory remarks which caused her to become distressed again. When the

---

[59] [2008] HJAC 18, para [22] (emphasis added).
[60] For a critique of this case, see section 6.30 below.
[61] [2009] HCJAC 28; 2009 SCL 829; 2009 SCCR 506. For a commentary, see (2009) *Scottish Criminal Law* (Aug) 829.

paramedics asked him to calm down, the appellant told them that the matter was none of their business, swore at them and refused to leave. The paramedics and their patient were alarmed, and the sheriff found as a fact that this reaction was a reasonable one in the circumstances. The appellant left when the police were called, and the incident lasted about 5 minutes. The appellant argued that it had been recognised in *Paterson* that an act in a private dwelling could only be a breach of the peace if it was likely to cause a serious disturbance, if discovered. It was suggested that the sheriff had not applied his mind to the issue of serious disturbance to the wider community. In refusing the appeal, the court reiterated: "The fact that the conduct itself occurs on private property is not a decisive feature of the crime".[62] What was important was whether the conduct, judged objectively, was genuinely alarming and disturbing and threatened serious disturbance to the community, but the community could consist of members of the public who were likely to see or hear that conduct from a public or private place, including persons in the same flat where the incident took place. This suggests that the two paramedics constituted "the community". However, the court added that it was

> "reasonable to suppose that there would be persons passing by the flat and living in the surrounding flats. Some may have observed the ambulance parked at the scene. In that context, were any member of the public to hear shouting and swearing, of the nature and duration found by the Sheriff, being apparently directed towards the occupant of the flat where the paramedics were in attendance or towards the paramedics themselves, then he would be likely to be genuinely alarmed. Such conduct would threaten serious disturbance to the community".[63]

This suggests that the community aspect required the potential for alarm by persons other than those present in the flat. References to passers-by or neighbours who "may have" observed something or who "would be likely to be" alarmed are highly speculative.

Four months later, in the first of two cases involving Mark Harris, **3.11** the public/private distinction was again at issue. In *Harris v HM Advocate*[64] (2009) the accused had faced two charges of breach of the peace, based on veiled threats he made to police officers, in

[62] 2009 SCCR 506 at 510, para [11], per Lord Carloway.
[63] *Ibid* at 511, para [12].
[64] [2009] HCJAC 80; 2010 JC 245; 2009 SLT 1078; 2010 SCL 56; 2010 SCCR 15. For a useful summary, see F Stark, "Breach of the Peace Revisited (Again)" (2010) 14 *Edin LR* 134. Commentaries on the case include: C Stephen, "Recapturing the Essence of Breach of the Peace: *Harris v HM Advocate*" (2010) 1 *JR* 15; C Shead, "Breach of the Peace: 'A Reconsideration'" (2009) *Scottish Criminal Law* (June) 560.

separate incidents, to the effect that he knew about aspects of their personal lives, such as where they lived.[65] In each case, only the officer in question and the accused were party to these conversations, which took place in a police station, and a Full Bench of the appeal court held that this did not amount to a breach of the peace since it lacked the necessary element of potential public disturbance. In doing so, the Court overruled *Young v Heatly*[66] but opined that it was "unnecessary ... to seek to give definitive guidance as to what public element would be sufficient" for breach of the peace.[67] This lack of guidance resulted in several further appeals, one of which was the second *Harris* case: *HM Advocate v Harris*[68] (2010). On this occasion the accused faced, *inter alia*, six charges of breach of the peace. The first two charges libelled that he had sent numerous letters and text messages to his former girlfriend (the first complainer), and to the girlfriend's daughter (the second complainer) respectively. The third charge involved repeatedly phoning the first complainer, and the fourth libelled the sending of what were described as "various items designed to cause distress and embarrassment" (it seems these were newspaper articles) to the legal firm where the daughter worked. The fifth of these charges narrated that the accused had arranged for a mobile tracking device to be fitted to the first complainer's car without her knowledge, and had used this to follow her to various locations, to her fear and alarm. The final charge was similar to this, but narrated that the accused had fitted a tracking device to a second car "for the purpose of harassment" of the complainers, and "to their fear and alarm". The first three and the sixth of these charges were dismissed as irrelevant by the appeal court. The requirement for conduct to threaten serious disturbance to the community meant that "communication at a distance of a message which passes wholly privately between individuals cannot, without more, be a relevant foundation for a breach of the peace".[69]

3.12   The impact of the first *Harris* case on the definition of breach of the peace was raised in *Bowes v Frame*[70] (2010), in which the

---

[65] The facts of the case are similar to those of *Friel v Carnegie* 1999 GWD 13–1410, in which the accused had told the complainer "that he knew where he lived and that he would come to his house and harm him and his family". He was found guilty of breach of the peace.

[66] 1959 JC 66; 1959 SLT 250; [1959] Crim LR 438. See section 2.6 above.

[67] 2010 JC 245 at 254, para [25].

[68] [2010] HCJAC 102; 2011 JC 125; 2010 SCCR 931.

[69] 2011 JC 125, at para [20], per LJ-G Hamilton. This could now be charged as a breach of the Criminal Justice and Licensing (Scotland) Act 2010, s 38: see section 4.8 below.

[70] *Sub nom Bowes v McGowan* [2010] HCJAC 55; 2010 JC 297; 2010 SLT 683; 2010 SCL 761; 2010 SCCR 657.

accused was a taxi driver who had been contracted to drive the 14-year-old complainer from her school to the residential home in which she lived. He had pled guilty to breach of the peace by making "comments of a sexual nature" to the girl in the course of the journey. These mainly consisted of him asking whether she had a boyfriend, and questioning her about her sex life and contraceptive practices. The complainer became very alarmed and upset and reported the incident on arrival at the home. The accused tried to have his guilty plea suspended on the basis that in light of the decision in *Harris (No 1)* his behaviour could not be considered to amount to a breach of the peace, since the remarks had been made in a vehicle in which only the complainer and the accused were present. In other words, the incident took place in private, similar to the case of *Young* v *Heatly* which had been overruled by *Harris*. However, the appeal court in *Bowes* upheld the conviction, stressing that

> "there was plainly a realistic risk of the conduct being discovered, as indeed occurred within a very short period of time following upon it, when its occurrence was reported to those who, in furtherance of a public duty, were responsible for the care of the complainer".[71]

Somewhat surprisingly, the appeal court also stated that the *Harris* case had not changed the definition of breach of the peace.[72]

The appeal court again stressed that "breach of the peace must have a public element" in *Angus* v *Nisbet*[73] (2010). The charge libelled that the accused had stopped his car and passed a piece of paper to the girl who delivered his newspapers, asking her to keep in touch with him, and providing his mobile phone number. The complainer, who was aged 14 at the time,[74] testified that she was scared and had telephoned her mother. The appeal court found that the necessary "public element" was present in these circumstances:

3.13

> "[W]e have no difficulty in concluding that the conduct did have a public element. It was an interaction between relative strangers, at the initiative of only one of them, which took place in a public street. It may be that what is said [*sic*] was not overheard by any third party and that what was done (the handing over of a piece of paper) would have appeared as an entirely obscure act, even had it been observed. Nevertheless, what was said and done was said and done in public."[75]

---

[71] 2010 JC 297 at 306, para [22], per Lord Osborne.

[72] For a critique of this case, see section 6.10 below, and F Stark, "Bowes v McGowan: Cause for Fear and Alarm" (2010) *Scottish Criminal Law* (Aug) 721.

[73] 2011 SC (JC) 69; [2010] HCJAC 76; 2010 SCCR 873.

[74] The judgment of Lord Brodie gives her age as 15 but since her date of birth is given as 10 September 1994, she would have been 14 on the date of the offence (11 June 2009).

[75] 2011 SC (JC) 69 at 72, para [13], per Lord Brodie.

In determining whether the test in *Smith* v *Donnelly* had been satisfied the court held that it had to be assumed that the "notional reasonable person should be taken as being aware of the whole circumstances" – in this case, the content of the note. Nevertheless, the court held that while the appellant's conduct was "puzzling" and "not something that a prudent person who did not wish to excite suspicion would have done", it did not amount to a breach of the peace.[76]

3.14   That the law was less than clear following *Harris (No 1)* is also illustrated by *Russell* v *Thomson*[77] (2010). The accused had been convicted of a breach of the peace which narrated that he had repeatedly harassed the headmistress of his children's school by sending her a threatening letter, via her solicitors, and entering the school playground and refusing to leave. The headmistress had obtained an interdict against the appellant, during the course of which he had passed her solicitor a handwritten letter indicating that the appellant's voice would be the last thing she would hear before being committed to hell. After the granting of the interdict the appellant had entered the playground and had spoken to teachers outside classrooms. The headmistress had asked him to leave, but he had ignored her, causing her alarm and distress. The Scottish Criminal Case Review Commission assessed the case and concluded that in light of both *Harris* cases, the sending of the letter could not amount to a breach of the peace. The Commission argued that it was "difficult to characterise the applicant's actions as 'severe'" and it was "not apparent how [these actions] threatened serious disturbance to the community".[78] It did not consider that this behaviour "could reasonably be viewed as meeting the test for breach of the peace".[79] However, the appeal court had little sympathy with this argument; it had

> "no difficulty in holding that the sending of a threatening letter to the headmistress of a primary school followed by an appearance by the sender at the door of that school at the start of the day, when parents, teachers (including the headmistress) and children could be expected to be present, is conduct which satisfies the dual test in *Smith (P)* v *Donnelly* and thus amounts to a breach of the peace".[80]

---

[76] 2011 SC (JC) 69 at para [15]. For a critique of the case, see section 6.10 below.
[77] [2010] HCJAC 138; 2011 JC 164; 2011 SCL 295; 2011 SCCR 77.
[78] Para 47 of the SCCRC's Report, quoted by the appeal court in 2011 JC 164 at para [12].
[79] *Ibid.*
[80] *Ibid* at para [21], per Lord Carloway.

It continued:

> "[T]his was behaviour which, looked at objectively, would be genuinely alarming and disturbing, in its context, to any reasonable person observing the scene as well as to those directly involved. It would threaten serious disturbance to the community, notably that of the staff of the school and any parents in the vicinity who might have been aware of the background."[81]

In *Hatcher* v *Harrower*[82] (2010) the appellant was convicted of a **3.15** breach of the peace which consisted of shouting and swearing at his wife in the family home, and placing her in a state of fear and alarm. As Lord Bonomy noted:

> "It was inevitable that the debate would soon move to the question whether severe oral abuse of, and unruly behaviour towards, one domestic partner by another over an extended period within the confines of the family home can amount to a breach of the peace, and more particularly whether in a given case that conduct did constitute a breach of the peace."[83]

The appeal court found that the accused's conduct had not threatened serious disturbance to the community. The complainer testified that two of the couple's children, aged 12 and 15, were present in the house throughout the incident, but the appeal court took the view that the threat of disturbance to the children did "not contain any element that can be characterised as 'public'"[84] and disagreed with the sheriff's view that the children could be "considered as members of the community or public".[85] It is worth comparing *Hatcher* v *Harrower* – with the case of *M'Arthur* v *Grosset*[86], decided in 1952. Here, the charge was that

> "within the living room of the dwelling-house ... occupied by you, you did bawl and shout, throw articles of furniture about said living room, put your wife ... in a state of fear and alarm, conduct yourself in a disorderly manner and commit a breach of the peace".

The case was reported on a procedural point, but there was no suggestion that this did not amount to a beach of the peace. It is, however, of interest to note that Lord Justice-General Cooper referred to this as a breach of the peace "of an apparently trivial character".[87] The law has come a long way in its handling of domestic abuse in

---

[81] 2011 JC 164 at para [26]. For a critique of this case, see section 6.9 below.
[82] [2010] HCJAC 92; 2011 JC 90; 2011 SCL 114; 2010 SCCR 903.
[83] [2010] HCJAC 92, para [1].
[84] *Ibid*, para [5].
[85] *Ibid*. The case is discussed in (2010) 107 (Oct) *Criminal Law Bulletin* 5.
[86] 1952 JC 12.
[87] *Ibid* at 13.

the 60 years since that case was decided, and it is both ironic and unfortunate that the redefining of breach of the peace created a gap in the protection of one spouse from verbal attack or threats of violence by the other. This was recognised by Lord Bonomy:

> "[I]f there is a lacuna in the law and domestic partners are not protected by the criminal law where one abuses the other in a way that would cause serious upset and distress to a reasonable person, but does so in private, then it is for Parliament and not the court to decide whether the law should be changed to criminalise such conduct."[88]

It was, of course, the appeal court itself which effectively *decriminalised* such behaviour by emphasising the need for "public" disorder. As we shall see in Chapter 4, the Scottish Parliament subsequently enacted legislation to close this loophole, and this provides that abusive or threatening behaviour is an offence irrespective of where it takes place, and whether or not it involves serious disturbance to the community.[89]

3.16   As previously noted, in *WM v HM Advocate*[90] (2010) the appellant was convicted of serious sexual assaults against his two sons, and also of two charges of breach of the peace. The latter charges libelled that over a period of several years the accused had threatened to harm the boys if they told anyone about the sexual abuse. In quashing the breach of the peace convictions, the court of appeal stressed that the references in *Paterson* to the fact that the accused's behaviour "if discovered" was likely to cause a serious reaction among the complainer's family ought not to be taken to encompass a third party receiving an account of behaviour at a different place and time: a "realistic risk of the conduct being discovered" was to be

> "understood as referring to the risk of the conduct of the accused being come upon, that is to say being seen or heard, by a third party (or parties) or being brought to their attention, while that conduct continues or in the immediate aftermath of the conduct having come to an end. ... There may, however, be borderline cases where the reporting to third parties is so immediately related in time and place to the conduct complained of that it can be regarded as part of the same event. *Bowes v Frame* may have been such a case. There was no such immediacy and proximity in the present case".[91]

Paterson was also distinguished on the basis that his conduct took place in a public place ("a stationery [*sic*] vehicle on a public road

---

[88] [2010] HCJAC 92 at para [5].
[89] See section 4.8 below.
[90] [2010] HCJAC 75; 2011 JC 49; 2010 GWD 26-488. See section 1.4 above.
[91] [2010] HCJAC 75, para [15]. This case is critiqued at section 6.10 below.

with the driver's door open")[92] in the first charge, and "in close proximity"[93] to adult members of the complainer's family ("albeit in a private house")[94] in the second. Whether such narrow distinctions are entirely satisfactory is explored in Chapter 6 below.[95]

ARTICLES 10 AND 11

According to Art 10(1) of the European Convention on Human Rights: **3.17**

> "Everyone has the right to freedom of expression. This right shall include freedom to hold opinions and to receive and impart information and ideas without interference by public authority and regardless of frontiers ..."

and Art 11(1) provides:

> "Everyone has the right to freedom of peaceful assembly and to freedom of association with others ...".

However, both Arts 10(2) and 11(2) allow restrictions to be imposed in the interests of, *inter alia*, national security, or public safety, for the prevention of disorder or crime, for the protection of health or morals, or for the protection of the rights of others. In addition, Art 11(2) provides that lawful restrictions may be imposed on the exercise of these rights by members of the armed forces, the police or the administration of the State. The European Court of Human Rights has emphasised that such restrictions must be "proportionate to the legitimate aim pursued".[96] It has been suggested that:

> "This means that even if a policy which interferes with a Convention right might be aimed at securing a legitimate aim of social policy, for example the prevention of crime, this will not in itself justify the violation if the means adopted to secure the aim are excessive in the circumstances."[97]

The magistrate hearing the case at first instance in *Smith* v *Donnelly* had commented that the appellant's behaviour in lying on a roadway had the potential to "disrupt national security" since the naval base could "hold Trident nuclear weapons".[98] He also emphasised that

---

[92] [2010] HCJAC 75, para [14].
[93] *Ibid.*
[94] *Ibid.*
[95] See section 6.10 below.
[96] *Handyside* v *United Kingdom* (1979–80) 1 EHRR 737 at 754.
[97] J Wadham, H Mountfield *et al, Blackstone's Guide to the Human Rights Act 1998* (6th edn, 2011) at para 2.110.
[98] Quoted by Lord Coulsfield: 2002 JC 65 at 66, para [5].

her protest could have put public safety at risk in respect of drivers on the road (and also the protesters themselves). This behaviour contravened the rights and freedoms of others. Although the appeal court repeated these comments, it was not addressed on the Art 10 arguments and confined its decision to those relating to Art 7.

3.18　　The case of *Lucas v United Kingdom*[99] (2003) also involved a peaceful demonstration at Faslane, resulting in a conviction for breach of the peace. The European Court of Human Rights considered

> "that the definition of the offence of breach of the peace as stipulated in *Smith (P) v Donnelly* is sufficiently precise to provide reasonable foreseeability of the actions which may fall within the remit of the offence. The concept of breach of the peace has been clarified by the Scottish courts recently and in *Smith (P) v Donnelly*, the High Court, in formulating its definition, had regard to the requirement of certainty in the Convention. The court notes that ... the test set down in Scottish law has the objective standard of the reasonable person. In *Larissis and Others v Greece* ... the court stated that considering the need to avoid excessive rigidity and to keep pace with changing circumstances, many laws are inevitably couched in terms which, to a greater or lesser extent, are vague and considered that this in itself does not disclose a violation of the certainty required by the Convention (in relation to article 7). With this in mind, the court finds that the current definition is formulated with the degree of precision required by the Convention and it provides sufficient guidance to individuals as to the consequences of their actions."[100]

In *Jones v Carnegie*[101] the appeal court accepted that the actions taken against the accused were indeed an interference with their Convention rights, but held that the prosecutions were based on the provisos in Arts 10(2) and 11(2), and the convictions were accordingly upheld; the rights to freedom of expression and freedom of assembly do not entitle protestors to commit a breach of the peace.

3.19　　Nevertheless, some older cases in which the accused's exercise of freedom of expression was held to be a breach of the peace may no longer be illustrative of the approach the courts are likely to take in future. Christie suggested that "to attend a meeting called for the support of a certain objective with the intention of vigorously opposing that objective may result in a charge of breach of the peace"[102] but conceded that the circumstances had to be "special",

---

[99] (App no 39013/02) (2003) 37 EHRR CD 86. See also *Jones v Carnegie* 2004 SCCR 361 in which the *Lucas* case is described at paras [3] and [12], and in the commentary at 377–383.

[100] (2003) 37 EHRR CD 86 at 89. For a discussion of the case, see: "Police Powers: Arrest of Anti Nuclear Demonstrators for 'Breach of the Peace' in Scotland" (2003) 4 *EHRLR* 464.

[101] 2004 JC 136; 2004 SLT 609; 2004 SCCR 361.

[102] Christie, para 2.54.

and cited the case of *Sleigh and Russell* v *Moxey* (1850) in support of this.[103] The renewed emphasis on freedom of expression following the incorporation of the ECHR suggests that the circumstances would have to be special indeed before opposition of this nature would be regarded as a breach of the peace; the mere fact that the accused "were out of sympathy with their audience" is likely to be insufficient.[104] In *Duffield* v *Skeen*[105] (1981) the two accused had shouted pro-IRA slogans such as: "Support your IRA", "Hands off Ireland", and "Brits out of Ireland", outside Celtic Park football stadium. The trial judge based the conviction on the fact that while a "small section of Celtic supporters" were "sympathetic with the sentiments of the slogans", a "large section" were "disgusted" by this. Similarly, in *Alexander* v *Smith*[106] (1984) the appellant had attempted to sell *Bulldog,* a newspaper of the National Front political party, to football supporters as they made their way to Tynecastle football ground. The police witnesses testified that some of the crowd "seemed incensed" by the appellant's behaviour. The appeal court upheld the conviction without delivering a formal opinion. It seems unlikely, and certainly undesirable, that the court would give so little consideration to the potential human rights issues in a future case such as this.

Indeed, that the appeal court is mindful of the need to take account of Convention rights is illustrated by *Dyer* v *Brady*[107] (2006) in which the accused were charged with breach of the peace by chaining themselves together as part of a peaceful protest during a G8 summit.[108] The sheriff had sustained a submission that there was no case to answer, and this was upheld by the appeal court, since there was "no evidence of anyone being alarmed or distressed" by the accused's "very low key protest" which was "at all times peaceful".[109] Prior to *Smith* v *Donnelly*, there is little doubt that this type of behaviour could have been successfully prosecuted as a breach of the peace. This approach cannot, however, be taken too far: in *Quinan* v *Carnegie*[110] (2005)

3.20

---

[103] (1850) J Shaw 369.

[104] Christie, para 2.54.

[105] 1981 SCCR 66. The case is discussed also at section 2.5 above.

[106] 1984 SLT 176.

[107] [2006] HCJAC 72; 2006 SLT 965; 2006 SCCR 629; 2006 GWD 31-664. See section 3.7 above.

[108] The G8 or "Group of 8" is an informal forum for governments of eight industrialised nations, namely the UK, USA, Russia, Japan, Italy, Germany, France and Canada. They hold an annual 3-day meeting, and this was held in Gleneagles, Perthshire, Scotland in 2005.

[109] 2006 SLT 965 at para [19].

[110] [2005] HCJAC 24; 2005 1 JC 279; 2005 SLT 707; 2005 SCCR 267; 2005 GWD 22-394.

the appellant was an MSP who was convicted of breach of the peace when he sat on the roadway outside Faslane Naval Base, obstructed the traffic and refused to desist. He argued that his status as an elected representative meant that interference with his right to freedom of expression by the imposition of a criminal sanction could only be justified if this was necessary in a democratic society and proportionate, as required by Art 10(2). However, the appeal court held that there was no basis on which to find that it was disproportionate to apply the law to the appellant in the same way as to other members of the public.

A NARROWER DEFINITION

3.21 It is clear that the renewed emphasis on Convention rights raises a question mark over whether some types of behaviour would now be regarded as breaches of the peace, even where these behaviours were frequently prosecuted as such, prior to *Smith* v *Donnelly*. Thus, for example, playing football in the street at night[111] or urinating in public[112] may be unlikely to provoke the required "serious disturbance". In *Borwick* v *Urquhart*[113] (2003) the charge libelled that the accused had used a video camera to film a 13-year-old girl who was unconscious (due to having consumed alcohol supplied by the accused):

> "... when she had vomited and urinated over herself and thereafter [did] show said film to other persons and did thereby put her and her family in a state of embarrassment and distress ...".

There seems little doubt that this would have been a breach of the peace pre-*Smith* v *Donnelly*, but Borwick's appeal against conviction was upheld, Lord Coulsfield stating shortly:

> "As the charge narrates, the appellant videoed the girl in a drunken and distressed state. The charge itself however only states that this conduct was to the distress and embarrassment of the girl and her family. The sheriff's findings show that he accepted a Crown submission that the breach of the peace lay in the taking of the video, not in the later showing of it, but his findings do not go beyond holding that one of the other girls at the party was upset and that [the complainer] herself was angry and embarrassed when she understood what had happened. In the light of the decision of this court in *Smith* v *Donnelly* it is clear that these findings do not justify a conviction for breach of the peace. The sheriff very rightly regarded the appellant's conduct as highly

---

[111] See *Cameron* v *Normand* 1992 SCCR 866.
[112] See *Hepburn* v *Howdle* 1998 JC 204; 1998 SLT 808; 1998 SCCR 363; 1998 GWD 8-141.
[113] 2003 SCCR 243.

reprehensible but that is not, it is now clear, sufficient for a conviction on this charge."[114]

He did not expand on what was lacking in this case; it may have been that causing distress and embarrassment is an insufficient basis for breach of the peace, or that there needed to be at least the potential for the wider public to be disturbed by the accused's behaviour. In *Lindsay* v *HM Advocate*[115] (2005) the sheriff had defined breach of the peace for the jury as:

"creating a disturbance of some kind, behaving in such a way as might reasonably be expected to cause an ordinary person to be alarmed, upset or annoyed or tempted to provoke a disturbance of the peace".[116]

The appeal court held that the sheriff had "referred to too low a test. It is not enough, for example, to point to conduct which is simply annoying".[117] Interestingly, the court also referred to the possibility that some forms of conduct could be "too trivial to be dignified as breach of the peace".[118]

CAUSING DISTURBANCE

The case of *Gherhardt* v *Lord Advocate*[119] (2010) involved an **3.22** extradition request from Romania. The "double criminality" rule requires that the conduct to be prosecuted in the requesting country must also constitute a criminal offence in the country being asked to extradite an accused, and each charge must be considered separately for this purpose. Gherhardt had been convicted in absence by a Romanian court of four charges, the third of which libelled that he had "illegally entered into the residence of the [complainers] ... refusing to leave at their request".[120] It is likely that this would have constituted a breach of the peace under Scots law in the era before *Smith* v *Donnelly*. However, according to the appeal court:

---

[114] 2003 SCCR 243 at para [13].

[115] [2005] HCJAC 66; 2005 1 JC 332; 2005 SCCR 515.

[116] 2005 SCCR 515, quoted at para [18].

[117] *Ibid* at para [20]. Compare *Gallocher* v *Weir and Patrick* (1902) 4 F (J) 93; (1902) 10 SLT 215 in which the charge libelled that the accused's behaviour "did ... annoy the lieges ...".

[118] 2005 SCCR 515. The appeal court held, however, that the misdirection had not resulted in a miscarriage of justice.

[119] [2010] HCJAC 35; 2010 JC 208; 2010 SLT 1010; 2010 SCL 943; 2010 SCCR 572; 2010 GWD 15-291.

[120] A breach of Art 192, para 2 of the Romanian Criminal Code. The accused had been sentenced to 4 years' imprisonment in respect of this charge.

"We do not agree with the sheriff's view that such conduct constitutes a breach of the peace. That view appears to involve the proposition that any trespass on private property accompanied by a refusal to leave when requested to do so constitutes a breach of the peace. In our opinion it is clear that the crime of breach of the peace requires the presence of an element of disturbance to the public peace ...".[121]

As we have seen, the courts frequently emphasise that behaviour can constitute a breach of the peace if it is "likely to cause" a disturbance to the public peace, rather than actually causing a disturbance. Many cases fall into the former category but *Gifford* v *HM Advocate*[122] (2011) is a rare exception to this. The two appellants and seven others had engaged in a protest on an airport runway. They had built a structure out of metal fencing on a taxiway of an airport, locked themselves to it and refused to leave. The airport had to be closed. The appeal court noted:

"Airline passengers and oil workers were consequently deprived of their flights or delayed, causing stress, anxiety and anger. Some 500–600 passengers were delayed within the terminal building. Some passengers shouted at airport staff; some were reduced to tears."[123]

Thus the accused's behaviour caused an actual disturbance, rather than merely being likely to cause such a disturbance. Relying on both *Harris* cases, one ground of appeal put forward by the appellants was that the sheriff ought to have upheld the defence submission that there was "no case to answer", on the basis that since the protest could not be seen by members of the public, "the conduct in question occurred in private and there was no realistic risk of it being discovered".[124] This argument was given short shrift by the appeal court, which held that the authorities cited by the appellants were

"not in point. They were concerned with situations in which the conduct in question did not cause or threaten disturbance to the public peace. In the present case, there was ample evidence of disturbance to the public peace. The fact that the persons whose conduct caused that disturbance were not visible to the general public is of no consequence".[125]

The appellants also argued that the sheriff had failed to direct the jury appropriately, since he ought to have instructed them to

---

[121] [2010] JC 208, para [11], per Lord Eassie.
[122] [2011] HCJAC 101; 2012 SCL 267; 2011 SCCR 751; 2011 GWD 36-741.
[123] 2012 SCL 267 at 270, para [3], per Lord Reed.
[124] *Ibid* at 271, para [9].
[125] *Ibid* at 271, para [10].

consider whether categorising certain conduct as a breach of the peace would violate the accused's Convention rights, in particular Arts 10 and 11. Again, this point was dealt with in short compass by the appeal court. Referring to *Jones* v *Carnegie*[126] and *Quinan* v *Carnegie*[127] the court held:

> "According to the consistent case law of this court the Convention rights to freedom of expression and freedom of assembly do not entitle protestors to commit a breach of the peace ...".[128]

MENS REA

Although the appellant in *Smith* v *Donnelly* argued that the *mens rea* required for breach of the peace was uncertain, this was not addressed by the appeal court, and there is no mention of *mens rea* in Lord Coulsfield's revised definition. Jones and Christie note that the *mens rea* of breach of the peace "has never been determined in any reported case"[129] and that it is "uncertain" what it might be.[130] They conclude that since breach of the peace is a common law crime, "it must be assumed that strict liability ... is not applicable ...".[131] Gane, Stoddart and Chalmers likewise note that its *mens rea* "has only rarely been considered, and at times the offence appears to be almost one of strict liability",[132] while Gordon suggests that "some degree of negligence" may suffice.[133] In practice, the courts find that if a reasonable person would have realised that certain behaviour was likely to result in a breach of the peace, then the accused ought to have foreseen this possibility. Thus in *Ralston* v *HM Advocate*[134] (1989) a prisoner who had engaged in a protest on the roof of his prison claimed that he lacked *mens rea*: he had not intended to breach the peace but merely to draw attention to conditions in the prison. The appeal court affirmed that so long as his conduct was deliberate, and was in fact likely to cause a disturbance, that was

3.23

---

[126] 2004 JC 136; 2004 SLT 609; 2004 SCCR 361, discussed at section 3.5 above.
[127] [2005] HCJAC 24; 2005 1 JC 279; 2005 SLT 707; 2005 SCCR 267; 2005 GWD 22-394, discussed at section 3.20 above.
[128] 2012 SCL 267 at 272, para [15].
[129] T H G Jones and M G A Christie, *Criminal Law* (2012) at para 12.17.
[130] *Ibid*. See also M G A Christie, *Breach of the Peace* (1990) where the author concluded that even if there was some authority suggesting that breach of the peace required *mens rea*, it was "completely uncertain what form that *mens rea* should take" (at para 2.28).
[131] Jones and Christie (n 129 above).
[132] C H W Gane, C N Stoddart and J Chalmers, *A Casebook on Scottish Criminal Law* (4th edn, 2009), para 16.07.
[133] Gordon (2001), para 41.09.
[134] 1989 SLT 474; 1988 SCCR 590.

sufficient. In *Butcher* v *Jessop*[135] (1989) the appeal court agreed with
the Crown's contention that there was:

> "[N]o need to infer that an accused intended to commit a breach of the peace;
> it was enough that his actions were such that the court of first instance was
> entitled to regard them objectively as constituting a breach of the peace."[136]

That the courts do not look too closely for *mens rea* in cases
involving breach of the peace has a long history: in *Deakin* v *Milne*[137]
(1882) the fact that members of the Salvation Army had no intention
of disturbing the peace as a result of parading through the streets
was irrelevant to their liability, since they knew that the parade was
likely to provoke a counter-demonstration. Lack of nefarious intent
may, however, lead to a lesser sentence: in *Buttercase* v *Russell*[138]
(1999) the appellant had fired a blank cartridge from a shotgun over
the head of a police officer, in the belief that he was protecting his
property from thieves. The appeal court halved the number of hours
of community service imposed by the sheriff for this breach of the
peace, noting that the appellant had no malicious intent.

3.24   One of the very few cases to have explicitly addressed *mens rea* is
Hughes v *Crowe*[139] (1993). The accused had played loud music and
made loud banging noises in his flat early on a Saturday morning,
causing considerable disturbance to the occupants of the flat below.
Commenting on this case, Gordon pointed out: "Although the court
say that *mens rea* is necessary for breach of the peace, they do not
say what *mens rea* is."[140] The court seems to have taken the view that
the accused must have been aware that his behaviour, at that time
on a weekend, would adversely affect his neighbours. There was,
however, no evidence that the accused actually knew that the other
flat was occupied. This seems to suggest that objective recklessness,
or perhaps merely negligence, is all that is required; he ought to have
been aware of the likely effects of his behaviour, therefore is treated
as if he acted with that knowledge.[141] It is rare for the Crown to

---

[135] 1989 JC 55; 1989 SLT 593; 1989 SCCR 119. See also section 2.8 above.

[136] 1989 SCCR 119 at 129, per LJ-C Ross. He later stated (at 130): "what the sheriff
had to do ... was to determine whether the actings complained of were deliberate,
and, if so, whether they amounted to breach of the peace ...". See also *McKenzie* v
Normand 1992 SLT 130; 1992 SCCR 14.

[137] (1882) 5 Coup 174; (1882) 10 R (J) 22.

[138] 1999 GWD 21–992.

[139] 1993 SCCR 320.

[140] *Ibid* at 324. That there is a *mens rea* requirement for breach of the peace is also
clear from the case of *Ross* v *HM Advocate* 1991 JC 210; 1991 SLT 564; 1991
SCCR 823, which established that those in a state of automatism lack *mens rea*. The
case is discussed briefly at section 3.40 below.

[141] For a critique of the courts' approach to *mens rea*, see section 6.2 below.

specify that an accused intended to cause a disturbance.[142] Stephen Gough, the so-called "Naked Rambler", has spent more than 6 years in prison as a result of multiple prosecutions, mainly for breach of the peace, for walking naked in Scotland.[143] The precise wording of the complaint in a recent trial has not been reported, however in a newspaper account of the case a Crown Office spokesman is quoted as saying:

> "Mr Gough *intentionally caused shock and alarm* to children and their parents. The evidence in this case clearly established that despite repeated police requests not to do so, he was determined to deliberately walk naked past a busy children's play-park in Fife. He *knew that in doing so he would provoke anger and upset*."[144]

Gough's repeated prosecution is highly controversial,[145] and it is clear from these comments that Crown Office is well aware of this controversy.

MOTIVE AND UNDERLYING INTENT

Evidence of a good motive, or that the accused lacked a bad motive, **3.25** is generally not relevant to liability.[146] Thus in declaring, *obiter*, that it would be a breach of the peace to run the wrong way on an escalator, crowded with people, the appeal court did not distinguish between a person "acting out of high spirits or to escape the police or just for bravado".[147] The irrelevance of motive is clear from *Ralston* (above), and also from *Palazzo* v *Copeland*[148] (1976), in which the

---

[142] See, however, the discussion at section 3.31 below.

[143] For a recent prosecution, see "Naked rambler Stephen Gough jailed for five months", *BBC News*, 13 September 2012, available at: http://www.bbc.co.uk/news/uk-scotland-edinburgh-east-fife-19585483.

[144] *Ibid* (emphases added). His case is discussed further at sections 6.28–6.29 below.

[145] See S Brocklehurst, "Naked Rambler: the UK's oddest legal stand-off", *BBC News*, 5 October 2012, available at http://www.bbc.co.uk/news/magazine-19625542. He was released from jail in October 2012, but by December 2012 was facing prosecution in Oxford Crown Court: see "Rambler Stephen Gough wants to stand trial naked", *BBC News*, 13 December 2012, available at: http://www.bbc.co.uk/news/uk-england-20714088.

[146] It should be noted, however, that some statutory provisions now require evidence of particular motivations to be established. See, eg, the Criminal Law (Consolidation) (Scotland) Act 1995, s 50A, discussed further at section 4.2 below.

[147] *Harris* v *HM Advocate* 1993 JC 150 at 160; 1993 SCCR 559 at 570. See also *Woods* v *Normand* 1992 SCCR 805: "Even if one assumes that the appellant had good motives ... what he and his companions indulged in went far beyond what was justified by the circumstances and was of such a nature as to constitute a breach of the peace" (*ibid* at 807 per LJ-C Ross).

[148] 1976 JC 52.

accused fired a shotgun out of his window in order to prevent some youths from further disturbing the peace. Lord Justice-General Emslie held that "the fact that the appellant's motive was the sound one of trying to stop a breach of the peace is irrelevant".[149] Mention has already been made of *Deakin v Milne*.[150] The Lord Justice-Clerk was at pains to point out:

> "In the opinion which I have formed in this case I do not desire to say anything that could for a moment be considered to reflect on the motives or objects of the persons whose conduct has here been brought in question [ie members of the Salvation Army]. I believe that many of them are respectable persons, who are sincere in the work that they have undertaken, and that many of the opinions that they promote are laudable. With that matter, however, we have nothing to do. The question relates to the preservation of the order and peace of the burgh."[151]

Lord Craighill added:

> "However much the purity of motives, or however strong the desire to do good, it is not a right thing that the results, however laudable and good, should be attained by means leading to such evils. When these persons saw that the first result of their proceedings was to bring about almost with certainty a breach of the public peace they should have desisted."[152]

In *Stewart v Lockhart*[153] (1990) the (male) accused was convicted of breach of the peace for dressing in women's clothing near the "red light" district of Aberdeen. The justice noted:

> "There was certainly no evidence that the appellant was in the area for any unlawful or dishonest purpose but I did not consider that the appellant's intention was relevant and in this I had regard to the case of *Ralston v HM Advocate*. It was the appellant's intention to appear to be female whatever his purpose or motive."[154]

3.26   In the context of motive, Christie discussed the case of *Shannon v Skeen*[155] (1977) in which two private detectives, hired to check how often employees of a vending machine company serviced and emptied its machines, were charged with a breach of the peace. The complaint libelled that the accused had persistently followed a female employee while she drove to various machines, collecting

---

[149] 1976 JC 52 at 53. See also *Donaghy v Tudhope* 1985 SCCR 118.
[150] (1882) 5 Coup 174; (1882) 10 R (J) 22. See section 3.23 above.
[151] (1882) 10 R (J) 22 at 26.
[152] *Ibid* at 27–28.
[153] 1991 SLT 835; 1990 SCCR 390. See section 2.5 above.
[154] 1990 SCCR 390 at 391.
[155] 1977 SCCR Supp 180.

money. The sheriff found as a fact that the complainer had been "very alarmed" and "was frightened that she was going to be robbed". He also noted that "this was a very natural fear, and must have been obvious" to the accused.[156] The appeal court found the charge to be a relevant one, thus the only question was "whether in the circumstances proved and demonstrated by the findings in fact guilt of breach of the peace was made out". In a very short judgment it held:

> "Without going into the question in any greater detail in this case we are satisfied that the findings in fact do not contain sufficient material to have justified a conviction of breach of the peace ...".[157]

Christie has suggested that this must have been due to the fact that, as *bona fide* detectives, their motive in behaving as they did meant that they could not be guilty of breaching the peace.[158] This seems rather an odd explanation, since the accused's behaviour in persistently following the employee was intentional, and the sheriff was clear that they must have appreciated the effect their behaviour was having. It is, however, difficult to come up with anything more plausible, since the appeal court's decision is so brief. Whether the decision reached in that case was the correct one is highly doubtful.

In *HM Advocate v Carson*[159] (1997) the appeal court noted, **3.27** without comment, that "it was accepted on behalf of the Crown that intention or motive was irrelevant to a charge of breach of the peace",[160] but this must mean only that there is no *requirement* for the Crown to show either intention to breach the peace, or a reprehensible motive. A bad motive or nefarious underlying intent may, however, merit an increased sentence,[161] and legislation has now provided that certain types of bad motives, such as those based on racial or religious prejudice, merit increased punishment.[162] It was noted earlier that a charge of breach of the peace may be included

---

[156] 1977 SCCR Supp 180 at 181.

[157] *Ibid* at 182.

[158] Christie, para 2.30.

[159] 1997 SLT 1119; 1997 SCCR 273; 1997 GWD 12-498.

[160] 1997 SCCR 273 at 274, per Lord Prosser.

[161] Christie cited the case of *MacGivern v Jessop* 1988 SCCR 511 in support of the suggestion that a bad motive serves as an aggravation (para 2.71). See section 1.3 above.

[162] See the Crime and Disorder Act 1998, s 96(2) (offence motivated by racial prejudice) and the Criminal Justice (Scotland) Act 2003, s 74(2) (offence motivated by religious prejudice). Offences motivated by prejudice based on a victim's sexual orientation, transgender identity or disability are treated as aggravated by virtue of the Offences (Aggravation by Prejudice) (Scotland) Act 2009. These provisions are discussed further at section 3.32 below.

by the Crown in order to demonstrate motive in relation to other crimes charged on the same complaint or indictment.[163] In contrast, in *McKendrick* v *HM Advocate*[164] (1999) the third charge – assault with intent to rape – explained a possible motivation for the first charge – breach of the peace by threatening a different female complainer with violence and trying to force his way into her house. In similar vein, in a case involving abduction and assault, the appeal court remarked, albeit *obiter*:

> "One can figure cases where a comparatively minor breach of the peace might lead to a sentence of life imprisonment where the breach of the peace is simply a symptom of a much more serious underlying state of affairs."[165]

An example of this is *LBM* v *HM Advocate*[166] (2011) in which the accused had engaged two schoolgirls aged 10 and 11 in conversation and asked if he could tickle their legs. He tried to entice them into a car. In the course of an interview with a social worker who was compiling a social enquiry report for the court, the appellant described himself as a "recovering paedophile". There were no previous convictions libelled against him, but he volunteered that he had engaged in similar conduct on two occasions in the 1990s, had begun grooming young girls in internet chat rooms since 2000 in order to commit sexual offences, and had been frequenting an area near a primary school with that intention. In imposing an Order for Lifelong Restriction on the appellant, the appeal court emphasised the motivations of the accused in carrying out this breach of the peace.[167]

3.28   We noted earlier that that the appeal court had ruled in *HM Advocate* v *Forbes*[168] (1994) that it was not competent for the Crown to include details of acts which the accused had not yet committed, but which it was alleged that he or she was intending to commit, as part of the libel for breach of the peace. Despite this decision, the Crown has made further attempts to include aspects of an accused's

---

[163] At section 1.4 above.

[164] 1999 SCCR 33.

[165] *Robertson* v *HM Advocate* 1997 SCCR 534 at 541, per Lord Sutherland.

[166] [2011] HCJAC 96; 2012 SLT 147; 2012 SCL 74; 2011 GWD 34-715.

[167] An Order for Lifelong Restriction (OLR) may be imposed by the High Court where someone is convicted of an offence involving serious violence or a sexual offence, or (as was the case here) where the court determines that there was a "significant sexual aspect" to the offender's behaviour in committing the offence (Criminal Procedure (Scotland) Act 1995, s 210A(10)). A sheriff can remit a case to the High Court if satisfied that an offender presents a substantial and continuing risk to public safety. The OLR provides for lifelong supervision. See s 210F of the 1995 Act.

[168] 1994 JC 71; 1994 SCCR 163, discussed at section 2.9 above.

underlying intentions in the narrative of the charge. As previously noted,[169] in *HM Advocate* v *Greig*[170] (2005) the charge libelled

"having been placed on the sex offenders register for life ... for offences of lewd and libidinous practices against young children, [you] did conduct yourself in a disorderly manner and knowing that there was likely to be a large number of children at a fireworks display there, dress yourself in such a manner as to be easily mistaken for a steward or first aid officer, position yourself adjacent to all the public facilities there, place a police officer who was in attendance at said event, to whom you are known and who was aware of the conviction aforesaid, in a state of fear and alarm for the safety of children and the public and did commit a breach of the peace".[171]

Sheriff Davidson reserved judgment as to whether this breached s 101 of the Criminal Procedure (Scotland) Act 1995, which prohibits references being made to an accused's previous convictions before the return of the verdict, unless this is competent "in support of a substantive charge".[172] However, he held that it was not a relevant charge of breach of the peace:

"Going to a fireworks display in a public park, dressing oneself in a manner as to be easily mistaken for a steward or first aid officer and standing near the toilets, which seems to me to be the specification of the overt conduct said to comprise this breach of the peace, does not in my opinion meet the requirements of being 'flagrant' on the hypothesis that, apart from the police officer with his special knowledge, no ordinary reasonable person was actually alarmed, nor does it appear to me to be conduct which presents as genuinely alarming and disturbing in its context to any reasonable person, if one excludes from that reasonable person the background knowledge possessed by the particular police officer."[173]

One can contrast this with the approach taken in *Angus* v *Nisbet*[174] (2010). It may be recalled that the appellant in that case had passed a piece of paper to a 14-year-old girl who delivered his newspapers, asking her to keep in touch with him, and providing his mobile phone number. In *Greig* the public's lack of knowledge about the appellant's previous convictions meant that there was nothing

---

[169] See section 3.3 above.

[170] 2005 SCCR 465.

[171] The reference to the police officer being placed "in a state of fear and alarm for the safety of children and the public" is an interesting one: it raises the issue of whether causing vicarious fear and alarm may suffice for a breach of the peace. I am indebted to Robin White for pointing this out.

[172] Criminal Procedure (Scotland) Act 1995, s 101(2).

[173] 2005 SCCR 465 at 471–472. For a critique of the use of the term "flagrant", see section 6.7 below.

[174] 2011 SC (JC) 69; [2010] HCJAC 76; 2010 SCCR 873. See section 3.13 above.

overtly disturbing about his behaviour, hence there was no breach of the peace. In *Angus* v *Nisbet* the appeal court noted that there was

> "nothing on the face of the interaction between the appellant and [the complainer], which, if it had been observed and overheard by a third party standing in the street, was in any way alarming or disturbing".[175]

Nevertheless, the court held that this, of itself, was not conclusive:

> "Such a notional third party would not be apprised of all the information giving the interaction its context, including the fact that [the complainer] and the appellant were effectively strangers one to the other, and, as Lord Coulsfield explained [in *Smith* v *Donnelly*], conduct has to be seen in its context. Agreeing, as we see it, with the approach of the sheriff, we regard it as necessary ... to assume that the notional reasonable person should be taken as being aware of the whole circumstances."[176]

It therefore had to be assumed that the "notional reasonable person" would have been aware of the contents of the note.

3.29   The Crown abandoned its appeal in *Greig*, but again included future intentions – and a previous conviction – as part of the narrative in *HM Advocate* v *Murray*[177] (2007). The first charge libelled:

> "... having been convicted after trial on a charge of assault to severe injury and danger of life, having assaulted a 13-year-old boy by striking him with a hammer and burying him in a shallow grave and having been sentenced to eight years detention in a young offender's institute [*sic*] ... [you did] ... conduct yourself in a disorderly manner, state to [a social worker] ... that you had been recently in possession of a hammer while behaving in a manner which may lead police officers to search you and with the intention of assaulting said police officers with said hammer, display a hammer to him and thereafter threaten to sexually assault and murder a child, further state that while in an area in Falkirk to the prosecutor unknown, you had seen a boy of 11–12 years whom you considered to be a possible victim and that said crime would be committed at a distance from your home, that you would dig the grave deep and in doing this you would avoid detection and prosecution for said crime and you did place said [social worker] in a state of fear and alarm for the safety of the lieges and you did commit a breach of the peace".

The second charge was in broadly similar terms, referring this time to alarming two social workers. The sheriff at first instance upheld a challenge to these charges on the basis that they breached s 101. He held that the revelation of the conviction in the context of the charges would be "grossly prejudicial" to the accused and that

---

[175] 2011 SC (JC) 69 at 72, para [15], per Lord Brodie.
[176] *Ibid* at 72–73, para [15].
[177] 2007 SCCR 271. This charge was referred to in section 3.3 above.

such prejudice "could not be cured by any direction of law".[178] Commenting on the case, Gordon doubted whether the facts libelled amounted to a breach of the peace at all:

> "The criminal law is not intended to inhibit probationers from telling their social workers about their fantasies and/or fears about what they may do … and the whole matter seems to have been one for medical or social work intervention, rather than for the criminal law. The charge is somewhat of a throwback to the earlier view that if something happens which causes concern or should not have happened, it must be a crime, and if one cannot think of any other crime which suits the situation it must have been a breach of the peace."[179]

The facts of *Murray* are rather similar to those in the case of *Macdonald* v *HM Advocate*,[180] (2008) decided nearly 7 months later. As previously noted,[181] the accused in that case had been convicted of sexually assaulting a child and was charged with two breaches of the peace which libelled that he had alarmed a psychologist by telling her that he intended to commit a sexually violent crime. The appeal court held that the charges were not competent ones, since "the context of the interview does not lend itself to the definitions of breach of the peace".[182] This reflects the approach taken by Gordon in his commentary on *Murray*.

ART AND PART LIABILITY

Breach of the peace can be charged on an art and part basis where 3.30 the accused engaged in behaviour which was part of a prior plan involving two or more accused, or was a reasonably foreseeable consequence of the plan. It need not have been part of the plan that a breach of the peace be occasioned, but there must have been agreement to engage in the behaviour in question. In *MacNeill* v *Robertson*[183] (1982) the trial judge stated that

> "responsibility for the acts of others only arises if it is proved affirmatively that there was a common plan and that the accused was a party to the common plan. I am satisfied that a person may be guilty of breach of the peace, art and part, in accordance with that basic principle".[184]

---

[178] 2007 SCCR 271 at para [34]. The Crown appeal was abandoned. For a commentary on the case, see A D Vannet, "Disclosure of previous convictions in the charge" (2008) *Scottish Criminal Law* (March) 271.

[179] 2007 SCCR 271 at 282.

[180] [2008] HCJAC 5; 2008 JC 262; 2008 SCCR 181.

[181] See section 3.8 above.

[182] 2008 JC 262 at 263, per Lord Johnston.

[183] 1982 SCCR 468.

[184] *Ibid* at 469–470. See also *Montgomery* v *Herron* (1976) SCCR Supp 131.

A more recent example is the case of *Rooney* v *HM Advocate*[185] (2007) in which five accused were charged with murder and attempted murder, and also that they did:

> "Whilst masked and whilst acting along with others whose identities are to the prosecutor meantime unknown, conduct [themselves] in a disorderly manner, smash windows and doors there, force entry to said house, threaten violence, place [the residents of the house] in a state of fear and alarm and commit a breach of the peace."[186]

Four of the five accused were convicted of this charge. As well as specifying that a named accused was "acting along with others", it is competent for a charge to state that the accused "did form part of a disorderly crowd"[187] or "form part of a mob of evilly disposed persons".[188] Breaches of the peace involving multiple accused are not infrequent occurrences. Few, however, involve as many as *Stirling* v *Herron*[189] (1976) in which there were 65 accused, who were prosecuted in batches of five, six and seven at a time. A bill of suspension was taken by one accused on the basis that he did not receive a fair trial, since the trial judge had already convicted the first batch of accused. While the appeal court in that case gave short shrift to the argument that "justice is not seen to be done if the same judge presides over two or more trials in this anthology",[190] it may well be the case that more recent interpretations of the requirements of a "fair trial" would lead to a different result were a similar challenge to be taken in future.[191] Christie raised the issue

---

[185] [2007] HCJAC 1; 2007 SCCR 49; 2007 GWD 8-138.

[186] Similar examples include: *Brown* v *HM Advocate* 2000 SCCR 736 ("while acting with another person whose identity to the prosecutor is meantime unknown"); and *McLean* v *Buchanan* 2001 SC (PC) 1; 2001 SLT 780; [2001] HRLR 51; 2001 SCCR 475; [2001] 1 WLR 2425, in which the charge of breach of the peace narrated that the crime was committed by the two named accused "while acting with others whose identities were unknown".

[187] "Form part of a disorderly crowd" (*MacNeill* v *Robertson* 1982 SCCR 468; *Tudhope* v *Donaldson* 1983 SCCR 443; *Bradford* v *McLeod* 1985 SCCR 379; *MacGivern* v *Jessop* 1988 SCCR 511; (1988) 133 Sol Jo 211; *Hawkins* v *Carmichael* 1992 SCCR 348; *Brodie* v *HM Advocate* 1993 JC 92; 1993 SCCR 371; *Robertson* v *HM Advocate* 1996 SCCR 243). See also *Boyle* v *HM Advocate* 1993 SLT 577; 1992 SCCR 824 ("while acting along with other persons ... form part of a disorderly crowd"); *Winnik* v *Allan* 1986 SCCR 35 ("form part of a crowd of noisy and disorderly persons"); *Tait* v *Allan* 1984 SCCR 385 ("form part of a noisy and disorderly crowd of approximately 200 persons").

[188] *Kilpatrick* v *HM Advocate* 1992 JC 120.

[189] 1976 SLT (Notes) 2; but see *Tait* v *Allan* (note 187 above).

[190] 1976 SLT (Notes) 2 at 4. See also *McDevitt* v *McLeod* 1982 SCCR 282 in which the chairman of the bench of justices was present on a boat in which a breach of the peace had taken place, but the appeal court refused to quash the conviction.

[191] See ECHR, Art 6(3): the "right to a fair trial" necessitates an independent and

of whether reporters and television crews could be charged art and part if they remained during a planned breach of the peace "and by their presence gave (additional?) impetus to its implementation (or, indeed, development)".[192] The emphasis now given to freedom of expression and of assembly by Arts 10 and 11 of the ECHR suggests that, other than in extreme circumstances, the courts would be reluctant to impinge on the media's freedom to report in this way.

AGGRAVATIONS

Christie noted that breach of the peace offences may be aggravated, **3.31** either by specifying in the libel that the accused intended to commit a breach of the peace, or by other circumstances such as "the occasion of the behaviour and the susceptibility of one's audience".[193] In respect of the first of these, he cited the case of *Dougall* v *Dykes*[194] (1861) in which the complaint averred that the accused's behaviour had been "wilful and malicious". A rare modern example is the case of *Macdonald* v *HM Advocate*[195] (2008) in which both breach of the peace charges narrated that the accused's behaviour had been "for the purpose of causing fear and alarm" to the complainers.[196] Offences can now be aggravated if committed while the accused is on bail,[197] or if there was a "significant sexual aspect" in its commission. The latter process, which may lead to registration on what is commonly known as the "sex offenders' register", began with the Sex Offenders Act 1997 which made it an offence for certain categories of convicted sex offenders to fail to provide details of their names and addresses to the police, and to update this information, as required. The current provisions are contained in the

---

impartial tribunal. This has been interpreted as requiring judges to appear objective, as well as actually to be objective. See *R* v *Bow Street Metropolitan Stipendiary Magistrate, ex p Pinochet Ugarte (No 2)* [2000] 1 AC 119; [1999] 2 WLR 272: "In any case where the impartiality of a judge is in question the appearance of the matter is just as important as the reality" ([2000] 1 AC 119 at 139, per Lord Nolan).

[192] Christie, para 2.46.

[193] *Ibid*, para 2.71. He also suggested that the status of the victim could act as an aggravation (at para 2.73).

[194] (1861) 4 Irv 101.

[195] [2008] HCJAC 5; 2008 JC 262; 2008 SCCR 181.

[196] 2008 SCCR 181 at 182. The case was discussed further at section 3.8 above. See also the case of the "Naked Rambler" at section 3.24 above.

[197] By virtue of the Criminal Procedure (Scotland) Act 1995, s 27(3). For examples in relation to breach of the peace, see *Connal* v *Crowe* 1996 SCCR 716; *Halcrow* v *Shanks* [2012] HCJAC 23; 2012 SLT 579; 2012 SCL 517; 2012 GWD 8-144 (discussed at section 1.3 above). For difficulties associated with this, see *Cochrane* v *Heywood* 1998 SCCR 331.

Sexual Offences Act 2003[198] and give the court discretion to impose these requirements in crimes such as breach of the peace. This has been used in many breach of the peace convictions,[199] covering a wide variety of behaviours, including: attempting to have sexual intercourse with a bicycle;[200] displaying one's underwear in public;[201] and indecent exposure and masturbation in public.[202]

3.32   A recent case involving a breach of the peace aggravated by the context in which it occurred is *Divin* v *HM Advocate*[203] (2012). The appellants had incited a riot using Facebook. Although the appeal court reduced the sentences imposed by the sheriff, it agreed with her view that "the context in which a crime is committed is of relevance to assessing its gravity and the culpability of those involved".[204] Here, the context was that the accused had posted their Facebook messages during a time of rioting and public disorder in several English cities. Reference has already been made to the "Naked Rambler".[205] The police had adopted a new policy of allowing Gough to "go on his way" and arrest him only "if his behaviour was gratuitous".[206] However, in July 2012 he walked naked past a children's park in Dunfermline, despite repeated requests from police to choose an

---

[198] Section 80 of and Sch 3, para 60 to the 2003 Act, as amended by the Sexual Offences (Scotland) Act 2009, Sch 5, para 5(d).

[199] For recent examples, see: *Cottam* v *AB* 2010 SCCR 669; *Halcrow* v *Shanks* [2012] HCJAC 23; 2012 SLT 579; 2012 SCL 517; 2012 GWD 8-144 (discussed at section 1.3 above); *Hay* v *HM Advocate* [2012] HCJAC 28; 2012 SLT 569; 2012 SCCR 281; 2012 GWD 8-142 (discussed at section 4.11 below); and the unreported cases of *Bourouba* (2010) 107 (Oct) *Criminal Law Bulletin* 5 (in which the accused was ordered to register as a sex offender for 10 years), and *Childs* (unreported, 10 September 2009, HCJ Appeal, discussed by K Phillips in "Breach of the Peace – Significant Sexual Aspect" (2009) 102 (Dec) *Criminal Law Bulletin* 7).

[200] Case of *Robert Stewart*, Ayr Sheriff Court (unreported, 2007, but see http://news. bbc.co.uk/1/hi/scotland/glasgow_and_west/7098116.stm). This is discussed further at sections 6.16 and 6.28 below.

[201] Unreported, but see "Pink thong fetish flasher jailed", *BBC News*, 23 October 2009, available at: http://news.bbc.co.uk/1/hi/scotland/glasgow_and_west/8322441. stm. (Note that the wearer was male. The Crown's request for forfeiture of the pink thong was granted.)

[202] *McGuire* v *Dunn* [2012] HCJAC 86, 2012 GWD 23-473. It was reiterated in that case that in determining whether there was a "significant sexual aspect" a court must consider whether the sexual aspect is "important enough to merit attention as indicating an underlying sexual disorder or deviance from which society is entitled to be protected" (*Hay* v *HM Advocate* [2012] HCJAC 28, at para [52], citing *Wylie* v *M* 2009 SLT (Sh Ct) 18; 2009 SCL 223; 2008 GWD 40-605, per Sheriff Pyle at para [13]).

[203] [2012] HCJAC 81; 2012 SCL 837; 2012 GWD 19-395. See section 1.3 above.

[204] *Ibid* para [20], per Lord Mackay of Drumadoon.

[205] See section 3.24 above.

[206] S Brocklehurst, "Naked Rambler: the UK's oddest legal stand-off", *BBC News*, 5 October 2012, available at http://www.bbc.co.uk/news/magazine-19625542.

alternative route. This illustrates Christie's point about "occasion of the behaviour and the susceptibility of one's audience".[207] It has also been increasingly recognised that crime victims often experience greater harm where the accused has been motivated by some form of *animus* against a group to which that victim belongs.[208] Thus, for instance, we now have statutory aggravations which provide increased sentences for offences motivated by racial[209] or religious[210] prejudice, and these have been applied in cases involving breaches of the peace.[211] Indeed, a review of the operation of the legislation relating to religious aggravations found that in 95 per cent of such cases the accused was charged with, and found guilty of, committing a breach of the peace.[212] Offences motivated by prejudice based on a

---

[207] Christie, para 2.71.

[208] For a detailed discussion, see N Chakraborti and J Garland, *Hate Crime: Impact, Causes and Responses* (2009).

[209] Crime and Disorder Act 1998, s 96(2): "An offence is racially aggravated ... if – (a) at the time of committing the offence, or immediately before or after doing so, the offender evinces towards the victim (if any) of the offence malice and ill-will based on the victim's membership (or presumed membership) of a racial group; or (b) the offence is motivated (wholly or partly) by malice and ill-will towards members of a racial group based on their membership of that group." See also the Criminal Law (Consolidation) (Scotland) Act 1995, s 50A ("racially aggravated harassment"), discussed further at section 4.2 below.

[210] Criminal Justice (Scotland) Act 2003, s 74(2). The wording is similar to the offence aggravated by racial prejudice, discussed above.

[211] Racially aggravated: *Dyer* v *Hutchison* [2006] HCJAC 45; 2006 JC 212; 2006 SLT 657; 2006 SCCR 377; *Martin* v *Howdle (sub nom Martin* v *Bott)* [2005] HCJAC 73; 2006 JC 35; 2005 SLT 730; 2005 SCCR 554; 2005 GWD 20-357; *Anderson* v *Griffiths* 2005 1 JC 169; 2005 SLT 86; 2005 SCCR 41; 2004 GWD 38-778; *Waugh* v *HM Advocate* 2005 SLT 451; 2005 SCCR 102; 2005 GWD 10-149; *HM Advocate* v *Kelly* 2010 SCCR 86; *Cowan* v *PF Falkirk* 2003 Scot (D) 7/9; *McLean* v *Buchanan* 2001 SC (PC) 1; 2001 SLT 780; [2001] HRLR 51; 2001 SCCR 475; [2001] 1 WLR 2425; *Clark* v *HM Advocate* 2000 SCCR 736. In the second and third of these cases a breach of the peace conviction was substituted on appeal for a charge of aggravated harassment. See also "Golfer David Drysdale fined for assault in McDonalds in Edinburgh", *BBC News*, 27 November 2012, available at: http://www.bbc.co.uk/news/uk-scotland-edinburgh-east-fife-20510096. Drysdale pled guilty to assault and racially aggravated breach of the peace. For a case of breach of the peace aggravated by religious prejudice, see *Dyer* v *Von and Hume* [2008] HCJAC 9; 2008 SCCR 265. For breach of the peace aggravated by both racial and religious prejudice, see *Walls* v *Brown* [2009] HCJAC 59; 2009 JC 375; 2009 SLT 774; 2009 SCL 973; 2009 SCCR 711; 2009 GWD 23-370; and: "Six charged with breach of the peace over antisemitic website", 16 May 2012, available at: http://local.stv.tv/glasgow/100111-six-charged-with-breach-of-the-peace-after-anti-semitic-website-discovered/3.

[212] K Doyle, *Use of Section 74 of the Criminal Justice (Scotland) Act 2003 – Religiously Aggravated Reported Crime: An 18 Month Review* (Scottish Executive Social Research, 2006), para 3.2. This is available at: http://www.scotland.gov.uk/Publications/2006/11/24133659/0.

victim's sexual orientation, transgender identity or disability are also treated as aggravated.[213]

ATTEMPTED BREACH OF THE PEACE

3.33   Christie considered this and concluded that "the way in which breach of the peace is defined leaves no scope for attempt".[214] He cited in support of this *Montgomery* v *McLeod*[215] (1977) in which a disturbance in a car park led the police to order a crowd of youths to disperse. One youth refused to leave and was arrested for breach of the peace on the basis that his behaviour might encourage the others to return to the scene. As Christie noted, if there was a crime of attempted breach of the peace "then surely the circumstances of this case afforded a realistic opportunity for its use",[216] yet the accused was convicted of the completed crime. Under the revised definition provided in *Smith* v *Donnelly*, it remains the case that "attempted breach of the peace" is not a possible charge: since there need not be actual alarm or disturbance but merely the potential to cause such alarm or disturbance, it seems that to "attempt to commit" a breach of the peace *is to* commit a breach of the peace. If it were to be shown that a number of accused had planned to cause a public disorder (for example, by expressing their intention to abseil from the roof of the Scottish Parliament), but had not implemented their plan, this could be charged as a conspiracy to commit a breach of the peace. But of course, as with all criminal conspiracies, this requires agreement between two or more individuals, thus expression of a similar plan on the part of one person alone would not be an offence at all. The breach of the peace in *Harvie* v *Harman*[217] (2010) involved an art student who sent a letter to a gallery informing them that he had selected the gallery for a project, entitled "brick", which involved him throwing something through the gallery window. He thereafter threw a pole through the window, and showed a recording of this incident at another gallery. Had he been apprehended following the writing of the letter, but before the damaging of the window, it is unlikely that he could have been convicted of breach of the peace

---

[213] By virtue of the Offences (Aggravation by Prejudice) (Scotland) Act 2009, s 1 (disability); and s 2 (sexual orientation and transgender identity). These provisions mirror the wording used in relation to racially aggravated offences: see n 209 above. See "Derek Riordan fined for homophobic abuse of Edinburgh bouncers", *BBC News*, 23 November 2012, available at: http://www.bbc.co.uk/news/uk-scotland-edinburgh-east-fife-20461818.
[214] Christie, para 2.47.
[215] 1977 SLT (Notes) 77; (1977) SCCR Supp 164.
[216] Christie, para 2.47.
[217] 2010 GWD 1-3.

– unless, of course, the sending of the letter in itself was judged sufficient to cause a "public disturbance". Given the decision in the first *Harris* case, this is now open to question.[218]

DEFENCES

Most defences, such as alibi,[219] non-age,[220] mental disorder[221] and coercion/necessity,[222] apply to breach of the peace as to other crimes, and raise no specific issues.[223] A few words are, however, required in respect of some other defences.

3.34

Factual errors

It has been suggested that it is incorrect to refer to error as a defence, since "it is merely an application of the rule that the prosecution must prove all the relevant elements of the offence".[224] In practice, an error of fact will only exculpate if it has affected the accused's *mens rea* and is both genuine and reasonable. Christie suggested that the type of error which might provide a defence could be the giving of a Nazi-style salute or a "pro-Hitler" speech to an audience of Jewish people, mistakenly believed by the accused to be members of the National Front,[225] but he conceded that this is doubtful. A moment's reflection suggests that many of those convicted of breach of the peace were in error as to the likelihood that their behaviour might cause alarm to others. Mention has already been made of *Duffield* v *Skeen*[226] (1981) in which the two accused shouted pro-IRA slogans

3.35

---

[218] *Harris* v *HM Advocate* [2009] HCJAC 80; 2010 JC 245; 2009 SLT 1078; 2010 SCL 56; 2010 SCCR 15, discussed at section 3.11 above. The student could have been prosecuted for a breach of the Criminal Justice and Licensing (Scotland) Act 2010, s 38. See section 4.8 below.

[219] For cases in which alibis were tendered in relation to charges of breach of the peace, see *Anderson* v *HM Advocate* 1974 SLT 239 and *Benson* v *Tudhope* 1986 JC 107; 1987 SLT 312; 1986 SCCR 422. See also *Winter* v *HM Advocate* 2002 SCCR 720; 2002 GWD 19-621.

[220] See now the Criminal Procedure (Scotland) Act 1995, s 41A, as inserted by the Criminal Justice and Licensing (Scotland) Act 2010, s 52, which prohibits the prosecution of any child under the age of 12.

[221] Previously referred to as "insanity": see the Criminal Procedure (Scotland) Act 1995, s 51A, as inserted by the Criminal Justice and Licensing (Scotland) Act 2010, s 168. See also the case of *Smith* v *M* 1984 SLT (Sh Ct) 28; 1983 SCCR 67.

[222] Christie discussed coercion as a defence to breach of the peace, at para 2.82.

[223] For a detailed discussion of defences, see J Chalmers and F Leverick, *Criminal Defences and Pleas in Bar of Trial* (2006).

[224] P Charleton, P A McDermott and M Bolger, *Criminal Law* (1999), para 18.01. See also P H Robinson, *Structure and Function in Criminal Law* (1997), pp 68–69.

[225] Christie, para 2.85.

[226] 1981 SCCR 66, discussed at section 3.19 above.

outside Celtic Football Park. The sheriff summarised their defence as being that they

> "were expressing political views to people who they expected would share their views. The appellant Duffield accepted he would be unlikely to try and sell this newspaper and shout these slogans outside, say, Ibrox Park. However, he said, 'I don't think it would offend people attending Celtic Park. A lot of people attending Celtic Park seem to have some support for the republican movement in Ireland.'"[227]

It may be, then, that the accused made an error as to the likely reception they would receive from the fans, but this did not prevent their convictions from being upheld. In *Buttercase* v *Russell*[228] (1999) the appellant had fired a shotgun over the head of a police officer. The report of the case is very brief, but it seems that he may have believed that he was protecting his property from thieves. This error did not prevent his behaviour from being a breach of the peace, but may have contributed to the reduction in sentence by the appeal court.

Errors of law

3.36   Christie cited *HM Advocate* v *Gollan*[229] (1883) as a case in which a jury recommended clemency due to the accused's "ignorance of the law".[230] The accused had breached the peace by trying to stop others from fishing on a Sunday, in the belief that desecration of the Sabbath was an unlawful activity. This was treated by the court as a mitigating factor. A more recent case is *Quinan* v *Carnegie*[231] (2005) in which the appellant believed that his status as a Member of the Scottish Parliament meant that the law relating to breach of the peace applied in a different way to him than to others. If this was an error of law, it availed him naught.

Self-defence

3.37   In *Derrett* v *Lockhart* (1991)[232] the charge against the two accused libelled that they had committed a breach of the peace by struggling and fighting with each other, causing injuries to each other.

---

[227] 1981 SCCR 66 at 67–68.
[228] 1999 GWD 21–992. The case is discussed briefly at section 3.23 above.
[229] (1883) 5 Coup 317.
[230] Christie, para 2.95.
[231] [2005] HCJAC 24; 2005 1 JC 279; 2005 SLT 707; 2005 SCCR 267; 2005 GWD 22-394. See section 3.20 above.
[232] 1991 SCCR 109.

The appeal court noted that "where a charge of breach of the peace is expressed in the sort of language in which this complaint was expressed, that is a situation in which a plea of self-defence will be open".[233] In his commentary to the case, Gordon noted that the appeal court seemed to suggest that self-defence would only be available where the wording of the charge made clear that fighting was alleged. He suggested that the Crown could not prevent the accused from trying to establish self-defence merely by omitting any reference to fighting or assault in the charge, and this must surely be correct.[234] As we have seen,[235] the greater specification now being provided in breach of the peace charges means that any allegation of "fighting" is now likely to be made explicit in the charge.

Provocation

In *MacNeill* v *McTaggart*[236] (1976) the court at first instance   3.38
acquitted the accused of breach of the peace by fighting, on the ground that he had been provoked. The Crown appeal was upheld, the court holding that: "It is not the law that provocation can be pled in exculpation of a charge of breach of the peace."[237] While provocation is not a complete defence it can, however, lead to a lesser sentence[238] so long as the accused's conduct is the immediate response to the provocation.[239]

Self-induced intoxication

Hume tended to view this as an aggravating factor, but did suggest   3.39
that it might act in mitigation of sentence if words were spoken due to "drunkenness".[240] It was not uncommon for such pleas in mitigation to be offered, but the Scottish Parliament has now taken a firm stance against this position: s 26 of the Criminal Justice and Licensing (Scotland) Act 2010 provides:

---

[233] 1991 SCCR 109 at 111, per LJ-C Ross.
[234] See *Butcher* v *Jessop* 1989 SCCR 119, discussed at section 2.8 above.
[235] See section 3.2 above.
[236] (1976) SCCR Supp 150.
[237] *Ibid* at 151.
[238] *Leys* v *Higson* 1999 GWD 34-1626.
[239] *Gallocher* v *Weir and Patrick* (1902) 4 F (J) 93; (1902) 10 SLT 215: "It is a fixed principle of our criminal law that it is not competent in a criminal case to appeal to provocation caused by words uttered several days before the crime took place" ((1902) 4 F (J) 93 at 94). For a possible example of a breach of the peace committed due to provocation, see *Kheda* v *Lees* 1995 SCCR 63.
[240] Hume, i, 46–47 See also Christie, para 1.23 where he suggests that this might form the basis for a plea in mitigation to certain minor forms of breach of the peace.

"(1) Subsection (2) applies in relation to an offender who was, at the time of the offence, under the influence of alcohol as a result of having voluntarily consumed alcohol.

(2) A court, in sentencing the offender in respect of the offence, must not take that fact into account by way of mitigation."

Nevertheless, intoxication may continue to be of relevance to breach of the peace. In *Heatherall* v *McGowan*[241] (2012) the accused put forward in mitigation that he had been intoxicated at the time of the offence; this was to negate the inference that his breach of the peace (involving indecent exposure) had a "significant sexual aspect", thus avoiding the notification requirements of the Sexual Offences Act 2003.[242] This was accepted by the appeal court.

Automatism

3.40   Intoxication by alcohol or other drugs, which is not self-induced, or other semi-conscious states may form the basis of the defence of automatism. The leading case is *Ross* v *HM Advocate*[243] (1991) which established that a loss of control could only exculpate if it was unforeseeable, and resulted from an external factor, rather than an underlying medical condition. A detailed description of this defence is outwith the scope of this book, but it should be noted that the appeal court quashed Ross's convictions on all charges – one of which was a breach of the peace. Since the court ruled that automatism negates *mens rea*, as opposed to impacting on the "voluntariness" of the *actus reus*, this case puts paid to any suggestion that breach of the peace could be a strict liability offence.[244]

CONCLUSIONS

3.41   The law has changed considerably since the turn of the 21st century. The increased focus on human rights following the incorporation of the European Convention on Human Rights into domestic law has led to greater specification being given of the conduct alleged to constitute a breach of the peace,[245] and we now find highly detailed charges.[246] Mindful of the guarantees provided in Arts 10 and 11 of the Convention, the appeal court has quashed some convictions

---

[241] [2012] HCJAC 25; 2012 SLT 583; 2012 SCL 492; 2012 GWD 8-141. See section 1.6 above.
[242] See further at section 3.31 above.
[243] 1991 JC 210; 1991 SLT 564; 1991 SCCR 823.
[244] See section 3.23 above.
[245] See section 3.2 above.
[246] See section 3.3 above.

where the accused had engaged in peaceful protests,[247] but it might have been hoped that a broader range of conduct would be treated as legitimate exercises of freedom of expression, rather than breaches of the law. While the reiteration in *Smith* v *Donnelly* that neither swearing at, nor refusal to co-operate with, the police is necessarily a breach of the peace[248] is a welcome narrowing of the scope of the crime, in large part this hope has not been fulfilled.[249] It is fair to say that the requirement in *Smith* v *Donnelly* that conduct be "severe" and have the potential to cause "serious disturbance" has provided a narrower definition. It is, however, a pity that the *mens rea* required for the crime remains a neglected aspect.[250] In *Bowes* v *Frame* the appeal court reviewed the development of the law from *Smith* v *Donnelly* through *Jones* v *Carnegie* and *Paterson* v *HM Advocate* to the first *Harris* case. It concluded:

> "In the light of the cases that we have just considered, we do not think that it can be said that, in any sense, *Harris* v *HM Advocate* effected a change in the law. What was involved in that case was a consideration of the application to the particular circumstances of the case of the principles explained in *Smith* v *Donnelly* and the other cases referred to. Of course, what was done in *Harris* v *HM Advocate* was to disapprove of the reasoning in *Young* v *Heatly* and, in consequence, overrule the decision in that case. It does not appear to us that that aspect of the decision can be considered as, in any sense, effecting a change in the law."[251]

As this chapter has demonstrated, however, *Harris* has in fact narrowed the ambit of breach of the peace still further, albeit somewhat equivocally, since the Crown must now demonstrate that the accused's conduct had the potential not merely to cause disturbance, but to cause a *public* disturbance.[252] Whether the current definition of breach of the peace resulting from this plethora of cases is a satisfactory one is considered in Chapter 6. One criticism that relates to the use of the crime is that the Crown resorts to it when other, possibly more pertinent, charges could be used instead.[253] In recent years the Scottish Parliament has enacted several offences to cover conduct which might otherwise have been prosecuted as breach of the peace. These are considered in the following chapter.

---

[247] See section 3.20 above.
[248] See sections 3.6 and 3.7 above.
[249] Consider, eg, the continued prosecution of the "Naked Rambler". This is discussed further at sections 6.28–6.29 below.
[250] See section 3.23 above.
[251] 2010 JC 297 at 305, para [20]; 2010 SCCR 657 at 665.
[252] See section 3.11 above.
[253] See sections 6.21–6.23 below.

CHAPTER 4

STATUTORY DEVELOPMENT

INTRODUCTION

Several forms of behaviour which had hitherto been prosecuted as **4.1** breach of the peace have been further specified in legislative provisions. Thus, making grossly offensive, indecent, obscene or menacing phone calls is now a statutory offence,[1] as is "kerb crawling".[2] This raises a general question about the relationship between statutory offences and common law crimes. In the English case of *R v Rimmington and Goldstein*[3] (2006) Lord Bingham stated that, as a matter of good practice, the prosecution ought to libel statutory offences in preference to common law ones:

> "Where Parliament has defined the ingredients of an offence, perhaps stipulating what shall and shall not be a defence, and has prescribed a mode of trial and a maximum penalty, it must ordinarily be proper that conduct falling within that definition should be prosecuted for the statutory offence and not for a common law offence which may or may not provide the same defences and for which the potential penalty is unlimited."[4]

No such good practice or respect for the primacy of statutes seems to operate in Scots law; the Crown frequently prosecutes a wide range of behaviours as breach of the peace when there is an (arguably more apposite) statutory offence.[5] This chapter focuses on those offences

---

[1] See the Communications Act 2003, s 127. A similar offence was previously contained in the Telecommunications Act 1984, s 43(1)(a). The latter was charged as an alternative to breach of the peace in *Jackson* v *HM Advocate* 1991 SCCR 206.

[2] Prostitution (Public Places) (Scotland) Act 2007, s 1. This was charged as a breach of the peace in *Lauder* v *Heatly* 1962 (unreported, but see Christie, para 3.29).

[3] [2005] UKHL 63; [2006] 1 AC 459; [2005] 3 WLR 982; [2006] 2 All ER 257; [2006] 1 Cr App R 17; [2006] HRLR 3; [2006] UKHRR 1; [2006] Crim LR 153.

[4] [2006] 1 AC 459 at 479, para [30]. See also section 6.24 below.

[5] This is discussed further at sections 6.21–6.23 below.

which have the greatest potential to impact on the prosecution's use of breach of the peace.

CRIMINAL LAW (CONSOLIDATION) (SCOTLAND) ACT 1995

Section 50A: racially aggravated conduct

4.2 The Criminal Law (Consolidation) (Scotland) Act 1995 was amended in 1998[6] to make it an offence to pursue a racially aggravated course of conduct which amounts to harassment of a person.[7] The conduct must be intended to amount to harassment or be such that it would appear to a reasonable person to amount to harassment.[8] It is also an offence under this section to act in a manner which is racially aggravated and which causes, or is intended to cause, alarm or distress.[9] This second offence does not require conduct on more than one occasion. Conduct is racially aggravated if immediately before, during or immediately after its commission the accused evinces malice and ill-will towards the complainer, based on the latter's membership (or the accused's presumption that the complainer is a member) of a racial group; or is motivated (wholly or partly) by malice and ill-will towards members of a racial group based on their membership of that group.[10] A recent prosecution under this section is *Donnachie v Robertson*[11] (2012) in which the appellant put his hands down his trousers before rubbing them on an Israeli flag belonging to a Jewish student.[12] The reference to motivation in this provision is an interesting one; as previously discussed, an accused's motive is generally irrelevant to their liability, though a good motive or a particularly bad motive may influence sentencing.[13] In *Donnachie* the appellant stated that his behaviour had been motivated by political views and was not intended to be a personal attack on the complainer, nor an anti-Semitic attack. A lack of malice towards Jews was not a defence, in this instance, since the section defines a racial group as a

---

[6] By the Crime and Disorder Act 1998, s 33.

[7] A "course of conduct" requires conduct on at least two occasions: Criminal Law (Consolidation) (Scotland) Act 1995, s 50A(6).

[8] *Ibid*, s 50A(1)(a).

[9] *Ibid*, s 50A(1)(b). "Conduct" includes speech, and "harassment" includes causing the person alarm or distress: *ibid*, s 50A(6).

[10] *Ibid*, s 50A(2).

[11] [2012] HCJAC 53; 2012 GWD 17-347.

[12] It appears that the charge was a breach of this section, despite the case summary on Westlaw and newspaper accounts referring to this as a breach of the peace: see "St Andrews student sentenced for Israel flag racism", *BBC News*, 13 September 2011, available at: http://www.bbc.co.uk/news/uk-scotland-edinburgh-east-fife-14897612.

[13] See section 3.25 above.

group of persons defined, *inter alia,* by nationality[14] thus the appellant's conviction was based on his stated antipathy towards Israelis, and his (mistaken) presumption that the complainer was an Israeli.[15]

SEXUAL OFFENCES (SCOTLAND) ACT 2009[16]

Section 6: coercing a person into looking at a sexual image

Although this offence is entitled "coercing a person into looking at **4.3** a sexual image", it is defined as "causing" someone to look at such an image, without that person's consent, or without any reasonable belief in consent.[17] The accused must act for sexual gratification, or to humiliate, distress or alarm the complainer. In the (unreported) case of *Christopher Walker* (2009), the accused pled guilty to a breach of the peace by sending a phone video message containing footage of his genitals to a stranger, having incorrectly dialled his girlfriend's phone number.[18] The ruling in the first *Harris* case means that in future such cases could no longer be charged as breach of the peace, since they involve private communications.[19] It should be noted, however, that the requirements of s 6 may not be fulfilled by the facts of the *Walker* case; the accused's intention was not to humiliate, distress or alarm the recipient, nor was the video sent for his own sexual gratification. Rather, it seems that it was sent for the gratification of the recipient. This may mean that similar behaviour in future could not be prosecuted as either the common law crime or the statutory offence.

Sections 23 and 33 of the Act provide similar offences to s 6 where **4.4** the person being coerced into looking at the images is a "young child" or an "older child", respectively.[20] Section 23 could now be used in circumstances such as that narrated in the breach of the

---

[14] Criminal Law (Consolidation) (Scotland) Act 1995, s 50A(6).

[15] *Ibid*, s 50A(2)(a).

[16] For a detailed description of the various provisions in the 2009 Act, see J Chalmers, *The New Law of Sexual Offences in Scotland: Supplement I to Volume II of Gordon's Criminal Law* (2010).

[17] Section 6(3) defines a "sexual image" as "an image (produced by whatever means and whether or not a moving image) of (a) [the accused] engaging in a sexual activity or of a third person or imaginary person so engaging, (b) [the accused's] genitals or the genitals of a third person or imaginary person".

[18] See "Genital video caller avoids jail", *BBC News*, 4 March 2009, available at: http://news.bbc.co.uk/1/hi/scotland/tayside_and_central/7924271.stm.

[19] [2009] HCJAC 80; 2010 JC 245; 2009 SLT 1078; 2010 SCL 56; 2010 SCCR 15. See section 3.11 above.

[20] A "young child" is defined throughout the Act as someone under the age of 13, and an "older child" as someone who is 13 or older but younger than 16.

peace charge in *Webster* v *Dominick*[21] (2003), which libelled that the accused had placed two girls aged 9 and 10 in a state of fear and alarm, by persistently following them and inducing them "to view material showing naked female and male persons".[22]

Section 7: communicating indecently

4.5   This is committed when a person sends a sexual written communication to a non-consenting person, or directs a sexual verbal communication at that person. Again, this must be for sexual gratification, or to humiliate, distress or alarm the other person.[23] Since breaches of the peace which involve a private communication between the accused and the complainer now fall foul of the "public disorder" element required by the first *Harris* case, this section may be used in future to prosecute many such cases. Thus it could be charged in circumstances such as those of *Dudley* v *HM Advocate*[24] (2004), in which the accused telephoned several women and, *inter alia*, asked them about their underwear and directed them to undress. Depending on what exactly was said by the accused (and the reports do not always make this clear) it also may apply to cases such as *MacNab* v *McDonald*[25] (1972) (use of "obscene language"); *Sinclair* v *Annan*[26] (1980) ("indecent remarks towards two ladies"); *Benson* v *Tudhope*[27] (1986) ("indecent suggestions"); *McLachlan, Petitioner*[28] (1987) ("obscene offensive remarks"); *Gibson* v *Heywood*[29] (1997) (police officer asking female complainer questions "of an indecent and personal nature", and "making indecent and personal comments" to her); *Kearney* v *Ramage*[30] (2007) ("sexually explicit comments"); and *Anoliefo* v *HM Advocate*[31] (2012) ("inappropriate and sexual remarks" and "indecent remarks").

---

[21] 2003 SCCR 525.

[22] The accused was charged with shameless indecency or alternatively breaches of the peace. (These were also the alternatives charged in *Usai* v *Russell* 2000 SCCR 57.) While *Webster* v *Dominick* redefined and renamed the former as "public indecency", the breach of the peace charges were accepted as being both competent and relevant.

[23] As with s 6, there are similar offences in ss 24 and 34 of the Act where the person with whom the accused is communicating is a child.

[24] 2004 Scot (D) 36/11.

[25] (1972) SCCR Supp 28.

[26] 1980 SLT (Notes) 55.

[27] 1986 JC 107; 1987 SLT 312; 1986 SCCR 422.

[28] 1987 SCCR 195.

[29] 1997 SLT 101.

[30] 2007 SCCR 35. See section 1.5, n 48 above.

[31] [2012] HCJAC 110; 2012 GWD 31-628. See section 6.20 below.

Section 8: sexual exposure

This offence is committed where a person exposes his or her 4.6
genitals in a sexual manner to another person, intending that
person to see them, and in order to obtain sexual gratification, or
humiliate, distress or alarm that other person. This may be prosecuted in cases such as *Hutchison* v *HM Advocate*[32] (1998); *Beattie*
v *HM Advocate*[33] (2008); and *Heatherall* v *McGowan*,[34] *Halcrow*
v *Shanks*[35] and *McGuire* v *Dunn*[36] (all 2012) in which indecent
exposure was treated as a breach of the peace.

Section 9: voyeurism

Voyeurism is given a broad definition in the Act, and includes one 4.7
person observing another where the latter is engaging in a "private
act".[37] The legislation provides that a person is "doing a private
act" if in a place "which in the circumstances would reasonably be
expected to provide privacy" and, *inter alia*, "the person's genitals,
buttocks or breasts are exposed or covered only with underwear".[38]
This could now be used instead of breach of the peace in cases such
as *MacDougall* v *Dochree*[39] (1992) in which the accused spied on
women who were using sun-beds in a leisure centre. Breach of the
peace was charged in the (unreported) case of *James Jardine* (2009),
who squatted in the aisles of a supermarket and took photographs
up women's skirts using a mini camera.[40] Since the victims in this
case were not "doing a private act", the statutory offence would
not have applied. However, the 2009 Act has since been amended
so that voyeurism includes operating equipment or recording an
image beneath the victim's clothing in order to observe the victim's
genitals or buttocks or the underwear covering these parts of the

---

[32] 1998 SLT 679; 1997 SCCR 726; 1998 GWD 1-12.
[33] [2008] HCJAC 73; 2009 JC 88; 2009 SLT 151; 2009 SCL 266; 2009 SCCR 106;
2009 GWD 5-76. See section 6.20 below.
[34] [2012] HCJAC 25; 2012 SLT 583; 2012 SCL 492; 2012 GWD 8-141. See section
1.6 above.
[35] [2012] HCJAC 23; 2012 SLT 579; 2012 SCL 517; 2012 GWD 8-144. See section
1.3 above.
[36] [2012] HCJAC 86.
[37] Sexual Offences (Scotland) Act 2009, s 9(1). Similar offences in ss 26 and 36 apply
where the voyeurism involves child complainers.
[38] Sexual Offences (Scotland) Act 2009, s 10.
[39] 1992 JC 154; 1992 SLT 624; 1992 SCCR 531.
[40] See "Probation over skirt photographs", *BBC News*, 15 October 2009, available
at: http://news.bbc.co.uk/1/hi/scotland/glasgow_and_west/8308945.stm. See also
Elphick v *HM Advocate* (unreported, August 7, 2002) (HCJ Appeal), discussed by
K Phillips in (2002) 60 (Dec) 5 *Criminal Law Bulletin*.

body, in circumstances where the genitals, buttocks or underwear would not otherwise be visible.[41] This could now be prosecuted in cases such as *Jardine*. The common law offence has been charged where the accused has not gone beyond preparation to the actual perpetration of one of these statutory offences. An example of this is the case of *Jude* v *HM Advocate*[42] (2012) in which a breach of the peace charge narrated that the accused had secreted a mobile phone in the complainer's bathroom "with the intention of taking indecent photographs of her".[43] The 2009 Act could now be used in similar cases, since it is an offence to install equipment with the intention of committing any of the offences in the section.[44]

CRIMINAL JUSTICE AND LICENSING (SCOTLAND) ACT 2010

Section 38: behaving in a threatening or abusive manner

4.8 In order to constitute an offence under this section, the behaviour must be such as would be likely to cause a reasonable person to suffer fear or alarm, and the accused must intend to cause fear or alarm or be reckless as to this.[45] The section represents a codification of one type of breach of the peace; indeed, the courts have referred to this as "the statutory breach of the peace".[46] The behaviour does not need to occur more than once,[47] can be in a public or private place, and need not involve serious disturbance to the community. In introducing an amendment to the Bill to include this provision, Kenny MacAskill, MSP, the Cabinet Secretary for Justice, stated that this was:

---

[41] Sexual Offences (Scotland) Act 2009, s 9(4A) and s 9(4B), added by the Criminal Justice and Licensing (Scotland) Act 2010, s 43(2)(a).

[42] [2012] HCJAC 65.

[43] At the conclusion of the evidence the Advocate Depute withdrew the libel in respect of several charges, including this one. For an analysis of voyeurism offences, see A A Gillespie, "'Up-skirts' and 'Down Blouses': Voyeurism and the Law" [2008] *Crim LR* 370.

[44] Sexual Offences (Scotland) Act 2009, s 9(4A), as amended by the Criminal Justice and Licensing (Scotland) Act 2010, s 43(2)(b)(i) and (ii).

[45] Section 38(2) provides a defence if the behaviour was "reasonable" in the particular circumstances. A person being attacked who responds with verbal abuse could presumably rely on this defence.

[46] *Harvey* v *HM Advocate* [2012] HCJAC 80, at para [5], per Lord Carloway. See also *Reilly* v *Robertson* [2012] HCJAC 76; 2012 GWD 20-423, at para [5]; *Young* v *McLintock* [2012] HCJAC 104; 2012 GWD 26-544, at para [7].

[47] Criminal Justice and Licensing (Scotland) Act 2010, s 38(3)(b)(i).

"intended to address the uncertainty about the scope of the common-law offence of breach of the peace that arose as a result of the appeal court's decision in *Harris* v *Her Majesty's Advocate*. In that case, the court ruled that a public element to the offending behaviour is required for the offence of breach of the peace to be committed. Although the judgment does not affect the majority of breach of the peace cases, which take place in public, we are concerned that it will make it more difficult for the criminal law to intervene, where that is appropriate, in domestic abuse cases that involve threatening or abusive behaviour but in which there is no evidence of physical violence that would enable a charge of assault to be libelled, as such cases often lack an obvious public element".[48]

Section 38 is an important provision which could be used in future instead of breach of the peace in many cases, such as those similar to *Bennett* v *HM Advocate*[49] (2006) in which the breach of the peace libelled that the accused had shouted, sworn and uttered threats to his victim, before then assaulting him. It could also cover the conduct of the accused in *Robertson* v *Vannet*[50] (1999), *Friel* v *Carnegie*[51] (1999), *McGraw* v *HM Advocate*[52] (2004), *Russell* v *Thomson*[53] (2010) and *Anoliefo* v *HM Advocate*[54] (2012). Since the behaviour need not involve, or be likely to cause, a public disturbance, this closes the gap in the law identified in *Hatcher* v *Harrower*[55] (2010), resulting from the first *Harris* case.[56] One commentator has suggested that this could also apply to situations such as that in *Bowes* v *Frame*[57] (2010), on the basis that "sexually explicit and inappropriate conversation, between an adult and a child, amounts

---

[48] *Scottish Parliament Official Report*, 30 June 2010, available at: http://www.scottish.parliament.uk/parliamentarybusiness/28862.aspx?r=5608&mode=html.

[49] [2006] HCJAC 3; 2006 SCCR 62.

[50] 1999 SLT 1081; 1998 SCCR 668. The accused had made threatening telephone calls.

[51] 1999 GWD 13–1410. The accused had told the complainer "that he knew where he lived and that he would come to his house and harm him and his family". See section 3.11, n 65 above.

[52] 2004 SCCR 637. See section 6.4 below.

[53] [2010] HCJAC 138; 2011 JC 164; 2011 SCL 295; 2011 SCCR 77. See section 3.14 above. The case is critiqued at section 6.9 below.

[54] [2012] HCJAC 110; 2012 GWD 31-628. See section 6.20 below.

[55] [2010] HCJAC 92; 2011 JC 90; 2011 SCL 114; 2010 SCCR 903. See section 3.15 above. See also *Harper* v *Higson* 2000 GWD 37-1396, in which the accused shouted and swore at his wife in her bedroom, and threatened to "smash her face in" and kill her.

[56] *Harris* v *HM Advocate* [2009] HCJAC 80; 2010 JC 245; 2009 SLT 1078; 2010 SCL 56; 2010 SCCR 15, discussed at section 3.11 above.

[57] [2010] HCJAC 55; 2010 JC 297; 2010 SLT 683; 2010 SCL 761; 2010 SCCR 657. See section 3.12 above. The case is critiqued at section 6.10 below.

to abuse".[58] Anecdotal evidence suggests that this has now become the charge used by the Crown in preference to breach of the peace.[59]

Section 39: stalking

4.9 This offence requires that the conduct in question occur on more than one occasion, but is otherwise widely defined.[60] It includes following a person; contacting, or attempting to contact them by any means; publishing any statement or other material about someone, or which purports incorrectly to be from that person; monitoring a person's use of the internet, e-mail or any other form of electronic communication; entering any premises, loitering in any place; interfering with any person's property, giving anything to anyone, or leaving anything where it may be found by, given to or brought to the attention of the person; watching or spying on someone; or acting in any other way that a reasonable person would expect would cause the other person to suffer fear or alarm.[61] The *mens rea* is defined such that the accused must intend to cause the complainer to suffer fear or alarm, or alternatively know, or ought in all the circumstances to know, that engaging in the course of conduct would be likely to cause fear or alarm. It is a defence to a charge of stalking for the accused to show that the course of conduct was authorised by virtue of any enactment or rule of law, was engaged in for the purpose of preventing or detecting crime, or was reasonable in the particular circumstances.[62]

4.10 Although the term "harassment" is not used in this legislation, it is apparent that repeatedly harassing someone falls within the definition of stalking. Several breach of the peace cases which involved repeated harassment would now be covered by this provision.[63] Thus in *McAlpine* v *Friel*[64] (1997) the two breach of the peace charges narrated that, over a 2-year period, the (female) accused had

---

[58] (2011) (Jan) *Scottish Criminal Law* 54 at 69.

[59] For the impact of this offence on the number of breaches of the peace now being prosecuted, see section 4.15 below.

[60] For a critique of the law prior to this enactment, see S Middlemiss and L Sharp, "A Critical Analysis of the Law of Stalking in Scotland" (2009) (73)1 *Journal of Criminal Law* 89; R Mays, "'Every Breath You Take … Every Move You Make': Scots Law, the Protection from Harassment Act 1997 and the Problem of Stalking" (1997) 6 *JR* 331.

[61] Criminal Justice and Licensing (Scotland) Act 2010, s 39(6).

[62] *Ibid*, s 39(5)(a)–(c). It is conceivable that the last part of this defence might be available to someone in the position of the accused in *Shannon* v *Skeen* 1977 SCCR Supp 180: see section 3.26 above.

[63] See *Flanigan* v *Napier* 1999 GWD 14-637 (in which the accused persistently followed his former cohabitee), and *Morris* v *HM Advocate* 2000 GWD 29-1124.

[64] 1997 SCCR 453; 1997 GWD 22-1074.

sent letters and packages to the complainer, had followed her and had stared at her, causing her fear and alarm.[65] In *Elliott* v *Vannet*[66] (1999) the complaint libelled that the 46-year-old accused had frequented a fast food outlet, harassing the 16-year-old complainer, an employee there, by repeatedly staring at her, speaking to her, and presenting unwanted gifts to her, placing her in a state of fear and alarm. More recently, in *Johnstone* v *HM Advocate* (2012)[67] the first charge libelled:

> "[Over a two year period] ... you did conduct yourself in a disorderly manner and did pursue a course of conduct which amounted to harassment of a person, namely, a medical practitioner, Doctor AB, ... and did:
> (a) on various occasions ... take video recordings or similar and photograph images of said Doctor AB without her knowledge or consent and store same on your computer;
> (b) ... follow said Doctor AB to her home address ... and did deliver a package addressed to her containing an anonymous handwritten note and brooches through the letterbox of her home;
> (c) ... enter an office used by said Doctor AB and did steal a key belonging to her;
> (d) ... steal 2 wing mirrors and 3 wiper blades from [a] motor vehicle ... belonging to said Doctor AB;
> (f) [*sic*] ... steal 2 wing mirrors and 3 wiper blades from said motor vehicle ... ;
>
> and you did thus harass said Doctor AB and did place her in a state of fear and alarm for her safety and did commit a breach of the peace".

Such behaviours could in future be prosecuted under s 39.

By contrast, in *Thomson* v *HM Advocate*[68] (2009) the accused **4.11** was indicted for several charges, the more serious of which involved the attempted abduction of four young girls, and the indecent assault of another. The indictment also included two charges of breach of the peace. The first libelled that he followed "C" (aged 10) in his motor car, and the second that, on the same day but in a different street, he had followed "C and L" (whose ages were both given as 11) and had spoken to "C". Given the different ages given for "C", it seems that this initial was used for two different complainers. Since each act of stalking related to a different girl, s 39 would not apply,

---

[65] See also *Egan* v *Normand* 1997 SCCR 211; *Shepherd* v *HM Advocate* 1999 GWD 31-1479.
[66] 1999 GWD 22-1033. See also *McKenzie* v *Normand* 1992 SLT 130; 1992 SCCR 14.
[67] 2012 JC 79; 2011 SLT 1257; 2011 SCL 825; 2011 SCCR 470; 2011 GWD 24-552. Note the allegations of theft within this breach of the peace (paras (c), (d) and (f)).
[68] [2009] HCJAC 1; 2009 SLT 300; 2009 SCL 376; 2009 SCCR 415; 2009 GWD 2-34.

though it might be argued that his behaviour was "threatening" and thus within s 38. Likewise the case of *Hay v HM Advocate*[69] (2012) recounts that the accused had pled guilty to an indictment which included several breaches of the peace involving repeatedly following girls in his car, and staring at them, to their fear and alarm. All the girls were aged between 14 and 16 and were not known to the accused. Only two of the girls were named, the rest being referred to as "unaccompanied females". The appeal related to the appropriateness of the accused being subject to the notification requirements of the Sexual Offences Act 2003,[70] but what is of interest for present purposes is that the accused "stalked" different victims hence there was not a "course of conduct" in respect of each one.[71] It may be, then, that the Crown will have to continue to rely on breach of the peace in these types of situations – unless the legislation is amended to require only one incident, or to include a course of conduct involving different complainers.[72] By contrast, the same accused was found guilty of several breaches of the peace, charged on summary complaint, which included three charges relating to the same flat and involved loitering outside it, and repeatedly staring through a window. Although this was said to be "to the fear and alarm of the lieges", the report makes clear that they related to the same complainer. In future, s 39 could be used for this type of behaviour.

OFFENSIVE BEHAVIOUR AT FOOTBALL AND THREATENING COMMUNICATIONS (SCOTLAND) ACT 2012

Section 1: offensive behaviour at regulated football matches

4.12   This offence was designed primarily to criminalise the singing of sectarian songs at football matches. It is an offence to express hatred of, or stir up hatred against, a person or group of persons based on their membership (or presumed membership) of a religious group, a social or cultural group with a perceived religious affiliation, or a group defined by colour, race, nationality, ethnic or national origins, sexual orientation, transgender identity, or disability.[73] The

---

[69] [2012] HCJAC 28; 2012 SLT 569; 2012 SCCR 281; 2012 SCL 492; 2012 GWD 8-142.

[70] See further at section 3.31 above.

[71] Section 39 of the 2010 Act refers to it being an offence "where A stalks another person ('B')".

[72] For a suggestion to this effect, see section 6.34 below.

[73] Offensive Behaviour at Football and Threatening Communications (Scotland) Act 2012, s 1(2)(a) and (4). See "Ayr United fan faces Dumfries offensive

behaviour must occur at a "regulated football match",[74] but this is given an extended definition such that it includes a place, other than domestic premises, where a match is being televised.[75] Behaviour is defined as occurring at such a match if occurs in the ground where the regulated football match is being held on the day on which it is being held; while the accused is entering or leaving that ground; or during a journey to or from the regulated football match.[76] It also includes behaviour which is directed towards, or is engaged in together with, another person who is in the ground, entering or leaving the ground or travelling to or from the match.[77] It is an offence if the proscribed behaviour is motivated by hatred of such a group, or is threatening, or is such that a reasonable person would be likely to consider offensive.[78] The behaviour must be likely to incite public disorder, or would be likely to incite public disorder[79] but for the fact that measures are in place to prevent public disorder, or those likely to be incited to disorder are not, in the event, present or are not present in sufficient numbers.[80] This is intended to prevent the accused from asserting that one team's supporters greatly outnumbered those of the other, or the police had a strong presence at the match, thus that disorder was in fact unlikely.[81]

Section 6: threatening communications/communicating religious hatred

It is an offence under this section to communicate material to someone which consists of, contains or implies, a threat or an incitement, to carry out a seriously violent act against a person, or against persons of a particular description, and which would

4.13

---

singing charge", *BBC News*, 2 April 2012, available at http://www.bbc.co.uk/news/uk-scotland-south-scotland-17584972.

[74] Offensive Behaviour at Football and Threatening Communications (Scotland) Act 2012, s 2(1) defines "regulated football match" in accordance with the Police, Public Order and Criminal Justice (Scotland) Act 2006, s 55(2).

[75] Offensive Behaviour at Football and Threatening Communications (Scotland) Act 2012, s 2(3).

[76] *Ibid*, s 2(2)(a). Compare *Ferguson* v *McFadyen* 1999 GWD 22-1051 (breach of the peace committed when accused travelling home from a match).

[77] *Ibid*, s 2(2)(b). The maximum penalty if prosecuted under summary procedure is 12 months' imprisonment, and on solemn procedure is 5 years' imprisonment: s 1(6).

[78] *Ibid*, s 1(2)(b)–(e).

[79] *Ibid*, s 1(1)(b).

[80] *Ibid*, s 1(5).

[81] See the Explanatory Notes accompanying the Offensive Behaviour at Football and Threatening Communications (Scotland) Bill, available at: http://www.scottish.parliament.uk/S4_Bills/Offensive%20Behaviour%20at%20Football%20and%20Threatening%20Communications%20(Scotland)%20Bill/b1s4-introd-en.pdf.

be likely to cause a reasonable person to suffer fear or alarm. The accused must intend to cause fear or alarm, or be reckless as to this.[82] It is also an offence to communicate threatening material to someone which is intended to stir up hatred on religious grounds.[83] It is a defence to show that the communication of the material was, in the particular circumstances, reasonable.[84] In relation to the offence of stirring up hatred on religious grounds, it is specifically provided in s 7 that this offence does not apply to communications which are discussions or criticisms of religions or the beliefs or practices of adherents of religions, expressions of antipathy, dislike, ridicule, insult or abuse towards those matters, proselytising, or urging of adherents of religions to cease practising their religions.[85] The offence is defined broadly and encompasses communications made by post, internet websites, e-mail, blogs, podcasts etc.[86] It does not, however, extend to "unrecorded speech",[87] thus would not cover the situation in the first *Harris* case, in which the implied threats were spoken.[88] This exception is designed to protect individuals' freedom of speech, guaranteed by Art 10 of the European Convention on Human Rights.[89]

4.14   The Offensive Behaviour at Football and Threatening Communications (Scotland) Bill was subject to much criticism during its passage through the Scottish Parliament,[90] and it was felt that its provisions relating to football matches could largely be dealt with using the crime of breach of the peace. Sarah Christie concluded:

---

[82] Offensive Behaviour at Football and Threatening Communications (Scotland) Act 2012, s 6(1) and (2).

[83] *Ibid*, s 6(5). The penalties are the same as for s 1: see s 6(7) .

[84] *Ibid*, s 6(6).

[85] "Religions" is broadly defined to include "religions generally", "particular religions", and "other belief systems" (*ibid*, s 7(2)). This last term could include all sorts of groups; one wonders whether "white supremacists", "creationists" and "Moonies" would be considered to be religions, based on their belief systems. The right to freedom of religion under Art 9 of the ECHR has been held to include Druidism, Scientology, the Moon Sect and Divine Light Zentrum: see J Murdoch, *Freedom of Thought, Conscience and Religion* (2007) at pp 12–13.

[86] See the Explanatory Notes, (n 81 above) at p 6.

[87] Offensive Behaviour at Football and Threatening Communications (Scotland) Act 2012, s 8(2).

[88] See section 3.11 above.

[89] See section 3.17 above.

[90] See S Christie, "The Offensive Behaviour at Football and Threatening Communications (Scotland) Bill – Strong on Rhetoric but Weak on Substance?" (2011) 25 *SLT* 185; D McArdle, "Too Much Heat, Not Enough Light" (2011) 56(7) *JLSS* 9. See also K Goodall, "Tackling Sectarianism through the Criminal Law" (2011) 15(3) *Edin LR* 423.

> "the fact that [s 1 of] the Bill covers situations where behaviour is likely to, rather than actually does incite public disorder, takes us no further than the current common law".[91]

It does, however, give a more specific label to certain forms of sectarian misconduct. The Convenor of the Justice Committee drew a distinction between having a conviction for s 1 of this legislation, which would make clear that this related to sectarian behaviour, and a conviction for a breach of the peace:

> "If … we are looking at the bill as a deterrent in some respects, a stigma would attach to a person who was convicted under it, because they would not be able to say, for example, that they were convicted of breach of the peace when they fell down, kicked over some buckets and woke folk up."[92]

Kay Goodall has welcomed the provisions in the Act which relate to incitement to religious hatred, on the basis that "it is an insult to victims to subsume this under religiously aggravated breach of the peace".[93] This too reflects concerns that the behaviour of offenders should be accurately labelled.[94]

CONCLUSION

Many of the legislative changes described above have the potential significantly to reduce the Crown's reliance on common law breach of the peace, and ss 38 and 39 of the Criminal Justice and Licensing (Scotland) Act 2010 have already done so: there was a 34 per cent decrease in the number of breach of the peace offences being recorded by the police in the year following its coming into force.[95] Since these offences, and the relevant provisions of the Sexual

4.15

---

[91] S Christie (n 90 above) at 187. Examples of breaches of the peace occurring at or in football stadia include: *Wilson v Brown* 1982 SLT 361; 1982 SCCR 49; *MacGivern v Jessop* 1988 SCCR 511; *Huston v Buchanan* 1994 SCCR 512; *Hannah v Vannet* 1999 GWD 29-1380; *Wright v HM Advocate* 2000 GWD 34-1306; *Allison v Higson* 2004 SCCR 720 (see section 6.8 below); *Dyer v Hutchison* [2006] HCJAC 45; 2006 JC 212; 2006 SLT 657; 2006 SCCR 377; *Walls v Brown* [2009] HCJAC 59; 2009 JC 375; 2009 SLT 774; 2009 SCL 973; 2009 SCCR 711.

[92] *Justice Committee Official Report*: 22 June 2011, col 90, available at: http://www.scottish.parliament.uk/parliamentarybusiness/28862.aspx?r=6366&mode=pdf.

[93] K Goodall, "Tackling Sectarianism through the Criminal Law" (2011) 15(3) *Edin LR* 423 at 426.

[94] For the importance of "fair" or "accurate" labelling in criminal law, see sections 5.13 and 6.32 below.

[95] In 2009–10 more than 85,000 breaches of the peace were recorded by the police. In 2010–11, this had fallen to less than 57,000: see *Statistical Bulletin: Recorded Crime in Scotland 2010–11*, Table 2, available at: http://www.scotland.gov.uk/Publications/2011/09/02120241/0 at 18.

Offences (Scotland) Act 2009, may be committed in any locus, they avoid the public/private difficulties which resulted from the first *Harris* case. The Crown is, however, free to charge breach of the peace instead of many of these statutory provisions, even if the latter are arguably more apposite. While many of the reforms resulting from the enactment of the 2009 Act were long overdue – for instance, the legal definition of rape had been criticised for many years[96] – it would not be overly cynical to suggest that the creation of some of the other statutory offences represents ad hoc law reform: the Scottish Parliament reacting to media outcries over sectarianism, for instance.[97] However, on a more positive note, the willingness of the Scottish Parliament to enact new legislation – even where the overlap with common law breach of the peace is considerable – could equally be taken as an indication of a growing acceptance of the need for fairer/more accurate offence labelling, and clearer definitions, in Scottish criminal law. It is suggested that the Parliament should replace the current common law breach of the peace with a clearer and more precise statutory offence. Some thoughts on how this could best be achieved are discussed in Chapter 6, as part of a wider critique of the crime. Before embarking on this, however, consideration must be given to whether the proscription of a range of behaviours which "breach the peace" (or could lead others to breach the peace) can be justified by one or more theories of criminalisation. This is attempted in Chapter 5.

---

[96] See, eg, C H W Gane, *Sexual Offences* (1992); P R Ferguson, "Controversial Aspects of the Law of Rape: An Anglo-Scottish Comparison" in R F Hunter (ed), *Justice and Crime: Essays in Honour of the Right Honourable the Lord Emslie* (1993) at p 180.

[97] The Scottish Parliament enacted more than 400 offences in its first decade. For a critique, see P R Ferguson, "Criminal Law and Criminal Justice: An Exercise in Ad Hocery" in E E Sutherland, K E Goodall, G F M Little and F P Davidson (eds), *Law Making and the Scottish Parliament: The Early Years* (2011) at p 208.

CHAPTER 5

CRIMINALISING BREACHES OF THE PEACE

INTRODUCTION

As explained in Chapter 1, this book sets out to critique breach of **5.1** the peace[1] – but on what basis might this be done? Two types of critique may be offered, the first of which considers whether there ought to be an offence of breach of the peace at all. This question is addressed by considering various theories of criminalisation, and forms the basis of this chapter. The second type of critique applies these theories to Scots law, and considers whether, if there ought indeed to be an offence of breach of the peace, the crime is adequately defined and appropriately applied in practice. Chapter 6 addresses these issues. It might seem strange to question whether we ought to have an offence of breach of the peace *per se*. One can well see the advantages for a prosecutor in having a broadly drawn offence designed to preserve "good order" and the public peace. It should be borne in mind, however, that breach of the peace is not an offence as such under English law; it provides the police with authority to arrest someone or search premises, but does not lead to a conviction.[2] The situation is similar in Canadian law.[3]

CRIMINALISATION

One's views on whether a particular criminal prohibition is warranted, **5.2**

---

[1] See section 1.1 above.

[2] See G Williams, "Arrest for Breach of the Peace" [1954] *Crim LR* 578. Breach of the peace in English law is discussed further at section 6.25 below. There had been some debate as to its status, but it now seems settled that breach of the peace is a crime at common law in the Republic of Ireland: see *Thorpe* v *DPP* [2006] IEHC 319; [2007] 1 IR 502, discussed in A O'Neill, "Common Law Offence: Breach of the Peace: *Thorpe* v *DPP*" (2007) 71(1) *J Crim Law* 21.

[3] See J Esmonde, "The Policing of Dissent: The Use of Breach of the Peace Arrests at Political Demonstrations" (2002) 1:2 *JLE* 246.

or not, may be dependent on the answers to several underlying questions, such as: What are, or ought to be, the purposes of the criminal law? How might criminal sanctions be justified? What limiting factors should restrict the use of such sanctions? What values should criminal law embody? Once these wider issues have been addressed, one could then ask how a particular crime such as breach of the peace might be justified, and consider what state interest(s) the crime is designed to protect. Detailed consideration of these philosophical questions cannot be attempted in a specialist work such as this. However, a brief attempt to address them is required in order to place breach of the peace in its wider context.

5.3   The principles by which a state ought to determine which types of behaviour should be subject to criminal proscription are debated in the growing academic literature on criminalisation.[4] This literature often highlights the dangers of over-criminalisation; having too many crimes, it is suggested, leads to excessive punishment.[5] Valid though these arguments are, it should be borne in mind that there are also dangers inherent in *under*-criminalisation. In respect of a crime such as breach of the peace, failure on the part of a state to proscribe certain forms of anti-social behaviour (to use a broad term) risks reducing the quality of life of those who have to put up with that behaviour, leading to increased disorder, and even self-help. As Robert Force so aptly put it, the making of excessively loud noise, for example, can be prohibited "not only because of the public interest in tranquillity, but also because of the danger that someone whose tranquillity is unreasonably disturbed may decide to physically render the disturber unnoisy".[6] As long ago as 1883, the Scottish appeal court upheld a conviction for breach of the peace on the basis that the "real root" of the appellant's offence in interrupting a religious meeting was that his behaviour was "an interference with the liberty" of others.[7] The criminal law has to set limits on one person's behaviour in order to avoid clashes with the

---

[4] Recent examples include: R A Duff *et al* (eds), *The Structures of the Criminal Law* (2011); D J Baker, *The Right Not to be Criminalized: Demarcating Criminal Law's Authority* (2011); V Tadros, *The Ends of Harm: The Moral Foundations of Criminal Law* (2011); D Husak, *Overcriminalization: The Limits of the Criminal Law* (2008). See also S S Beale, "The Many Faces of Overcriminalization: From Morals and Mattress Tags to Overfederalization" (2004–5) *Am U L Rev* 747; S H Kadish, *Blame and Punishment: Essays in the Criminal Law* (1987) at pp 21–35; H Packer, *The Limits of the Criminal Sanction* (1969).

[5] See, in particular, D Husak, *Overcriminalization: The Limits of the Criminal Law* (2008).

[6] R Force, "Decriminalization of Breach of the Peace Statutes: A Nonpenal Approach to Order Maintenance" (1972) 46:3 *Tul L Rev* 367 at 369.

[7] *Hendry v Ferguson* (1883) 10 R (J) 63 at 65.

interests or rights of others – but it must endeavour to do so in the least restrictive way possible.[8]

MORALISM AND PATERNALISM

Legal moralism

Proponents of legal moralism believe that the criminalisation of **5.4** conduct may be justified if that conduct is inherently immoral, irrespective of whether it causes direct harm to anyone.[9] Lord Devlin supported this; he argued that society had not merely a right but a duty to punish acts of "gross" immorality.[10] He believed that if the law failed to enforce a community's dominant morality this *would* risk a very serious harm indeed – that of social disintegration.[11] The link between crime and immorality is necessarily a close one, if only because both are concerned with preventing harm. In practice, of course, criminal law proscribes certain immoral behaviours (for example, murder, rape and theft) but not others (for example, in Scots law, adultery, breaking one's promises, and lying[12]). The debate over legal moralism is generally of little relevance in finding a justification for the Scottish crime of breach of the peace, however, some cases could be construed as involving the enforcement of morals, for example *Turner* v *Kennedy*[13] (1972) (distributing pamphlets advocating sexual freedom for school children); *Webster* v *Dominick*[14] (2003) (inducing children to view material showing nude people); *Stewart* v *Lockhart*[15] (1990) (male accused dressing in women's clothes near an area frequented by prostitutes). However, in each of these cases the prosecution of the accused can be better justified by other grounds, such as the prevention of harm.[16] In *Stewart* v *Lockhart*, though, the potential harm seems to have been

---

[8] Compare Joel Feinberg's view that criminal prohibitions are legitimate "only when they protect individual rights": J Feinberg, *The Moral Limits of the Criminal Law Volume 1: Harm to Others* (1984) at p 144. His work is discussed further at section 5.6 below.

[9] See J Feinberg, *The Moral Limits of the Criminal Law Volume 4: Harmless Wrongdoing* (1988) at p xx.

[10] P Devlin, *The Enforcement of Morals* (1965) at p 17.

[11] See also R P George, *Making Men Moral: Civil Liberties and Public Morality* (1993) at pp 5–6.

[12] Lying may be criminal in specific circumstances, for example if done under oath, or in an attempt to pervert the course of justice, or if the lie is told with a view to gaining some practical result (the basis of fraud).

[13] (1972) SCCR Supp 30.

[14] 2003 SCCR 525. See section 4.4 above.

[15] 1991 SLT 835; 1990 SCCR 390. See sections 2.5 and 3.25 above.

[16] The "harm principle" is discussed at section 5.6 below.

to the appellant himself, rather than to other people.[17] This leads us to a consideration of legal paternalism.

Legal paternalism

5.5 Those who advocate legal paternalism believe that a state may sometimes be justified in protecting people from themselves, and that this may include using the criminal law to attempt to prevent self-harming conduct. Most people accept that paternalistic criminal laws may be justified where they are designed to safeguard those who are vulnerable through ill health, mental deficiency or youth.[18] There is less enthusiasm when such laws impact on the choices of adults who are fully competent to determine their own best interests. In liberal states such as ours it is commonly felt that the state should not attempt to limit freedom of thought, and should interfere with freedom of speech or action only where absolutely necessary to safeguard the rights of others.[19] Whether paternalism is an appropriate basis for criminalising conduct is beyond the scope of this book, since the debates surrounding its use generally have little to offer in our search for a justification for criminalising breaches of the peace.[20] A more fruitful criminalisation theory focuses on the "harm principle" and the "offence principle".

THE HARM AND OFFENCE PRINCIPLES

5.6 Joel Feinberg's *The Moral Limits of the Criminal Law*[21] championed the "harm principle" (put simply, that the criminal law should focus on safeguarding certain "welfare interests"[22] which are under threat of harm from others' behaviours) and, to a lesser extent, the "offence principle" (that some forms of behaviour which cause serious offence to others can rightly be proscribed).[23] In respect of the first of

---

[17] This is discusssed further at section 6.14 below.

[18] See, eg, the Licensing (Scotland) Act 2005 which provides a number of offences relating to the sale or consumption of alcohol by children (ss 102–109), and the Tobacco and Primary Medical Services (Scotland) Act 2010, which proscribes the selling of tobacco products to persons under the age of 18.

[19] See the discussion on Arts 10 and 11 of the ECHR at section 3.17 above. For further discussion of the issues raised by legal paternalism, see J Kleinig, *Paternalism* (1983) and J Feinberg, *The Moral Limits of the Criminal Law Volume 3: Harm to Self* (1986).

[20] See, however, the further discussion on self-harm at section 6.14 below.

[21] J Feinberg, *The Moral Limits of the Criminal Law Volume 1: Harm to Others* (1984); *Volume 2: Offense to Others* (1985); *Volume 3: Harm to Self* (1986); and *Volume 4: Harmless Wrongdoing* (1988).

[22] Feinberg, *Harm to Others* at p 37.

[23] Feinberg, *Offense to Others* at p 1. See also Packer's view that the criminal

these principles, Feinberg was clear that "crimes against the person" and "crimes against property" could generally be justified on the basis that they involve "the direct production of serious harm to individual persons and groups".[24] The former group of crimes aims to prevent harm to individuals' bodily integrity,[25] including sexual integrity.[26] The latter proscribes misappropriations of property,[27] and its non-consensual damage or destruction.[28] The harm principle can also be employed to justify the protection of the environment (in the sense of ecology or nature, as well as one's physical surroundings more generally), and of other public areas such as parks and public transport, and Feinberg included among his welfare interests a "tolerable social and physical environment".[29] Many Scottish prosecutions for breach of the peace could be described as being designed to secure this.

Feinberg suggested that before criminalising a particular type   5.7 of behaviour, regard must be had to the risk the behaviour poses, risk being a compound of the magnitude of potential harm and the probability of the harm becoming manifest. Thus, "the greater the probability of harm, the less grave the harm need be to justify [state] coercion; the greater the gravity of the envisioned harm, the less probable it need be".[30] The importance of the conduct to the offender's way of life and the opportunities for alternative behaviours must be considered by a legislature before determining whether criminalisation is appropriate. Feinberg's approach corresponds to the liberal ideal that freedom from state interference is a positive good, perhaps one of the ultimate goods. The issue is, of course, how much interference is acceptable in any situation, and what type(s) of interference ought to be employed.[31] The Scottish breach of the

---

law should proscribe conduct that gives, or is likely to give, offence to innocent bystanders: H Packer, *The Limits of the Criminal Sanction* (1969) at p 306.

[24] Feinberg, *Harm to Others* at pp 10–11.

[25] Thus accounting for the crimes of assault, culpable and reckless injury, drugging, abduction, culpable homicide, murder etc.

[26] Thus accounting for the crimes of rape, sexual assault etc. See now the Sexual Offences (Scotland) Act 2009, some of whose provisions are described in sections 4.3–4.7 above. For the role of breach of the peace charges in safeguarding sexual integrity, see section 5.8 below.

[27] Thus accounting for the crimes of theft, robbery, fraud, embezzlement, and reset.

[28] Thus accounting for the crimes of vandalism, malicious mischief, and fire-raising.

[29] Feinberg, *Harm to Others* at p 37. Other interests included good health and "at least minimal income and financial security".

[30] *Ibid* at p 191.

[31] For the argument that criminal prohibitions are legitimate *only* when they protect individual rights see *ibid* at p 144. The European Convention on Human Rights reflects some of these concerns, and indeed the liberal values which prompt them. See section 3.1 above.

peace parts company with the liberal version of the offence principle, however, in so far as the latter requires conduct to occur *in public* before criminalisation can be contemplated. This is an issue which is considered further below.[32]

THE HARM PRINCIPLE APPLIED TO BREACH OF THE PEACE

5.8   Many forms of unacceptable sexual behaviour have been prosecuted as breach of the peace, including cases in which the accused: followed young girls in his car, to their fear and alarm;[33] tried to entice girls into his car;[34] spied on women who were using sunbeds in a leisure centre;[35] took photographs up women's skirts using a mini camera;[36] exposed his genitals in a sexual manner;[37] made sexual phone calls to strangers;[38] asked indecent and personal questions;[39] made indecent remarks;[40] and masturbated in front of an elderly female relative.[41] Since a core aim of the criminal law is the prevention of harm, the harm principle can be employed to justify the criminalisation of types of conduct which create an unacceptable risk of harm to others, as well as that which actually causes it.[42] Many of the sexual

---

[32] The application of the offence principle to breach of the peace is considered at sections 5.9–5.11, and the public/private issue at sections 5.12–5.13, below.

[33] *Thomson* v *HM Advocate* [2009] HCJAC 1; 2009 SLT 300; 2009 SCL 376; 2009 SCCR 415; 2009 GWD 2-34; *Hay* v *HM Advocate* [2012] HCJAC 28; 2012 SLT 569; 2012 SCCR 281; 2012 SCL 492; 2012 GWD 8-142. Both cases are described further at section 4.11 above.

[34] *LBM* v *HM Advocate* [2011] HCJAC 96; 2012 SLT 147; 2012 SCL 74; 2011 GWD 34-715. See section 3.27 above.

[35] *MacDougall* v *Dochree* 1992 JC 154; 1992 SLT 624; 1992 SCCR 531. See section 4.7 above.

[36] See "Probation over skirt photographs", 15 October 2009, *BBC News*, available at: http://news.bbc.co.uk/1/hi/scotland/glasgow_and_west/8308945.stm.

[37] *Hutchison* v *HM Advocate* 1998 SLT 679; 1997 SCCR 726; 1998 GWD 1-12; *Heatherall* v *McGowan* [2012] HCJAC 25; 2012 SLT 583; 2012 SCL 492; 2012 GWD 8-141 (see sections 1.6 and 3.39 above); *Halcrow* v *Shanks* [2012] HCJAC 23; 2012 SLT 579; 2012 SCL 517; 2012 GWD 8-144 (see section 1.3 above).

[38] *Dudley* v *HM Advocate* 2004 Scot (D) 36/11. See section 4.5 above.

[39] *Gibson* v *Heywood* 1997 SLT 101. See section 4.5 above.

[40] *Anoliefo* v *HM Advocate* [2012] HCJAC 110; 2012 GWD 31-628. See section 6.20 below.

[41] *Beattie* v *HM Advocate* [2008] HCJAC 73; 2009 JC 88; 2009 SLT 151; 2009 SCL 266; 2009 SCCR 106; 2009 GWD 5-76. See section 6.20 below.

[42] See A P Simester and A von Hirsch, "Rethinking the Offense Principle" (2002) 8 *LEG* 269; A von Hirsch, "Extending the Harm Principle: 'Remote' Harms and Fair Imputation" in A P Simester and A T H Smith (eds), *Harm and Culpability* (1996). For discussion of the issues raised by criminalising behaviours which do not cause harm, but merely the risk of harm, see Chapter 6 of R A Duff, *Answering for Crime: Responsibility and Liability in the Criminal Law* (2007).

behaviours just described threaten others' sexual integrity, and these others are often women or children. It could, of course, be argued that *all* breaches of the peace risk harm to others, by definition, since they risk (and on occasion actually cause) alarm or distress. But are these emotional states a sufficient "harm" to satisfy the harm principle? Louis Schwartz has suggested that "citizens may legitimately demand of the state protection of their psychological as well as their physical integrity",[43] justifying the law in proscribing the making of "loud noises, offensive odors, and tumultuous behavior disturbing the peace".[44] Jean Hampton has also suggested that a broad definition be given to harm, such that it include:

> "disruption of or interference in a person's well-being, including damage to that person's body, psychological state, capacities to function, life plans, or resources over which we take this person to have an entitlement".[45]

This rather begs the question: if we have already decided that someone has an entitlement to something then it seems uncontroversial to consider infringements of that entitlement to be a "harm" and worthy of protection. The central difficulty lies in determining which interests ought to be recognised as affording such an entitlement in the first place. In contrast to Hampton's more expansive approach, Feinberg excludes from his definition of "harm" various psychological states, such that one cannot complain of having being harmed merely because of being made to feel bored by another's behaviour, and he also excludes other transitory emotions including anger, alarm and embarrassment[46] – each of which has been libelled in charges of breach of the peace in Scotland. Thus the harm principle is generally interpreted as requiring physical harm rather than merely psychological upset, unless the latter leads to the former. Breaches of the peace which actually cause definite physical harm to others, or pose a real and substantial risk of such harm, may be justified by this principle, but in practice there are relatively few cases of this type. *Divin* v *HM Advocate*[47] (2012), in which the accused incited a riot using Facebook, may be one example of conduct which caused a real likelihood of serious physical harm to persons and their property. Within this category one could also put

---

[43] L B Schwartz, "Morals Offenses and the Model Penal Code" (1963) 63 *Colum L Rev* 669 at p 671.

[44] *Ibid.*

[45] J Hampton, "Correcting Harms versus Righting Wrongs: the Goal of Retribution" (1992) 39 *UCLA L R* 1659 at p 1662.

[46] Feinberg, *Harm to Others* at p 45.

[47] [2012] HCJAC 81; 2012 SCL 837; 2012 GWD 19-395 (see sections 1.3 and 3.32 above).

some cases involving discharging firearms,[48] or brandishing some types of weapon,[49] but if there had been a real risk of serious harm these cases would likely have been prosecuted as other crimes.

THE OFFENCE PRINCIPLE APPLIED TO BREACH OF THE PEACE

5.9   Hume's *Commentaries* included several chapters on "Offences Against the Public Police or Economy",[50] and he quoted the English writer William Blackstone as meaning by this

> "the due regulation and domestic order of the kingdom: Whereby the individuals of the State, like members of a well-governed family, are bound to conform their general behaviour to the rules of propriety, good neighbourhood and good manners; and to be decent, industrious, *and inoffensive*, in their respective stations".[51]

In exploring his "offence principle", Feinberg offers a thought experiment in which readers are invited to imagine that they are on a bus journey during which some of the other passengers engage in behaviours which might be regarded as highly offensive.[52] These behaviours are divided into those which engender: "affronts to the senses" (seeing, hearing or smelling); "disgust and revulsion" (behaviour that literally sickens the witness); "shock to moral, religious or patriotic sensibilities"; "shame, embarrassment and anxiety" (Feinberg suggests that these mainly concern nudity and fornication); and "fear, resentment, humiliation and anger". Depending on the circumstances, each of Feinberg's categories could form the basis – and indeed many have formed the basis – of

---

[48] *Palazzo v Copeland* 1976 JC 52. See also: "Teacher fined for firing pistol", *BBC News*, 12 May 2009, available at: http://news.bbc.co.uk/1/hi/scotland/edinburgh_and_east/8046375.stm.

[49] Cases of breach of the peace involving brandishing items include: *MacNeill v Robertson* 1982 SCCR 468; *Hamilton v Wilson* 1994 SLT 431; 1993 SCCR 9; *Paterson v Webster* 2002 SLT 1120; 2002 SCCR 734; and *Watson v Robertson* [2009] HCJAC 36; 2009 SCL 899. See in particular *Kidd and Tiffoney v HM Advocate* [2010] HCJAC 98; 2010 GWD 34-694 (brandishing a Samurai sword at police officers); and *Boyle v HM Advocate* 1993 SLT 577; 1992 SCCR 824 (where this led to murder).

[50] D Hume, *Commentaries on the Law of Scotland Respecting Crimes* (4th edn, 1844), Chaps XVIII–XXII. Christie has pointed out that "police" here may mean "policy", thus the offences listed are perceived to be "against public policy" (M G A Christie, *Breach of the Peace* (1990), para 1.18). Hume's discussion included incest, adultery, bigamy and clandestine marriage, fornication, drunkenness, and "unnatural lusts" (by which he meant sodomy and bestiality).

[51] *Hume*, i, 446 (emphasis added).

[52] Feinberg, *Offense to Others* at p 10.

conviction for breach of the peace in Scots law. Thus, the accused
who attempted to have sexual intercourse with a bicycle presumably
"affronted the senses" of the cleaner who discovered him so doing,[53]
and the cleaner may have also experienced "disgust and revulsion".
The notion of "affront to the senses" may lie behind the repeated
conviction for breach of the peace of the "Naked Rambler", or
perhaps his prosecution is based on shock to moral sensibilities.[54]
Such sensibilities may also be offended by the behaviour of those
who breach the peace by engaging in kerb crawling[55] or masturbation.[56] Heckling a church congregation and minister is an example
of behaviour which may offend against religious sensibilities,[57] as
is "shouting and screaming" at a religious meeting,[58] painting a
swastika on someone's property[59] or (again, depending on the circumstances) making a Nazi salute.[60] "Religious sensibilities" could have
been an issue in the recent case of *Donnachie* v *Robertson*[61] (2012)
which involved desecration of an Israeli flag belonging to a Jewish
student, but it seems the accused was motivated by anti-Israeli sentiments, rather than anti-Semitic ones. This case might appear to have
involved patriotic as well as religious sensibilities, but although
he had a brother in the Israeli Defence Force and felt a "sense of
connection with the State of Israel", the owner of the flag was not
in fact an Israeli citizen. Many examples could be given of breaches
of the peace occasioning "fear" or "anger", and the "Peeping Tom"
cases,[62] and those involving indecent exposure,[63] may lead others

---

[53] See the case of *Robert Stewart* (unreported, 2007), discussed at sections 6.16 and
6.28 below.
[54] His case is discussed further at sections 6.28–6.29 below. For an early breach of
the peace involving "nudity in the streets", see *James Ainslie* (1842) 1 Broun 25,
cited in J S More, *Lectures on the Law of Scotland: Volume II* (1864) at p 408.
[55] *Lauder* v *Heatly* 1962 (unreported, but see Christie, para 3.29).
[56] *Hutchison* v *HM Advocate* 1998 SLT 679; 1997 SCCR 726; 1998 GWD 1-12.
More recent cases include: *Kelly* v *HM Advocate* 2001 JC 12; *Beattie* v *HM Advocate*
[2008] HCJAC 73; 2009 JC 88; 2009 SLT 151; 2009 SCL 266; 2009 SCCR 106;
2009 GWD 5-76 (see section 6.20 below); *Halcrow* v *Shanks* [2012] HCJAC 23;
2012 SLT 579; 2012 SCL 517; 2012 GWD 8-144 (discussed at section 1.3 above).
[57] See "Church heckler jailed for breach", *BBC News*, 23 July 2008, available at:
http://news.bbc.co.uk/1/hi/scotland/tayside_and_central/7521925.stm. Similar, but
much older, cases include *Hugh Fraser* (1839) 2 Swin 436; *Dougall* v *Dykes* (1861)
4 Irv 101 (see section 3.31 above).
[58] *Hendry* v *Ferguson* (1883) 5 Coup 278; (1883) 10 R (J) 63.
[59] Unreported, but see *The Herald*, 7 January 1999.
[60] *Worsfold* v *Walkingshaw* 1987 SCCR 17.
[61] [2012] HCJAC 53; 2012 GWD 17-347. The case was discussed at section 4.2
above.
[62] *Raffaelli* v *Heatly* 1949 JC 101; 1949 SLT 284; *MacDougall* v *Dochree* 1992 JC
154; 1992 SLT 624; 1992 SCCR 531. See sections 2.5 and 4.7 above, respectively.
[63] *Hutchison* v *HM Advocate* 1998 SLT 679; 1997 SCCR 726; 1998 GWD 1-12;

to feel humiliation and resentment. The various accused who: took photographs by pointing a camera up women's skirts;[64] lay on the floor of a changing room in order to glimpse a teenage girl dressing;[65] and filmed and distributed a video of a couple having sex at a party[66] would each have caused humiliation and resentment on the part of their victims; one might go further and suggest that, particularly in the first two of these examples, such behaviour can be extremely unnerving and intimidating for victims.

5.10   It seems, then, that, in Scotland at least, the offence principle is a common basis for breach of the peace charges. Indeed Gordon has suggested that one function of breach of the peace "is simply to enable people to be punished for not behaving in a seemly manner".[67] Although Feinberg's approach to "offensive behaviour" may have appeared liberal when his books were published in the 1980s, society in the 21st century may be less tolerant of some forms of conduct. Andrew von Hirsch has observed that relatively innocuous activities such as begging, or being homeless and living on the street, may well cause general irritation or even "offence", thus Feinberg's theory offers little comfort to those who would argue against the criminalisation of such behaviours.[68] "Offensive behaviour" can quickly become a "catch-all": we label conduct "offensive", and then hold that *ipso facto* it merits criminalisation, without any real debate as to the ulterior reasons for considering it offensive in the first place. As well as asking: "Is this behaviour offensive?", perhaps we need to ask: "What is it about this behaviour that makes us regard it as offensive? And is it *so* offensive that it merits criminalisation?"

5.11   Von Hirsch has argued that general "offensiveness" is too broad a criterion for criminalisation, and has suggested that we focus on behaviours which cause offence by failing to treat others with proper respect.[69] Thus he proposes three categories of offensive behaviour which could warrant criminalisation, namely: (1) affronts

---

Usai v Russell 2000 SCCR 57; George v HM Advocate [2011] HCJAC 33; 2011 GWD 15-363.

[64] "Probation over skirt photographs", BBC News, 15 October 2009, available at: http://news.bbc.co.uk/1/hi/scotland/glasgow_and_west/8308945.stm.

[65] "Man spied on girl as she changed", BBC News, 6 January 2010, available at: http://news.bbc.co.uk/1/hi/scotland/tayside_and_central/8444008.stm.

[66] "Man fined £1,000 for teenage party sex video", BBC News, 14 April 2010, available at: http://news.bbc.co.uk/1/hi/scotland/south_of_scotland/8620284.stm.

[67] Mackay v Heywood 1998 SCCR 210 at 213.

[68] A von Hirsch, "The Offence Principle in Criminal Law: Affront to Sensibility or Wrongdoing?" (2000) 11(1) KCLJ 78 at p 82. For a critique of laws proscribing begging, see D J Baker, "A Critical Evaluation of the Historical and Contemporary Justifications for Criminalising Begging" (2009) 73(3) J Crim Law 212.

[69] Von Hirsch (n 68 above) at p 83.

to privacy; (2) insults; and (3) "unfair pre-emption of others' options concerning the use of shared public facilities and space".[70] His second ("insulting people") seems too broad a category, unless the insults are profound, but von Hirsch's first and third categories seem promising as potential rationales for proscribing certain forms of behaviour. Thus safeguarding privacy seems a legitimate basis on which to proscribe the conduct of the voyeurs in the cases mentioned in notes 62 and 64–66 above (although, in the case of the couple who were videoed while having sex at a party, it could be argued that those who choose to engage in such behaviours should hardly expect privacy). Applying von Hirsch's proposal to the "Naked Rambler", it may be suggested that his convictions were not justified in those cases in which prosecution was based on the fact that some people found his nakedness shocking or alarming. More recently, however, the police had suggested alternative routes for Gough – and had even offered to drive him there – so that he could avoid passing children's play parks. However, he refused to heed their requests and conviction in these circumstances seems justified. In von Hirsch's terminology, Gough's more recent behaviour failed to treat others with proper respect by amounting to an unfair pre-emption of their options over the use of public spaces. Criminalising those who play music at an excessively loud volume,[71] make other loud noises,[72] or urinate in a public fountain[73] may also be justified as safeguarding the equitable use of public facilities and spaces. However, whether the criminalisation of these various behaviours ought to be by way of *breach of the peace* – as has been the case – or by some other more specific offence is a different question. This is addressed further in Chapter 6.[74]

THE PUBLIC/PRIVATE DIVIDE

It is common for liberal theorists to distinguish between the "public" and the "private" spheres, and to contend that it is legitimate for the state to interfere in the former, but not generally the latter. As we have seen, many breaches of the peace involve behaviours which are felt by others to be "offensive". In relation to such types of

5.12

---

[70] Von Hirsch (n 68 above) at p 88.
[71] See *Hughes* v *Crowe* 1993 SCCR 320 (discussed at section 3.24 above).
[72] *Ibid*.
[73] Urinating in public was charged as breach of the peace (along with shouting and swearing) in *Hepburn* v *Howdle* 1998 JC 204; 1998 SLT 808; 1998 SCCR 363; 1998 GWD 8-141. This is also a statutory offence: Civic Government (Scotland) Act 1982, s 47.
[74] See sections 6.21–6.23 below.

behaviour, liberals generally argue that the criminal law ought to concern itself only with those which occur in public places. This is the approach taken by John Tasioulas:

> "... the space in which the offending behaviour is experienced must be public rather than private, that is, a domain in which the community as a whole has a substantial interest in regulating ... the nature of what might be experienced".[75]

The liberal demand for a private sphere which is immune from regulation by the state has been challenged by feminists who point out that the historical distinction between "the public" and "the private" meant that those who suffered verbal and physical abuse within the home – predominantly women and children – were often without legal remedy.[76] Domestic abuse was seldom prosecuted 30 years ago, in part at least due to the notion that this was a private matter which was not the concern of the criminal law. As Vanessa Munro explains:

> "The boundaries of public and private drawn and maintained in liberal theory emerge, under a feminist analysis, as deeply political and inherently constructed. Indeed, determinations of what counts as public and what counts as private are the result of a conscious process of decision making. The downside of this has been that those with power in society, typically men, have been able to relegate sexual and familial situations in which women are most vulnerable to the unregulated private sphere."[77]

The feminist critique does not demand that there be no distinction between the public and the private, or that the criminal law ought always to be enforced irrespective of the locus of the behaviour. Rather, the argument is that whether or not to criminalise certain behaviour cannot be determined simply by labelling something as a "public" matter (hence fit for criminalisation) or "private" (and thus free from proscription). The real debate should be about the values which are at stake if the behaviour at issue is, or is not, criminalised. While the "private" nature of the behaviour is a factor to

---

[75] J Tasioulas, in A von Hirsch and A P Simester, *Incivilities: Regulating Offensive Behaviour* (2006) 149–171 at p 151.

[76] See A M Jaggar, *Feminist Politics & Human Nature* (1983) at p 34; E Frazer and N Lacey, *The Politics of Community: A Feminist Critique of the Liberal-Communitarian Debate* (1993) at p 47; L Finley, "Breaking Women's Silence in Law: the Dilemma of the Gendered Nature of Legal Reasoning" (1989) 64 *Notre Dame L Rev* 886 at p 899. See also C A MacKinnon, *Women's Lives, Men's Laws* (2007) at p 262.

[77] V E Munro, "Dev'l-in disguise? Harm, Privacy and the Sexual Offences Act 2003" in V E Munro and C Stychin, *Sexuality and the Law* (2007) 1 at p 11. See also Frazer and Lacey (n 76 above) at p 72.

be considered in this, it should not be determinative.[78] Very many behaviours are criminalised irrespective of the locus in which they occur, for example intentional killings, assault, theft, robbery, rape, fraud, cruelty to animals etc. This needs to be borne in mind when we consider the requirement for actual or potential "public disturbance" in breach of the peace.[79] There may be good reasons for restricting the definition of this common law crime so that it applies only to "public disorders", but it is unfortunate that in doing so the appeal court created a gap in the criminal law such that victims of domestic abuse/abuse in private were without protection in the period between their ruling in the first *Harris* case in 2009, and the coming into force of s 38 of the Criminal Justice and Licensing (Scotland) Act 2010, more than 15 months later.[80]

One of our preliminary issues concerned the values which criminal **5.13** law ought to embody.[81] As noted previously, prominent among potential values is the rule of law.[82] This is a term with multiple meanings, but one of its central meanings is that criminal prohibitions should be of general application, relatively certain in their ambit, clearly expressed, adequately publicised, consistent with other laws, and prospectively applied. Article 7 of the ECHR has been interpreted as requiring precision in offence definitions,[83] and the concept of "fair labelling" is based on a similar concern to ensure that "widely felt distinctions between kinds of offences and degrees of wrongdoing are respected and signalled by the law" and that "offences should be divided and labelled so as to represent fairly the nature and degree of the law-breaking".[84] Thus offences must be fairly (or accurately) labelled to ensure that a conviction for a

---

[78] See R A Duff, *Answering for Crime: Responsibility and Liability in the Criminal Law* (2007) at pp 50–51. Lacey makes a similar point: "[A]rguments about public and private spheres are all too often hived off from their underlying liberal rationales and used as if we were simply *describing* spheres of activity, obscuring the normative premises of the argument." (N Lacey, *State Punishment: Political Principles and Community Values* (1998) at p 57 (emphasis in original)).

[79] This is considered further in Chapter 6.

[80] The case was decided on 22 July 2009, and s 38 of the 2010 Act came into force on 6 November 2010.

[81] See section 5.2 above.

[82] See section 1.8 above.

[83] See section 3.2 above.

[84] A Ashworth, *Principles of Criminal Law* (6th edn, 2009) at p 71; J Chalmers and F Leverick, "Fair Labelling in Criminal Law" (2008) 71 *MLR* 217. The term seems to have been coined by Glanville Williams in "Convictions and Fair Labelling" (1983) 42 *CLJ* 85, based on an idea of "representative labelling" which was described by Ashworth in "The Elasticity of *Mens Rea*" in C F H Tapper (ed), *Crime, Proof and Punishment: Essays in Memory of Sir Rupert Cross* (1981) at p 53.

particular offence accurately reflects what it was that the accused *did* that was reprehensible. As Jeremy Horder has put it:

> "[W]hat matters is not just that one has been convicted, but *of what* one has been convicted. If the offence in question gives too anaemic a conception of what that might be, it is fair neither to the [accused], nor to the victim. For the wrongdoing of the former, and the wrong suffered by the latter, will not have been properly *represented* to the public at large."[85]

Thus if behaviour is inaccurately labelled as a "breach of the peace" this will lead to misunderstandings about how the person convicted must have behaved.

CONCLUSION

5.14   This chapter has considered whether the criminalisation of conduct which "breaches the peace" can be justified by the harm and offence principles, and has also offered a critique of the liberal debate over the "public" and "private" spheres. While one may be able to appeal to one or other of these two principles in order to explain a particular case in which certain behaviour has been prosecuted as a breach of the peace, our discussion has demonstrated that it is in fact rather difficult to find a firm basis on which to justify this offence *per se*. Even if it is conceded that a certain type of behaviour merits proscription, whether this should be labelled as the crime of breach of the peace, or some other, more specific, offence requires further thought. We also need to consider whether the definition of breach of the peace, and its application in practice, are appropriate. These issues form the basis of the final chapter.

---

[85] J Horder, "Re-thinking Non-fatal Offences Against the Person" (1994) 14 *OJLS* 335, at p 351 (emphases in original).

CHAPTER 6

A CRITIQUE

INTRODUCTION

The analysis of the common law crime of breach of the peace under- **6.1** taken in Chapters 1–5 has led to the conclusion that it ought to be replaced with a more clearly defined statutory offence. Even if we assume that a crime of this nature can be justified by one or more principles of criminalisation, the Scottish version of breach of the peace can nevertheless be criticised on a number of grounds. It is neither adequately defined nor appropriately applied, and a review of its history reveals that its boundaries have always been unclear. Lord Justice-General Clyde noted in 1959 that its limits had "never been sharply defined".[1] Its expansionist nature was criticised by Gerald Gordon in 1967; he noted that convictions for breach of the peace could encompass "actings which are in themselves very far removed from the creation of a public disturbance".[2] In 1977, the appeal court declared that "There is no limit to the kind of conduct which may give rise to a charge of breach of the peace",[3] and in 1999 the court referred to it as an "amorphous offence".[4] In the United States, the constitutionality of several breach of the peace statutes has been successfully challenged for being overly broad and overly vague, thus violating the requirements of due process.[5] By contrast,

---

[1] *Young* v *Heatly* 1959 JC 66 at 70.
[2] G H Gordon, *The Criminal Law of Scotland* (1967) at p 927. See also the 2nd edition of this work (1978) at para 41-03.
[3] *Montgomery* v *McLeod* 1977 SLT (Notes) 77 at 77; (1977) SCCR Supp 164 at 165.
[4] *Paterson* v *Lees* 1999 SC (JC) 159; 1999 SCCR 231, per Lord Sutherland. The case concerned the crime of "shameless indecency", which all three judges in the appeal court also referred to as "amorphous": that crime was renamed and redefined in *Webster* v *Dominick* 2003 SCCR 525.
[5] See R Force, "Decriminalization of Breach of the Peace Statutes: A Nonpenal Approach to Order Maintenance" (1972) 46:3 *Tulane L Rev* 367 at p 370.

that it was somewhat vaguely defined has often been regarded by
the Scottish courts as one of its chief virtues. Academic writers have
frequently criticised this, with Sarah Oliver concluding:

> "the breadth and random use of the different criteria which will suffice for the
> conduct requirement suggest a degree of flexibility which may, on occasion,
> amount to insufficient certainty within the criminal law to accord with
> justice".[6]

Whether any particular behaviour would amount to a breach of the
peace has always been difficult to predict. According to Lord Justice-
Clerk Wheatley in *Carey* v *Tudhope*[7] (1984):

> "Each case will depend on its own circumstances. The facts of each case have
> to be looked at in the light of the surrounding circumstances in which they
> took place. In many cases it becomes a matter of judgment for the judge to
> decide whether in the context and atmosphere of what occurred the facts did
> constitute the offence of breach of the peace in the law of Scotland."[8]

Thus in a case in 1981, abusing solvents was not a breach of the
peace,[9] leading one commentator to state that: "Glue-sniffing ...
has the distinction of being one of the very few activities judicially
held not to constitute a breach of the peace".[10] However, the year
after this observation a glue-sniffer was successfully prosecuted[11] –
demonstrating that Crown Office operates on the premise that it is
legitimate for it to push the boundaries of offences. While this might
have been acceptable before Scotland had its own legislature, the
re-establishment of the Scottish Parliament means that the Crown
should now leave it to our elected representatives to determine which
types of behaviour merit criminalisation. Despite its redefinition in
Smith v *Donnelly*[12] (2001) and the refinements made in subsequent
cases such as the first *Harris* case (2009),[13] the boundaries of breach
of the peace remain less than clear, as evidenced by the number

---

[6] S A Oliver, "Recent Trends in Breach of the Peace" 1997 36 *SLT* 293 at p 296.
See also G Gordon, "Crimes without Laws?" 1966 *JR* 214; P R Ferguson, "Breach
of the Peace and the European Convention on Human Rights" (2001) 5 *Edin LR*
145. According to Gane *et al*: "The breadth of this offence is notorious" (C H W
Gane, C N Stoddart and J Chalmers, *A Casebook on Scottish Criminal Law* (4th
edn, 2009), para 16.02).
[7] 1984 SCCR 157.
[8] *Ibid* at 160.
[9] *Fisher* v *Keane* 1981 JC 50; 1981 SLT (Notes) 28.
[10] Commentary on *Ahmed* v *HM Advocate* 1983 SCCR 483 at 498.
[11] *Taylor* v *Hamilton* 1984 SCCR 393.
[12] 2002 JC 65; 2001 SLT 1007; 2001 SCCR 800.
[13] [2009] HCJAC 80; 2010 JC 245; 2009 SLT 1078; 2010 SCL 56; 2010 SCCR 15.
See section 3.11 above.

of cases taken to the appeal court.[14] The criticism that the crime remains ill defined relates particularly to its *mens rea*, but also to various facets of its *actus reus*.

MENS REA

As previous discussions have made clear, so long as the behaviour which constitutes the breach of the peace is intentionally done, there is no requirement for the Crown to show any intention to cause a disturbance.[15] Michael Christie's analysis of the case law led him to conclude that:

6.2

> "The role which *mens rea* plays and the form (if any) which it takes in breach of the peace remains, therefore, mysterious. Given the want of cogent authority on this issue, it would be better to assume that no particular form of dole is required and that no realistic defence can be mounted on the basis that one's client lacked *mens rea* …".[16]

While this may well be sound advice for solicitors, it reveals a most unsatisfactory state of affairs. That the *mens rea* of this commonly prosecuted crime remains uncertain is arguably the most serious indictment against it. Even if there were no difficulties with its *actus reus*, this lack of clarity in *mens rea* would itself justify the argument that breach of the peace requires to be redefined. Legislation ought to specify that there must be intention to breach the peace, or recklessness in failing to appreciate the likelihood that the behaviour in question would cause a disturbance. A decade ago, a small group of law professors drafted a Bill which, if enacted, would replace common law crimes with statutory offences. Although published under the auspices of the Scottish Law Commission, our *Draft Criminal Code for Scotland, with Commentary*[17] was an unofficial exercise, and while several of its provisions have been mirrored in subsequent legislation, the *Code* itself has not been enacted. It proposes replacing the current common law breach of the peace with several, more specific offences, including s 48 ("making unlawful threats"), s 49 ("violent and alarming behaviour") and

---

[14] Thus Lord Carloway referred to a "flurry of decisions on breach of the peace in recent times": *McIntyre* v *Nisbet* [2009] HCJAC 28 at para [10].

[15] See section 3.23 above.

[16] M G A Christie, *Breach of the Peace* (1990) at para 2.31.

[17] E Clive, P R Ferguson, C H W Gane and A A McCall Smith, *A Draft Criminal Code for Scotland, with Commentary* (2003) available at: http://www.scotslawcom.gov.uk/downloads/cp_criminal_code.pdf.

s 50 ("intrusive and alarming behaviour").[18] It offers a redefinition of breach of the peace itself in s 92:

> "A person who intentionally or recklessly causes a disturbance by acting in a way which a reasonable observer would regard as violent, aggressive, or disorderly is guilty of the offence of breach of the peace."

Recklessness is defined in s 10:

> "For the purposes of criminal liability –
> (a) something is caused recklessly if the person causing the result is, or ought to be, aware of an obvious and serious risk that acting will bring about the result but nonetheless acts where no reasonable person would do so;
> (b) a person is reckless as to a circumstance, or as to a possible result of an act, if the person is, or ought to be, aware of an obvious and serious risk that the circumstance exists, or that the result will follow, but nonetheless acts where no reasonable person would do so;
> (c) a person acts recklessly if the person is, or ought to be, aware of an obvious and serious risk of dangers or of possible harmful results in so acting but nonetheless acts where no reasonable person would do so."

While the essential elements of ss 48–50 have largely been enacted in subsequent legislation,[19] a provision similar to s 92 of the Code ought to be enacted in order to make clear the *mens rea* required for breach of the peace.

ACTUS REUS

6.3 There are several aspects of the *actus reus* which may be subject to critique. To reiterate the common law definition, the Crown must establish that there was conduct on the part of the accused which was "*severe* enough to cause alarm to ordinary people, *and* threaten *serious* disturbance to the community".[20] We must therefore consider the nature of disorderly conduct, the reference to "ordinary people", the conjunctive nature of the test, the meaning of "severe" (and of the alternative adjective used to describe conduct in some cases: "flagrant"), and the potential for serious disturbance to the community.

---

[18] See section 6.11 below.
[19] See the Criminal Justice and Licensing (Scotland) Act 2010, ss 38 and 39 (described at sections 4.8–4.11 above) and the Offensive Behaviour at Football and Threatening Communications (Scotland) Act 2012, s 6 (described at sections 4.12–4.14 above).
[20] *Smith* v *Donnelly* 2002 JC 65 at 71, para [17] (emphases added).

"Disorderly" conduct

While breach of the peace charges vary enormously in their 6.4
wording, the archetypal charge includes an averment that "you
… did conduct yourself in a disorderly manner". This may have
seemed an essential prerequisite given that breach of the peace
purports to be an offence of public (dis)order. However, in *Lees* v
Greer[21] (1996) it was held that the absence of these words was not
fatal to the relevancy of the charge. In *McGraw* v *HM Advocate*[22]
(2004) the jury deleted the reference to disorderly conduct so that
the conviction was for a charge which specified that the accused
"did utter threats of violence against [the two complainers] … and
commit a breach of the peace". One might have thought that this
was the common law charge of making "criminal threats",[23] but
the appeal court referred to the fact that the Criminal Procedure
(Scotland) Act 1995, in providing illustrations of breach of the peace
charges, "distinguishes between cases in which disorderly conduct is
alleged and cases in which there are threats causing a breach of the
peace".[24] The court concluded that

> "it is impossible to contend that disorderly conduct is of the essence of breach
> of the peace when Parliament itself has distinguished two classes of cases, one
> which includes disorderly conduct and the other does not".[25]

As Gordon points out in his commentary to the case, the court's
reliance on the wording of a schedule which merely provides
examples of charges was an "unsatisfactory basis for determining
relevancy".[26] Nevertheless, while it is clearly unnecessary for "disorderly conduct" to be libelled, the greater specification being given
in charges, as required by the ECHR, means that it ought to be
included if the Crown intends to lead evidence to this effect.[27]

"Ordinary people"

The reference in *Smith* v *Donnelly* to behaviour which could alarm 6.5
"ordinary people" reflects the terminology used in older cases.
Thus in *Ferguson* v *Carnochan*[28] (1889) "the lieges" was said to

---

[21] 1996 SLT 1096.
[22] 2004 SCCR 637.
[23] See G H Gordon, *The Criminal Law of Scotland* (3rd edn by M G A Christie,
2001), para 29.62 on.
[24] 2004 SCCR 637 at 639, per Lord Penrose.
[25] *Ibid.*
[26] *Ibid* at 640.
[27] Specification of charges is discussed in more detail at section 3.2 above.
[28] (1889) 2 White 278; 16 R (J) 93; 26 SLR 624.

mean either "ordinary people"[29] or "sober and reasonably minded people",[30] depending on which report of the case is consulted. These terms may not, of course, be synonymous, raising a further level of potential confusion. The criminal law usually imposes a standard of reasonable behaviour, hence, for example, a person who claims to have acted in self-defence generally has to show that he used no more than reasonable force. In contrast to this, in homicide cases the mitigating plea of provocation uses the standard of the "ordinary person" since it is assumed that no "reasonable person" would take human life, even if subject to extreme provocation. It seems in practice that "ordinary people" is treated as synonymous with "reasonable people" in the context of breach of the peace, but it is unfortunate that the latter expression was not used in the leading case. The *Jury Manual* suggests that judges ought to explain to jurors that in order to convict of breach of the peace they would have to be satisfied that the accused's conduct was, *inter alia,* "genuinely alarming and seriously disturbing to the *ordinary reasonable* person".[31] Should the courts attempt to further refine the definition, or the offence becomes a statutory one, it ought to be made clear that the standard is that of the reasonable person. In Canada, in cases of homicide provoked by prolonged domestic abuse, a context-sensitive version of the reasonable person is used.[32] This reflects the fact that the deceased may have behaved towards the accused in a manner which caused the later to apprehend serious injury from what may appear to an outside observer as relatively trivial: "just wait until I get you home" has a much more sinister implication to a person who has been abused for many years than the same words spoken in a different context. Scots law would do well to consider adopting a context-sensitive approach to the "reasonable person" in such cases, and perhaps also in appropriate cases of breach of the peace.

The conjunctive test

6.6 As previously discussed,[33] *Smith* v *Donnelly* specifies that the Crown

---

[29] (1889) 16 R (J) 93 at 94.

[30] (1889) 2 White 278 at 281.

[31] *Jury Manual* (Judicial Studies Committee for Scotland, Feb 2012), para 34.2, available at: http://www.scotland-judiciary.org.uk/Upload/Documents/JURYMANUALFeb12.pdf (emphasis added).

[32] See *Lavallee* v *R* [1990] 1 SCR 852; 22 CCC (3rd) 97 (SCC). See also J Meszaros, "Achieving Peace of Mind: The Benefits of Neurobiological Evidence for Battered Women Defendants" (2001) 23:1 *Yale J Law Fem* 117 at p 174: "the responses of the reasonable person could be enlarged to include the responses a reasonable person would have after enduring recent, chronic, and severe abuse".

[33] At section 3.4 above.

must establish both that there was conduct on the part of the accused which was severe enough to cause alarm to ordinary people, *and* that it threatened serious disturbance to the community."[34] This has since been referred to by the courts as affording a "conjunctive" test,[35] and one commentator has questioned whether "any other conjunction has ever enjoyed such prominence in the history of Scottish legal language".[36] Having to establish both elements has narrowed the ambit of breach of the peace but, as we have seen, this has caused confusion as to what is required to satisfy the requirement for "public" disorder.[37] It has also led to convictions being quashed on appeal where the sheriff had not made clear that the test is a conjunctive one.[38] It may be that Lord Coulsfield consciously used the conjunctive "and" rather than the disjunctive "or" as a means of narrowing the definition, in order to produce a definition of breach of the peace which was "of sufficient certainty to meet the requirements of the [European] Convention".[39] He did not, however, purport to be producing a radically different definition, but rather synthesising the definitions used in previous cases: "We therefore conclude that the definition of the crime found in the principal authorities does meet the requirements of the Convention."[40] It is noteworthy that in Christie's scholarly account of the case law he concluded that "a single definition" of breach of the peace was "impractical"[41] and therefore offered the following:

> "(1) breach of the peace consists of proven or admitted conduct on the part of the accused where there is also evidence that the conduct caused, or if allowed to continue would reasonably in all the circumstances have been likely to cause, by way of provocation of others or otherwise, real ... disturbance of the standing peace of the immediate and surrounding area where the conduct occurred; *and*, (2) breach of the peace *also consists of* proven or admitted conduct on the part of the accused from which, in all the circumstances, a court can reasonably infer that any reasonable person might be alarmed, upset, annoyed or suffer any other similar mental trauma as a result."[42]

---

[34] *Smith* v *Donnelly* 2002 JC 65 at 71, para [17] (emphasis added).

[35] See *Paterson* v *HM Advocate* [2008] HCJAC 18; 2008 JC 327; 2008 SLT 465; 2008 SCL 691; 2008 SCCR 605; *Hatcher* v *Harrower* [2010] HCJAC 92; 2011 JC 90; 2011 SCL 114; 2010 SCCR 903; *WM* v *HM Advocate* [2010] HCJAC 75.

[36] See the Commentary to *Paterson* v *HM Advocate* in (2008) *Scottish Criminal Law* 691 at p 704. The case is discussed at section 3.9 above.

[37] This public/private aspect is discussed further at sections 6.15–6.20 below.

[38] See *Anoliefo* v *HM Advocate* [2012] HCJAC 110; 2012 GWD 31-628.

[39] *Smith* v *Donnelly* 2002 JC 65 at 71, para [16].

[40] *Ibid* at 72, para [18].

[41] Christie, para 2.23.

[42] *Ibid* (emphases added).

Although Christie employed the conjunctive, it is clear that these definitions reflected alternative forms of breach of the peace: some behaviours cause, or could cause, disturbance of the peace "of the immediate and surrounding area" (ie of the community). Other behaviours were such that they would be likely to alarm the reasonable person. Either type could constitute a breach of the peace. It would have been preferable if the definition in *Smith* v *Donnelly* had reflected this disjunctive approach.

"Flagrant" conduct

6.7   In *Young* v *Heatly*[43] (1959) Lord Justice-General Clyde stated that in the absence of evidence of actual fear and alarm, breach of the peace required "flagrant" conduct.[44] This term has been used in many later cases,[45] including *Smith* v *Donnelly* itself,[46] in which Lord Coulsfield added:

> "'Flagrant' is a strong word and the use of that word points to a standard of conduct which would be alarming or seriously disturbing to any reasonable person in the particular circumstances."[47]

Dyer v *Hutchison*[48] (2006) was an appeal by stated case by the Crown, involving charges of racially aggravated breach of the peace at various football matches.[49] In each of three cases sheriffs had acquitted the respondents.[50] The Crown appeals were upheld in all cases, the appeal court holding that the sheriffs had set too

---

[43] 1959 JC 66; 1959 SLT 250; [1959] Crim LR 438.

[44] 1959 JC 66 at 70. The case is discussed at sections 2.6 and 3.11 above.

[45] For example, *Fisher* v *Keane* 1981 JC 50; 1981 SLT (Notes) 28; *Taylor* v *Hamilton* 1984 SCCR 393; *Stewart* v *Lockhart* 1991 SLT 835; 1990 SCCR 390 (discussed at sections 2.5 and 3.25 above, and critiqued further at section 6.13 below); *MacDougall* v *Dochree* 1992 JC 154; 1992 SLT 624; 1992 SCCR 531 (see section 4.7 above); *Wyness* v *Lockhart* 1992 SCCR 808; *Cameron* v *Normand* 1992 SCCR 866; *Hughes* v *Crowe* 1993 SCCR 320 (see section 3.24 above); *McMillan* v *Higson* 2003 SLT 573; 2003 SCCR 125 (discussed at section 3.7 above).

[46] 2002 JC 65.

[47] *Ibid* at 71, para [18]. See also *Jones* v *Carnegie* 2004 JC 136; 2004 SLT 609; 2004 SCCR 361.

[48] [2006] HCJAC 45; 2006 JC 212; 2006 SLT 657; 2006 SCCR 377.

[49] For further discussion of racially aggravated breaches of the peace, see section 3.32 above.

[50] Criminal Procedure (Scotland) Act 1995, s 175(3) provides that a prosecutor in summary proceedings may appeal to the High Court on a point of law against an acquittal.

much store by the need for the conduct to be "flagrant".[51] In *Dyer* v *Brady*[52] (2006) the court stated:

> "[W]e are not persuaded that the sheriff was wrong to sustain the submissions of no case to answer. At most, as the sheriff has said, this was a 'very low key protest'. It was at all times peaceful and, as we have noted, there was no evidence of anyone being alarmed or distressed. Nor, in that situation, do we consider that what the respondents were doing can be characterised as being 'flagrant'. In *Dyer* v *Hutchison* this Court suggested that the recurring use of the word 'flagrant' in recent cases may not always be helpful, but for present purposes we simply say, adopting the word used by Lord Coulsfield in the passage quoted earlier, that the conduct of the respondents was not in our view severe enough to cause alarm to ordinary people."[53]

Despite the court's misgivings about the helpfulness of the term, it has been used in several cases subsequent to this.[54] "Flagrant" seems to be used to describe behaviour which is so obviously likely to cause a disturbance/fear and alarm that no evidence of this effect need be given. It is word which may not be familiar to most lay people, and ought therefore to be avoided in judges' charges to juries.

"Severe" conduct

The reference to "severe" in Lord Coulsfield's definition is, with respect, rather an odd one. Synonyms for "severe" include "austere", "cruel", "Draconian", "hard" "harsh", "inexorable", "relentless", "rigid", "strict", "unbending" and "unrelenting",[55] none of which

6.8

---

[51] Gordon's commentary to the cases suggests that it demonstrates that breach of the peace "can still be used to criminalise any behaviour which the High Court regards as socially unacceptable" (2006 SCCR 377 at 389).

[52] [2006] HCJAC 72; 2006 SLT 965; 2006 SCCR 629; 2006 GWD 31-664. See sections 3.7 and 3.20 above.

[53] [2006] HCJAC 72, at para [19].

[54] See *Walls* v *Brown* [2009] HCJAC 59; 2009 JC 375; 2009 SLT 774; 2009 SCL 973; 2009 SCCR 711; 2009 GWD 23-370 (quoting sheriff McDonald, 2009 SCCR 711 at 714, para [8]); *McIntyre* v *Nisbet* [2009] HCJAC 28; 2009 SCL 829; 2009 SCCR 506 (sheriff citing *Smith* v *Donnelly* at 508, para [3]); *Paterson* v *HM Advocate* [2008] HCJAC 18; 2008 JC 327; 2008 SLT 465; 2008 SCL 691; 2008 SCCR 605 (charge to the jury by Sheriff Small, quoted in 2008 SCCR 605 at 615, para [23]). In *Russell* v *Thomson* [2010] HCJAC 138; 2011 JC 164; 2011 SCL 295; 2011 SCCR 77 the note of appeal stated: "The appellant has suffered a miscarriage of justice. The appellant's behaviour ... did not amount to a breach of the peace in that the appellant's behaviour was not serious *or flagrant* ...."(2011 SCCR 77 at 82–83, para [13] (emphasis added)). See also *HM Advocate* v *Greig* 2005 SCCR 465, discussed at section 3.28 above.

[55] *The New Collins Dictionary and Thesaurus*. The *Oxford English Dictionary* (available online at: http://oxforddictionaries.com) suggests "very great", "intense", "demanding great ability, skill, or resilience", "strict or harsh".

seems particularly apposite in this context – how can *conduct* comprising a breach of the peace be "severe"? In *Allison* v *Higson*[56] (2004) the accused, a spectator at a football match between Rangers and a European team, ran onto the pitch waving a Union Jack flag, when Rangers scored their first goal. The sheriff found that the appellant's actions "could reasonably have been expected to incite others to behave in a disorderly manner", with the potential to lead to "major crowd-control problems".[57] While this satisfies the second limb of the test (the potential for serious disturbance) it does not really address the first limb, namely whether the conduct itself was "severe" enough to cause alarm. The crowd were in jubilant mood following the goal, and it seems most unlikely that even the fans from the opposing team were alarmed by this display. Nevertheless, the appeal court upheld a conviction for breach of the peace. Reference has already been made to *Russell* v *Thomson*[58] (2010) in which the appellant was convicted of a breach of the peace involving sending a threatening letter to the headmistress of his children's school, entering the school playground and refusing to leave. As noted previously, the Scottish Criminal Case Review Commission assessed the case and concluded that the sending of the letter could not amount to a breach of the peace. As well as arguing that this was due to the private nature of the communication, the Commission also suggested that it was "difficult to characterise the applicant's actions as 'severe'".[59] Despite the lack of success of this argument, it is hard to see how other behaviours held to constitute a breach of the peace – such as the wearing of "inappropriate clothes",[60] the playing of bagpipes,[61] or the photographing of a drunk woman[62] – could be categorised as "severe conduct". It may be that "severe" in this context is being used to mean "outrageous" or "egregious". In practice, the requirement for severity (whatever it means) seems to be ignored at times by the courts. Nevertheless, while the courts

---

[56] 2004 SCCR 720.

[57] Finding 6, quoted *ibid* at 721, para [4].

[58] [2010] HCJAC 138; 2011 JC 164; 2011 SCL 295; 2011 SCCR 77. The case is discussed at section 3.14 above.

[59] Paragraph 47 of the SCCRC's Report, quoted by the appeal court in 2011 JC 164 at para [12].

[60] "Clothes claim head avoids court", *BBC News*, 10 July 2009, available at: http://news.bbc.co.uk/1/hi/scotland/north_east/8140198.stm. See also *Stewart* v *Lockhart* 1991 SLT 835; 1990 SCCR 390, discussed at sections 2.5 and 3.25 above and section 6.13 below.

[61] "Edinburgh buskers 'to pipe down'", *BBC News*, 12 June 2008, available at: http://news.bbc.co.uk/1/hi/scotland/edinburgh_and_east/7451328.stm.

[62] "Man fined for taking photograph", *BBC News*, 3 October 2008, available at: http://news.bbc.co.uk/1/hi/scotland/edinburgh_and_east/7651107.stm.

should operate a *de minimis* principle in respect of all crimes – and indeed the courts have on occasion referred to certain breaches of the peace as being particularly "trivial"[63] – the word "severe" ought not to form part of the definition of this crime.

Potential for "serious disturbance to the community"

It is unclear what is required to satisfy this part of the test. It seems to have been interpreted in cases subsequent to *Smith* v *Donnelly* to mean that behaviour which did not have the potential to affect the wider community – as opposed to the complainer(s) alone – could not constitute a breach of the peace. This seems to have been the view taken in the first *Harris* case,[64] (where the alarm likely to be caused to the police officers themselves was discounted), in *Macdonald*[65] (2008) (in which the averment that the accused's behaviour had caused fear and alarm to two psychologists – and indeed had been "for the purpose of causing fear and alarm"[66] – could not save the charge from being declared irrelevant), and in *Hatcher* v *Harrower*[67] (2010) (in which the fear and alarm caused to the appellant's wife, and the potential for this to have alarmed their children, was not enough for a "public disorder"). Harassing a headmistress was not sufficient in itself in *Russell* v *Thomson*[68] (above) but this breach of the peace conviction was upheld due to the likelihood of alarm being caused to parents, other teachers and pupils. This emphasis on disturbing persons other than the complainer(s) is also seen in the second *Harris* case[69] (2010). The relevant parts of the charges included averments that the accused did

    (1) "... repeatedly send or cause to be delivered numerous letters and text

6.9

---

[63] See *Lindsay* v *HM Advocate* [2005] HCJAC 66; 2005 1 JC 332; 2005 SCCR 515, in which the appeal court stated that some forms of conduct could be "too trivial to be dignified as breach of the peace" (at para [20]); *M'Arthur* v *Grosset* 1952 JC 12, involving a breach of the peace "of an apparently trivial character" (at 13); and *Craig* v *Herron* 1976 SCCR Supp 152, where the conduct was described as being "of a somewhat technical character and of trivial significance" (at 153). *Craig* v *Herron* is discussed at section 2.8 above.

[64] [2009] HCJAC 80; 2010 JC 245; 2009 SLT 1078; 2010 SCL 56; 2010 SCCR 15. See section 3.11 above.

[65] [2008] HCJAC 5; 2008 JC 262; 2008 SCCR 181.

[66] 2008 SCCR 181 at 182. See section 3.31 above.

[67] [2010] HCJAC 92; 2011 JC 90; 2011 SCL 114; 2010 SCCR 903. See section 3.15 above.

[68] [2010] HCJAC 138; 2011 JC 164; 2011 SCL 295; 2011 SCCR 77. See section 3.14 above.

[69] [2010] HCJAC 102; 2011 JC 125; 2010 SCCR 931. See section 3.11 above.

messages to [the first complainer] ... and did thereby harass, annoy, intimidate and frighten her ..."

(2) "... repeatedly send communications to [the second complainer at the firm of solicitors where she was employed] ... to her alarm and distress ..."

(3) "... for the purpose of causing annoyance, inconvenience or needless anxiety to [the first complainer] ... repeatedly telephone [her]..."

(4) "... cause to be sent and did send to various persons at [the firm of solicitors where the second complainer was employed] numerous envelopes containing various items designed to cause distress and embarrassment to [the second complainer], all to her fear and alarm and distress ...".

A distinction was drawn between the first three of these charges (offensive written materials and annoying phone calls, directed at the complainers: not relevant charges of breach of the peace), and the fourth charge (similar materials sent to one complainer's work colleagues: a relevant charge of breach of the peace). Curiously, although this fourth charge averred that fear, alarm and distress was caused only to the complainer, the court was able to salvage the charge by noting that it might be possible for the Crown to show that the employees who actually received the letters were also alarmed, and this could constitute "the necessary community element".[70] It seems that this is a distinction without a difference. A similar approach was taken in relation to the charges involving tracking devices. These libelled:

(1) "you ... did cause and arrange to be fitted to [the first complainer's] motor vehicle ... a mobile tracking device without [her] knowledge or consent ... did conduct yourself in a disorderly manner, use the information provided by said device to follow said [complainer] to various locations and make your presence known to her, all to her fear and alarm ... ;"

(2) "you ... did ... obtain and fit or cause to be fitted, to [a second vehicle] ... a mobile tracking device, for the purpose of harassment of [the two complainers] ... to their fear and alarm ...".

The first of these two charges was held to be a relevant one, but not the second. This was on the basis that in the first charge the accused was alleged to have used the information provided by the device to follow the complainer:

"to various (presumably public) places and make his presence there known to her. The particular circumstances in which these events occurred in public places may or may not amount to a breach of the peace. We are not in these circumstances prepared to hold that [this first charge] ... is irrelevant".[71]

---

[70] 2011 JC 125 at 134; 2010 SCCR 931 at 940, para [20].

[71] Ibid at para [21] (emphases added; first parenthesis in original).

Contrast the case of *Wilson* v *Brown*[72] in 1982:

> "It is well settled that a test which may be applied in charges of breach of the peace is whether the proved conduct may reasonably be expected to cause *any person* to be alarmed …".[73]

It is difficult to justify an approach which holds that alarming only one or two people is insufficient. Indeed, it is not clear how many people need to have been alarmed, or to have had the potential to have been alarmed, before it can be said that the accused's behaviour has disturbed "the community".

It may be recalled that in *Angus* v *Nisbet*[74] (2010) the accused's action in giving his phone number to a 14-year-old girl was regarded by the appeal court as "puzzling", but not a breach of the peace. By contrast, the remarks made by the taxi driver in *Bowes* v *Frame*[75] (2010) to a girl of the same age as the complainer in *Angus* did constitute a breach of the peace. *Bowes* v *Frame* was distinguished on its facts in *Angus* since the accused's comments in *Bowes* had "an explicitly sexual content".[76] Presumably the appeal court took the view that while there was evidence that the complainer in *Angus* was scared by the accused's behaviour, this was not likely to cause a wider disturbance. Certainly, the accused's conduct was less explicitly sexual than in *Bowes*, but it is submitted that the wider community would be disturbed by what lay behind the contact; many would consider it highly inappropriate for a 50-year-old stranger to give his phone number to a girl aged 14. And what of her parents' reaction: could the fact that they might well discover what had taken place and be alarmed by this be sufficient for a breach of the peace? Apparently not. Yet, as we have seen, in *Paterson*[77] (2008) it was the likely reaction of the parents of the 17-year-old complainer should they discover the accused's behaviour which constituted the necessary potential for serious community disturbance, the complainer's own reaction being insufficient. Fortunately, the complainer in *Bowes* had immediately reported the incident to her carers; as we saw in *WM* v *HM Advocate*[78] (2010) it was fatal to the breach of the peace in that

6.10

---

[72] 1982 SLT 361; 1982 SCCR 49, per Lord Dunpark.

[73] 1982 SCCR 49 at 51 (emphasis added).

[74] 2011 SC (JC) 69; [2010] HCJAC 76; 2010 SCCR 873; 2011 SCL 33.

[75] [2010] HCJAC 55; 2010 JC 297; 2010 SLT 683; 2010 SCL 761; 2010 SCCR 657. See section 3.12 above.

[76] 2010 JC 69; [2010] HCJAC 76, at para [16].

[77] [2008] HCJAC 18; 2008 JC 327; 2008 SLT 465; 2008 SCL 691; 2008 SCCR 605. See section 3.16 above.

[78] [2010] HCJAC 75; 2011 JC 49; 2010 GWD 26-488. See sections 1.4 and 3.16 above.

case that the young boys did not alert anyone about their father's threats until many years after he had sexually assaulted them. Even if the rationale for the crime is to proscribe behaviour which is likely to provoke a *public* disturbance, one must ask who is more likely to react in a way which disturbs the public peace: a mother whose young sons tell her that they have been repeatedly sexually abused by their father and threatened with violence should they reveal this (*WM*); or an employee of a residential home who learns that a taxi driver made sexual comments to a girl in the employee's care (*Bowes*)? It seems clear that the former is much more likely to be far more alarmed and upset than the latter, thus there is greater potential for the mother to react in a way which causes a disorder.

6.11 The "private" nature of the conduct in most sexual offences means that it is difficult in any event to obtain adequate evidence, but requiring a short time interval between the threats made in cases such as *WM* and the possibility of public disorder arising from their communication to a third party creates an additional barrier to successful prosecution. As previously noted, s 38 of the Criminal Justice and Licensing (Scotland) Act 2010 makes it an offence to engage in "threatening and abusive behaviour". This could be used in future to cover cases similar to that of *WM*.[79] In a case decided prior to *Smith* v *Donnelly*, namely *Biggins* v *Stott*[80] (1999), the two charges of breach of the peace libelled that the accused had invited a 13-year-old girl to accompany him to his flat, and had offered her money to do so, thereby placing her in a state of fear and alarm. If a similar case arose again, and the court applied *Angus* v *Nisbet*, it seems doubtful that this would now be a breach of the peace, there being no explicit sexual content to the accused's remarks.[81] If, however, the court chose instead to follow cases such as *Paterson* and *LBM* v *HM Advocate*[82] (2011) there is little doubt that, if discovered, such conduct by a mature man towards an adolescent girl is likely to cause a strong reaction among other adults, leading very possibly to serious disturbance thereafter. Although such behaviour might be prosecuted as a breach of s 38, this does not quite capture the essence of the wrongful conduct, which is more "alarming" than "threatening" or "abusive".[83] As noted previously, the *Draft*

---

[79] See section 4.8 above.

[80] 1999 JC 298; 1999 SLT 1037; 1999 SCCR 595; 1999 GWD 24-1136.

[81] It does, however, seem that the girl believed that the accused's intention was "to engage in sexual activity" with her: 1999 JC 298 at 299; 1999 SCCR 595 at 596.

[82] [2011] HCJAC 96; 2012 SLT 147; 2012 SCL 74; 2011 GWD 34-715. See section 3.27 above.

[83] See the discussion on fair labelling at sections 1.8 and 5.13 above.

Criminal Code proposes a range of offences which might be useful additions to the criminal calendar.[84] One of these, in s 50, provides:

> "(1) A person who by intrusive behaviour intentionally or recklessly causes another person fear, alarm or significant distress is guilty of the offence of intrusive and alarming behaviour.
> (2) For the purposes of this section – (a) intrusive behaviour includes stalking, following, watching and spying upon a person; and (b) behaviour includes an isolated act and a course of conduct."

Enactment of an offence such as this would criminalise the behaviours of the accused in *Bowes* v *Frame*,[85] *LBM* v *HM Advocate*, – and possibly even *Angus* v *Nisbet* – without resort to s 38 or breach of the peace.

REMOTE RISKS OF HARM

In our discussion in Chapter 5, we noted that the "harm principle" permits the criminalisation of conduct that creates a risk of harm, as well as that which actually causes harm.[86] The courts seem content to brand conduct as a breach of the peace even when the risk of harm is somewhat speculative. As previously noted,[87] the risk of harm can even be from a possible disturbance caused by *persons other than the accused.* The law generally punishes individuals who freely choose to act in a criminally wrongful manner. Criminalisation of a person on the basis that *others* might respond violently to that person is a departure from this principle. It is possible to envisage circumstances where the accused's behaviour is very likely to provoke immediate, serious violence by others: deliberately entering a "team" pub in the colours of a rival football team during a match and verbally abusing rival fans might be an example.[88] If the possibility of reprisals is more remote, however, it is arguable that the requirements of the harm principle have not been met. **6.12**

As previously discussed, in *Raffaelli* v *Heatly*[89] (1949) the accused was charged with breach of the peace by staring through a gap in curtains into a house late at night. Potential harm to others posed by the accused's behaviour was surely extremely remote. Andrew von Hirsch has suggested that **6.13**

---

[84] See section 6.10 above.
[85] [2010] HCJAC 55; 2010 JC 297; 2010 SLT 683; 2010 SCL 761; 2010 SCCR 657. See section 3.20 above.
[86] At section 5.8 above.
[87] See section 2.5 above.
[88] I am indebted to Claire McDiarmid for this example.
[89] 1949 JC 101; 1994 SLT 284, discussed at section 2.5 above.

"there is a moral reason for considering the behaviour of a 'Peeping Tom' as offensive – namely, that it is disrespectful to intrude into others' legitimate intimate sphere".[90]

But it would be inappropriate to criminalise conduct purely on the basis that it is "disrespectful"; this is too broad a criterion. Those who are referred to as "Peeping Toms" are generally being accused of having surreptitiously observed others' nudity, or others engaging in sexual activities, for the observer's sexual gratification.[91] While there may be sound reasons for criminalising this sort of behaviour – being spied on while naked or involved in sexual intimacy is a serious violation of privacy – it should be noted that in *Raffaelli* there was no evidence about what, if anything, was going on behind the curtains.[92] The conviction in that case was based on the view that the appellant's behaviour "might reasonably be expected to lead to the lieges being alarmed or upset or tempted to make reprisals at their own hand".[93] A similar approach was taken in *Stewart v Lockhart*[94] (1990). It will be recalled that the male accused was dressed as a woman in an area frequented by prostitutes.[95] This was found to be "likely to occasion a breach of the peace" on the basis that a (hypothetical) man who was looking for a prostitute could cause a disturbance/breach the peace on discovering Stewart's true gender.[96] While there was some evidence in *Raffaelli* that reprisals were likely – according to Lord Justice-Clerk Thomson, one complainer "was afraid to inform her own husband as to the situation in case he would through distaste be tempted into a breach of the peace"[97] – the risk of reprisals in *Stewart* was far more speculative. In any event, if others appear likely to breach the peace as a result of a person's behaviour, it is those others who ought to be

---

[90] A von Hirsch, "The Offence Principle in Criminal Law: Affront to Sensibility or Wrongdoing?" (2000) 11 *King's College LJ* 78 at 83.

[91] The term "Peeping Tom" is believed to derive from the legendary tale of Lady Godiva, who rode naked on a horse through the streets of Coventry in an attempt to persuade her husband not to continue levying high taxes on the townsfolk. According to the legend, the citizens of Conventry undertook to avert their eyes, but "Peeping Tom" betrayed her trust and looked as she rode by.

[92] Appropriate cases *must* now be dealt with by the statutory offence of voyeurism: see the Sexual Offences (Scotland) Act 2009 s 9(2), discussed at section 4.7 above.

[93] 1949 JC 101 at 101.

[94] 1991 SLT 835; 1990 SCCR 390.

[95] See sections 2.5 and 3.25 above.

[96] See also *Robert Fraser, The Scotsman*, 23 March 1978, cited in Gane, Stoddart and Chalmers, para 16.02. For a critique of *Stewart v Lockhart*, see para 16.04 of that work.

[97] 1949 JC 101 at 101.

arrested (or perhaps simply warned).[98] Although it is certainly not explicit in the case report that the appellant was actually soliciting at the time of his arrest, the case creates the impression that the appeal court was engaged in the enforcement of morals. While this perception may not be accurate, criminalising behaviour such as this without any recognition of the need to attempt to balance individual liberties against the need to secure public order leaves the court's decision vulnerable to such an interpretation. The case of *Kara* v *United Kingdom*[99] (1998) has clarified the rights of transvestites. Here, a male transvestite had been disciplined by his employers for breaching their dress code by wearing "female" clothes at work, including leggings, tights and halter tops. The European Commission on Human Rights held that a requirement for employees to dress "appropriately" to their gender could be regarded by an employer as necessary to safeguard its public image.[100] However, the Commission stressed that Kara could dress as he pleased outside work, since constraints imposed on a person's mode of dress constitute an interference with private life under Art 8 of the ECHR.[101] Any interference with this could also be challenged as a breach of freedom of expression, guaranteed by Art 10. As we have seen,[102] interference with this latter right is permissible "for the prevention of disorder or crime", but it is submitted that, if the circumstances of *Stewart* v *Lockhart* were to recur, there would now need to be clearer evidence of the likelihood of a disturbance, rather than mere speculation.

SELF-HARM

As we have seen,[103] the harm principle is generally interpreted as providing a justification for criminalising certain types of conduct which harm or risk harm *to others*, and the criminalisation of self-harming behaviours is often regarded as unwarranted legal **6.14**

---

[98] See also *Deakin* v *Milne* (1882) 5 Coup 174; (1882) 10 R (J) 22, discussed at sections 3.23 and 3.25 above.

[99] (1998) 27 EHRR CD 272.

[100] Prior to 1988, individuals who wished to claim that their rights under the European Convention on Human Rights had been breached had no direct access to the European Court of Human Rights. They had to apply to the Human Rights Commission, which would pass the case to the Court if it found the case to be well founded. Direct access to the Court by individuals became permitted in 1989 due to the enactment of Protocol 11 to the ECHR, and the Commission was abolished.

[101] See Gane, Stoddart and Chalmers, para 16.04.

[102] See section 3.17 above.

[103] See section 5.6 above.

paternalism.[104] As we noted previously, it is possible that one rationale for the arrest and subsequent prosecution of the accused in *Stewart* v *Lockhart* (above) was to protect him from the (possibly violent) reactions of others. In his note to the appeal court the Justice stated:

> "At the very least the appellant might [have been] shouted at and verbally abused and he was also in grave danger of being physically attacked. For this reason I found the appellant guilty of the charge as libelled."[105]

Another possible example of legal paternalism is *Colhoun* v *Friel*[106] (1996) which involved a peaceful protest. The appeal court noted:

> "[The appellant] had sat down on the tree deliberately while it was in the course of being cut up, and *he placed himself* and the workman *in a position of danger* by his refusal to move".[107]

The rationale for prosecuting as a breach of the peace the behaviours of those who threaten or attempt suicide,[108] or who engage in tomb-stoning[109] may be based, at least in part, on paternalistic concerns, and the only potential "harm" to others is that they might be fearful *for* the accused. This is surely insufficient. Given its controversial nature as a principle of criminalisation, it is submitted that it is rarely justifiable for conduct to be prosecuted for breach of the peace on the basis of legal paternalism, alone.

THE PUBLIC/PRIVATE DIVIDE, AND DISCOVERABILITY

6.15   As we have previously noted,[110] although breach of the peace is commonly regarded as a "public order" crime, until recently the courts paid little heed to the locus in which the conduct occurred. However, even before the first *Harris* case held that private commu-nications could not constitute a breach of the peace, the courts

---

[104] See section 5.5 above.

[105] 1990 SCCR 390 at 391.

[106] 1996 SLT 1252; 1996 SCCR 497.

[107] 1996 SCCR 497 at 499 (emphases added).

[108] See *John MacLean (The Scotsman*, 30 October 1979, cited in Gane, Stoddart and Chalmers, para 16.02) and cases referred to in Christie, para 3.33. More recent cases include *Blane* v *HM Advocate* 1991 SCCR 576; *Baker* v *MacLeod* 1998 GWD 11-540; and *Torbet* v *HM Advocate* 1998 SCCR 546.

[109] See "Youth charged over 'tombstoning'", *BBC News*, 1 June 2009, available at: http://news.bbc.co.uk/1/hi/scotland/tayside_and_central/8077061.stm. Tombstoning is "an extreme sport involving jumping from cliffs or other high objects into the sea" (*ibid*).

[110] See section 2.6 above.

had been reluctant to convict where behaviour took place in private and the accused had made efforts to ensure that it would not be discovered by others. One example of this is *Thompson* v *MacPhail*[111] (1989) in which the accused had locked himself into a toilet cubicle in a fast food restaurant. The manager of the premises became suspicious and called the police. They managed to open the door and caught the accused withdrawing a syringe from his arm. It is not known what the accused had been injecting; it may have been a controlled drug such as heroin, or a lawful drug, such as insulin. The appeal court held that this was not a breach of the peace; it was essentially a private act and the accused had done all he could to keep it private. Of course, each case must be determined on its own facts, and *Thompson* v *MacPhail* is not authority for the proposition that "shooting up" in the toilet of a restaurant will not amount to a breach of the peace. Nevertheless, the case did illustrate an important limitation on the crime: there is doubtless a range of conduct which could cause alarm to the reasonable person but which, if committed in private, ought not to be criminal. If, however, the accused's behaviour is likely to be discovered by a third party, and once discovered could reasonably be expected to cause alarm, then the conduct will be a breach of the peace.[112]

In *Bryce* v *Normand*[113] (1997) the accused had made a video **6.16** recording of his 15-year-old neighbour while she was undressing, without her knowledge. Although the girl had been unaware that she was being filmed, and only became aware of this about a month later, this was held to be a breach of the peace on the basis that such conduct could reasonably be expected to lead to alarm or disturbance, had it been discovered.[114] The importance of discoverability is also illustrated by the (unreported) case of *Robert Stewart* (2007), who pled guilty to a sexually aggravated breach of the peace[115] for simulating sex with a bicycle in the locked bedroom of the hostel in which he was living.[116] His case led to some debate on the merits of prosecuting such behaviour, and to the revelation

---

[111] 1989 SLT 637; 1989 SCCR 266.

[112] See also *MacDougall* v *Dochree* 1992 JC 154; 1992 SLT 624; 1992 SCCR 531, discussed at section 4.7 above.

[113] 1997 SLT 1351.

[114] See also *HM Advocate* v *Carson* 1997 SLT 1119; 1997 SCCR 273; 1997 GWD 12-498, in which the accused was charged with a breach of the peace which involved taking clandestine photographs of children at a primary school.

[115] See section 3.31 above regarding crimes aggravated by a "significant sexual aspect".

[116] See "Bike sex man is placed on probation", *BBC News*, 14 November 2007, available at: http://news.bbc.co.uk/1/hi/scotland/glasgow_and_west/7095134.stm, discussed at section 3.31 above.

that his was not the first prosecution for "simulating sex with an inanimate object",[117] a 38-year-old man having been arrested in 2002 for "simulating sex with a traffic cone in front of a crowd of people", and having been fined £100 in 1997 for "trying to have sex with a shoe in an Edinburgh street", and a teenager having sentence deferred in 2007 for "simulating sex on a pavement".[118] Although minimal details are available, it seems likely that the charge in each of these cases was breach of the peace. In contrast to the case of *Robert Stewart,* the locus in each of these other cases was a public place, thus the behaviours involved were a form of exhibitionism. It may have been determinative that Stewart's behaviour occurred in a hostel in which cleaners were permitted to open residents' rooms. If, however, we consider the public/private spheres, as described in Chapter 5,[119] it is hard to characterise his room in the hostel as, for him, anything other than his home – the embodiment of the private sphere. If he had not been homeless, but in his own "home", to which he had exclusive access, it is unlikely that his behaviour would have been discovered, far less prosecuted. Many people might find Stewart's behaviour shocking, or even offensive, but is this the sort of behaviour which ought to be proscribed by the criminal law?

6.17   Although the real issue is the likelihood of behaviour being discovered, rather than the "public"/"private" nature of the locus *per se,* it is curious how often the appeal court emphasises the public nature of the locus when upholding a conviction. Thus, as we have seen,[120] in *Paterson* v *HM Advocate,*[121] in which the two breaches of the peace involved sexual behaviour towards a 17-year-old girl, Lord Justice-General Hamilton stated:

> "it is important to notice that the conduct alleged in [one charge] occurred in a public place and that [the other] charge ... although on private property, occurred in relatively close proximity to where [the complainer's] parents were sitting in an adjacent room".[122]

In *Angus* v *Nisbet* the court "had no difficulty in concluding that the conduct did have a public element" since it "took place in a public street" and "what was said and done was said and done in public".[123] The wider public were unaware of the nature of the conversation,

---

[117] See "Bike case sparks legal debate", *BBC News*, 16 November 2007, available at: http://news.bbc.co.uk/1/hi/scotland/glasgow_and_west/7098116.stm.

[118] *Ibid.*

[119] At sections 5.12–5.13 above.

[120] At section 3.9 above.

[121] 2008 JC 327; 2008 SCCR 605.

[122] 2008 JC 327 at 336; 2008 SCCR 605 at 614–615 at para [22].

[123] 2011 SC (JC) 69; [2010] HCJAC 76 at para [13].

however, so it is difficult to see how these circumstances satisfy the need for a public element, if one does not rely on location.

Mention has already been made of *Bowes* v *Frame* in which **6.18** the accused taxi driver alarmed the 14-year-old complainer by making remarks of a sexual nature. In respect of the public/private dimension, the appeal court noted that the locus of the offences was "a publicly licensed taxi which was available for hire to members of the public" being driven on "several public roads".[124] According to the appeal court, this was "a different situation from one in which conduct that might be objectionable occurred in a private motor vehicle".[125] In relation to the potential discoverability of the behaviour, "there was plainly a realistic risk of the conduct being discovered, as indeed occurred within a very short period of time following upon it, when its occurrence was reported to those who, in furtherance of a public duty, were responsible for the care of the complainer".[126] If, however, reporting an incident is equivalent to "discoverability", then almost any behaviour has the potential for public disorder, even that in *Thompson* v *MacPhail*, since he may have recounted his behaviour to others, after the event.

When the Lord Advocate gave evidence to the Justice Committee **6.19** of the Scottish Parliament during its consideration of the Offensive Behaviour at Football and Threatening Communications (Scotland) Bill, one reason he gave for favouring the creation of the new offences in the Bill related to breach of the peace. He stated:

> "Over the past few years, the common-law crime of breach of the peace has been developing as a result of the European convention on human rights, which requires that a citizen knows what is criminal and what is not. The argument is that breach of the peace is ill defined and that the limits of the crime are not well enough defined for a citizen to know whether certain conduct is criminal or not. For example, recently – that is, in the past couple of years – it has been held that for breach of the peace to apply there must be a public element to it. For example, *conduct in a private dwelling house can no longer be a breach of the peace* …".[127]

Presumably, he meant that conduct in a private dwelling house is no longer a breach of the peace if the only persons alarmed or disturbed by it are within the house, and there is no reasonable likelihood that people outside the house would be alarmed or disturbed. If, however, the head of the Scottish prosecution service is indeed of the view that

---

[124] 2010 JC 297 at para [22].
[125] *Ibid.*
[126] *Ibid.*
[127] See *Justice Committee Official Report*, 22 June 2011, col 99, available at: http://www.scottish.parliament.uk/parliamentarybusiness/28862.aspx?r=6366&mode=pdf (emphasis added).

breach of the peace cannot now be committed in a private house (or presumably in any other private location) then the first *Harris* case has narrowed the definition of the crime considerably. If the Lord Advocate's views reflect Crown Office policy – and we must surely assume that they do – then breach of the peace will no longer be prosecuted where the locus is a private one. This provides a further illustration of the confused state of the current law.

6.20   Some cases in which a conviction for breach of the peace was obtained, or in which the accused pled guilty, would probably not now have a successful outcome for the prosecution. In *Wylie* v *M*[128] (2008), for example, the accused pled guilty to a charge of breach of the peace which libelled that he had repeatedly telephoned the complainer, making sexual comments to her, which placed her in a state of fear and alarm. In light of the first *Harris* case, however, it is unlikely that breach of the peace could be charged in similar circumstances in future, since the telephone conversations might be regarded as private communications: only the complainer (and possibly her mother) were alarmed.[129] In *Beattie* v *HM Advocate*[130] (2008) the accused was convicted of three offences, the last of which was a breach of the peace involving masturbating, in his own home, in front of an elderly relative. The appeal related to a point of evidence law,[131] but no issue was raised as to the relevancy of the breach of the peace charge. In *George* v *HM Advocate*[132] (2011) the appellant was convicted of 18 offences, including assault, sexual assault, and breaches of the peace, committed when he was an art teacher at a residential school. The breaches of the peace involved making indecent remarks and exposing himself on various occasions to pupils at the school. It is difficult to tell from the report of the case, but the facts seem similar to those in the (now overruled) case of *Young* v *Heatly*,[133] in terms of the "private" nature of the behaviour. In *Anoliefo* v *HM Advocate*[134] (2012) the appellant was convicted on indictment of six breaches of the peace, an assault

---

[128] 2009 SLT (Sh Ct) 18; 2009 SCL 223; 2008 GWD 40-605.

[129] This could now be charged as a breach of the Criminal Justice and Licensing (Scotland) Act 2010, s 38, depending on the nature of the comments.

[130] [2008] HCJAC 73; 2009 JC 88; 2009 SLT 151; 2009 SCL 266; 2009 SCCR 106; 2009 GWD 5-76 (also reported as *CAB* v *HM Advocate* and *B* v *HM Advocate*).

[131] Namely, the application of the *Moorov* doctrine. For a commentary on the evidential aspects of the case, see (2009) *Scottish Criminal Law* (Mar) 266–282.

[132] [2011] HCJAC 33; 2011 GWD 15-363. See section 3.11 above. These incidents occurred in the 1970s, and were prosecuted pre-*Harris*, in 2006.

[133] 1959 JC 66; 1959 SLT 250; [1959] Crim LR 438, discussed above at sections 2.6 and 3.11.

[134] [2012] HCJAC 110; 2012 GWD 31-628.

and a rape. All but the rape conviction were quashed on appeal. In relation to the breaches of the peace, the appeal court concluded:

"The trial judge did not direct the jurors fully as to the terms of the conjunctive test. In particular he did not direct them that they required to address and be satisfied that the conduct of the appellant had caused the risk of serious disturbance to the community. In our view that was a material misdirection."[135]

The court also noted that:

"The relevance of none of the charges of breach of the peace had been challenged in advance of the trial, nor was any submission made at the close of the Crown case that the appellant had no case to answer in respect of any of those charges of breach of the peace."[136]

The indictment averred a serious course of conduct: sexual remarks made to several women (charged as breaches of the peace), culminating in the rape of another. Yet it is clear that breaches of the peace such as these are vulnerable to challenge; in light of *Harris* they are likely to fall foul of the requirement that the accused's behaviour has the potential for "public/community disturbance". The offence of "threatening and abusive behaviour" in s 38 of the Criminal Justice and Licensing (Scotland) Act 2010 may be used by the Crown to prosecute similar cases, in future.[137]

APPLICATION: ALTERNATIVE CHARGES

As previously noted,[138] many forms of unacceptable sexual behaviour **6.21** have been prosecuted as breach of the peace. These have included cases in which the accused tried to entice young girls into his car;[139] made sexual phone calls to strangers;[140] asked indecent and personal questions;[141] made indecent remarks;[142] and masturbated in front of

---

[135] [2012] HCJAC 110 at para [11], per Lord Eassie. The conviction on the assault charge was dependent on the application of the *Moorov* doctrine. Since the convictions for breach of the peace were quashed, this charge also required to be set aside due to insufficiency of evidence. See *ibid* at para [4].
[136] *Ibid* at para [10].
[137] See section 4.8 above.
[138] See section 5.8 above.
[139] *LBM v HM Advocate* [2011] HCJAC 96; 2012 SLT 147; 2012 SCL 74; 2011 GWD 34-715. See section 3.27 above.
[140] *Dudley v HM Advocate* 2004 Scot (D) 36/11. See section 4.5 above.
[141] *Gibson v Heywood* 1997 SLT 101. See section 4.5 above.
[142] *Anoliefo v HM Advocate* [2012] HCJAC 110; 2012 GWD 31-628. See section 6.20 above.

an elderly female relative.[143] These behaviours are often committed in private and/or involve what is essentially a private communication from the accused to the complainers. The latter are often women or children. There is little doubt that the criminal law should proscribe these forms of conduct, but the offence of threatening and abusive behaviour more accurately describes the wrong being committed in such cases than does breach of the peace.[144] Thus a separate criticism that can be levied against breach of the peace relates to its application, and the fact that the Crown continues to prosecute a wide range of behaviours for this crime when there are (arguably more apposite) alternative offences. This raises issues of fair labelling.[145] As well as using breach of the peace for the range of sexual behaviours listed above, we see this in relation to cases which involve assaults.[146] In *Sproull v McGlennan*[147] (1999) the two accused pled guilty to charges of breach of the peace which libelled that they had assaulted the complainers, and had repeatedly punched and kicked them. At the time, the maximum sentence a sheriff could generally impose in respect of a common law crime prosecuted in summary procedure was 3 months' imprisonment,[148] but a sentence of up to 6 months' imprisonment could be imposed for an offence "inferring personal violence" where the accused had one or more previous convictions for a similar offence.[149] Each of the accused had at least one previous conviction for assault. Taking the view that they had pled guilty to a breach of the peace which included assault, the

---

[143] *Beattie v HM Advocate* [2008] HCJAC 73; 2009 JC 88; 2009 SLT 151; 2009 SCL 266; 2009 SCCR 106; 2009 GWD 5-76. See section 6.20 above.

[144] See section 4.8 above.

[145] For a recent example, see "Student admits splattering Nick Clegg with paint in Glasgow", *BBC News*, 20 February 2012, available at: http://www.bbc.co.uk/news/uk-scotland-glasgow-west-17102979. This could have been charged as assault or possibly vandalism. The concept of fair labelling is defined at section 5.13 above, and discussed further at section 6.32 below.

[146] For example, *HM Advocate v Hegarty* 2002 SCCR 1022: "kick [the complainer] on the body and knock her to the ground, all to her injury, and commit a breach of the peace". See also *Butcher v Jessop* 1989 JC 55; 1989 SLT 593; 1989 SCCR 119 (discussed at section 2.8 above); *Robb v HM Advocate* 1999 JC 223; and *Buttercase v Russell* 1999 GWD 21–992 (discussed at section 3.29 above). Note, however, *Johnstone v Lindsay* 1907 SC (J) 9; (1906) 14 SLT 429 in which it was stated that: "It would have been easy for the prosecutor here to have combined the two offences in one charge, *for assault is a breach of the peace*" ((1907) SC (J) 9 at 11 (emphasis added)).

[147] 1999 JC 105; 1999 SLT 402; 1999 SCCR 63; 1999 GWD 3-140. See also *Butcher v Jessop* 1989 JC 55; 1989 SLT 593; 1989 SCCR 119 and *Robb v HM Advocate* 1999 JC 223.

[148] By virtue of the Criminal Procedure (Scotland) Act 1995, s 5(2)(d).

[149] Criminal Procedure (Scotland) Act 1995, s 5(3). This provison was repealed by the Criminal Proceedings etc (Reform) (Scotland) Act 2007, s 43(b).

sheriff sentenced them to 4 months' imprisonment, and this was upheld on appeal.[150] Although Lord McCluskey expressed surprise that the Crown had included in the one libel "two distinguishable factual matters which would normally be treated as constituting separate offences, namely assault on the one hand and breach of the peace on the other"[151] and accepted that breach of the peace does not "in its nature necessarily infer personal violence",[152] he held that in the present case each appellant had assaulted someone, and that this obviously did infer personal violence.[153] In contrast to this, in *Youngson* v *Higson*[154] (2000) repeatedly pulling at the complainer's bike and threatening to assault her was not an offence which inferred personal violence. Similarly, in *Paterson* v *Webster*[155] (2002) it was held that a breach of the peace which averred that the appellant did "brandish two knives" and "threaten the lieges with violence" fell short of inferring personal violence because there was no averment that he had been menacing any particular person. Nevertheless, where there is sufficient evidence to prove an assault, it is submitted that it would be preferable for the Crown to libel this as a charge in its own right.

It may be that the Crown libelled breach of the peace rather than assault in some cases as part of a plea-bargaining or charge-bargaining process; an accused with previous convictions for assault may hope for a lesser sentence by pleading guilty to breach of the peace, rather than risk a trial for assault. It is noteworthy that the procurator fiscal in *Sproull* v *McGlennan* (above) agreed with the accused's solicitors that the sheriff had no power to impose a sentence in excess of 3 months, since the charge was breach of the peace, not assault. Now that the maximum summary sentence is 12 months' imprisonment,[156] and there is no power to increase this maximum for a second or subsequent offence involving violence, whether or not a breach of the peace inferred personal violence is of less relevance. The Crown has, however, continued to prosecute breach of the peace for conduct which could have been more appropriately charged as a different crime. An example of this is the case of *Cottam* v *AB*[157] (2010) in which the charge libelled that the accused had repeatedly placed his hand on the legs of the complainer, who

6.22

---

[150] See also *Adair* v *Morton* 1972 SLT (Notes) 70.
[151] 1999 JC 105 at 108; 1999 SCCR 63 at 66.
[152] *Ibid*.
[153] See also "Four Months for Breach of the Peace" (1999) 37 (Feb) *Crim LB* 2.
[154] 2000 SLT 1441; 2000 GWD 29-1125.
[155] 2002 SLT 1120; 2002 SCCR 734.
[156] Criminal Procedure (Scotland) Act 1995, s 5(2)(d), as amended by the Criminal Proceedings etc (Reform) (Scotland) Act 2007, s 43.
[157] 2010 SCCR 669.

was asleep on a train, "in an inappropriate manner" and repeatedly rubbed her thighs.[158] One is reminded of the argument by the Convenor of the Justice Committee in favour of a specific offence of "communicating religious hatred". As previously noted,[159] she pointed out that failure to enact that offence would mean that a person who engaged in sectarian behaviour would be prosecuted instead for breach of the peace, and could try to downplay this by saying that they were convicted of this because they "fell down, kicked over some buckets and woke folk up".[160] Similarly, from the perspective of the complainer and the wider public, the behaviour in *Cottam* v *AB* is neither accurately nor fairly labelled as a breach of the peace: it was clearly a sexual assault.

6.23   It is not only in assault-type cases that breach of the peace has been employed instead. This has also occurred in respect of breaches of road traffic legislation.[161] In *Black and Sneddon* v *HM Advocate*[162] (2006) the charge narrated that the two accused did "strike and break the windscreens of two cars ... and scratch and dent the bodywork of said vehicles, throw bottles at [a] house and thereby break a window and glass door panels there ...". This reads very much like vandalism[163] or the common law crime of malicious mischief, but was charged as a breach of the peace.[164] In *Burns* v *HM Advocate*[165] (2001) the charge of breach of the peace libelled that the accused had used the internet to "encourage others to commit indecent acts with children", which could have been charged as incitement to commit sexual assault. A somewhat bizarre example is *Winter* v *HM Advocate*[166] (2002) in which the

---

[158] The accused was placed on the sex offenders' register for 5 years.

[159] See section 4.14 above.

[160] *Justice Committee Official Report*: 22 June 2011, col 90, available at: http://www.scottish.parliament.uk/parliamentarybusiness/28862.aspx?r=6366&mode=pdf.

[161] *Craig* v *Herron* 1976 SCCR Supp 152 (discussed at section 2.8 above); *Smillie* v *Wilson* 1990 SLT 582; 1990 SCCR 133; *Horsburgh* v *Russell* 1994 JC 117; 1994 SLT 942; 1994 SCCR 237; *Austin* v *Fraser* 1998 SLT 106; 1997 SCCR 775; 1997 GWD 38-1929. See the Road Traffic Act 1988, s 2 (dangerous driving) and s 3 (careless or inconsiderate driving) for alternative offences to breach of the peace.

[162] [2006] HCJAC 11; 2006 SCCR 103.

[163] A statutory offence by virtue of the Criminal Law (Consolidation) (Scotland) Act 1995, s 52.

[164] See also *Walsh* v *Heywood* 2000 GWD 15–591; and "Guitars attacked for playing away", *BBC News*, 15 May 2009, available at: http://news.bbc.co.uk/1/hi/scotland/north_east/8052371.stm. For a recent example, see "Student admits splattering Nick Clegg with paint in Glasgow", *BBC News*, 20 February 2012, available at: http://www.bbc.co.uk/news/uk-scotland-glasgow-west-17102979.

[165] 2010 SC (PC) 26; 2009 SLT 2; [2009] 1 AC 720; [2009] 2 WLR 935.

[166] 2002 SCCR 720; 2002 GWD 19-621.

appeal court referred to "an unusual charge".[167] As previously noted,[168] this libelled:

> "... you did ... conduct yourself in a disorderly manner, pretend to [the complainer] ... that you had assaulted a person by repeatedly punching and striking that person on the face with a knife, smear your hands and said knife with red liquid, cause said [complainer] to believe that said red liquid was blood, clean said red liquid and fingerprints from said knife in [his] presence and place [him] in a state of fear and alarm and this you did in order to induce him to participate in crimes of violence and did thus commit breach of the peace".

This could have been charged as incitement to commit assault, or as fraud.[169] Other cases in which the Crown has prosecuted breach of the peace where a different and more appropriate offence could have been employed include those involving: brandishing what would otherwise be offensive weapons;[170] discharging an air pistol;[171] making hoax calls to the emergency services;[172] indecent exposure and/or masturbation;[173] playing loud music;[174] and urinating in a

---

[167] 2002 SCCR 720 at 722, per LJ-C Gill.

[168] See section 3.3 above.

[169] In one unreported breach of the peace case the acccused pretended to be a professional hairdresser and offered to cut women's hair (see *The Scotsman*, 7 December 1999). This could have been charged as fraud.

[170] *Watson* v *Robertson* [2009] HCJAC 36; 2009 SCL 899; *Kidd and Tiffoney* v *HM Advocate* [2010] HCJAC 98; 2010 GWD 34-694 (a Samurai sword). See the Criminal Law (Consolidation) (Scotland) Act 1995, s 47 (having an offensive weapon in a public place), and s 49 (having an article with a blade or point in a public place).

[171] "Teacher fined for firing pistol", *BBC News*, 12 May 2009, available at: http://news.bbc.co.uk/1/hi/scotland/edinburgh_and_east/8046375.stm. Such behaviour could contravene s 47 (*ibid*: offensive weapons), or constitute an assault, depending on the circumstances.

[172] "Man jailed over Pope visit Edinburgh Airport bomb hoax", *BBC News*, 31 March 2011, available at: http://www.bbc.co.uk/news/uk-scotland-edinburgh-east-fife-12923630. Bomb hoaxes are proscribed by the Criminal Law Act 1977, s 51. Making a hoax call related to fires, road traffic accidents or other emergencies is a contravention of the Fire (Scotland) Act 2005, s 85(1).

[173] *Beattie* v *HM Advocate* [2008] HCJAC 73; 2009 JC 88; 2009 SLT 151; 2009 SCL 266; 2009 SCCR 106; 2009 GWD 5-76 (see section 6.20 above); *Heatherall* v *McGowan* [2012] HCJAC 25; 2012 SLT 583; 2012 SCL 492; 2012 GWD 8-141 (see sections 1.6 and 3.39 above); *Halcrow* v *Shanks* [2012] HCJAC 23; 2012 SLT 579; 2012 SCL 517; 2012 GWD 8-144 (discussed at section 1.3 above); and *McGuire* v *Dunn* [2012] HCJAC 86. Public indecency is a common law offence: see *Webster* v *Dominick* 2003 SCCR 525. See also the offence of "sexual exposure" in the Sexual Offences (Scotland) Act 2009, s 8 (discussed at section 4.6 above).

[174] *Hughes* v *Crowe* 1993 SCCR 320 (see section 3.24 above). The Civic Government (Scotland) Act 1982, s 54(1) provides that any person who, *inter alia*, "operates any radio or television receiver, record player, tape-recorder or other sound producing device, so as to give any other person reasonable cause for annoyance, and fails to

public fountain.[175] It might be suggested that breach of the peace is the option favoured by the Crown when a case is at the lower end of the spectrum of wrongdoing.[176] Thus where fighting has not resulted in serious injury it might be regarded as more appropriate to prosecute for a (mere) breach of the peace, rather than for assault. As noted in Chapter 1, however, not all breaches of the peace involve minor wrongdoing.[177] Controversy was caused in 2009 when it was reported that a man who had threatened to blow up a mosque and behead Muslims was charged with breach of the peace.[178] Some Islamic groups claimed that this was a racist decision since an offence under terrorist legislation would have been more appropriate. It seems more likely that the attraction for the Crown in resorting to breach of the peace in this and other cases is the ease with which that crime may be proved. As we have seen, there is no need to prove actual disturbance, only that the conduct was reasonably likely to cause a disturbance, and there is no need to prove much by way of *mens rea*. If its *mens rea* requirement were to be tightened, such that intention or recklessness as to the causing of disorder was required, this would make it less likely that breach of the peace would be viewed by the Crown as an easy alternative.[179]

6.24   It is not uncommon for the Crown to libel a common law crime such as breach of the peace when a statutory offence is time barred.[180] As noted previously,[181] Lord Bingham in *R v Rimmington and Goldstein*[182] (2006) stated that the prosecution ought to libel statutory offences in preference to common law ones, as a matter of good practice. He continued:

---

desist on being required to do so by a constable in uniform, shall be guilty of an offence …".
[175] *Hepburn* v *Howdle* 1998 JC 204; 1998 SLT 808; 1998 SCCR 363; 1998 GWD 8-141. This is a statutory offence by virtue of the Civic Government (Scotland) Act 1982, s 47.
[176] This was the view expressed in H H Brown, "Breach of the Peace" (1895) 3 SLT 151 at 153: "trivial cases should be charged as a breaches of the peace, and more serious cases as substantive offences".
[177] See section 1.3 above.
[178] See M Howie, "Racist escapes terror charge after threat to behead and bomb Muslims", *The Scotsman*, 14 April 2009, available at: http://www.scotsman.com/news/racist-escapes-terror-charge-after-threat-to-behead-and-bomb-muslims-1-1034288.
[179] See section 6.2 above for an indication of how this might be done.
[180] See *HM Advocate* v *Roose* 1999 SCCR 259 (involving "shameless indecency"). Gordon has queried whether such attempts raise human rights issues: 1999 SCCR 259 at 261.
[181] See section 4.1 above.
[182] [2005] UKHL 63; [2006] 1 AC 459; [2005] 3 WLR 982; [2006] 2 All ER 257; [2006] 1 Cr App R 17; [2006] HRLR 3; [2006] UKHRR 1; [2006] Crim LR 153.

"I would not go to the length of holding that conduct may never be lawfully prosecuted as a generally-expressed common law crime where it falls within the terms of a specific statutory provision, but good practice and respect for the primacy of statute do in my judgment require that conduct falling within the terms of a specific statutory provision should be prosecuted under that provision unless there is good reason for doing otherwise."[183]

The ease with which a common law alternative may be proved due to its vague definition and minimal *mens rea* requirement would presumably not amount to "good reason". The Scottish appeal court ought to suggest to the Crown that Lord Bingham's approach be taken in relation to breach of the peace, at least.[184]

LESSONS FROM OTHER JURISDICTIONS

As well as reflecting on Lord Bingham's *dictum* (above), Scots law **6.25** could benefit from a consideration of other aspects of English law. As previously noted,[185] breach of the peace is not an offence as such in English domestic law;[186] rather it provides the police with authority to arrest someone or search premises.[187] An arrested person is then "bound over to keep the peace", but no conviction is recorded, since this is a civil matter. In *R v Howell*[188] (1981) the English Court of Appeal held that "disturbance" alone was insufficient to justify an arrest for breach of the peace.[189] The definition provided in that case reflects the harm principle[190] and bears repeating:

"[T]here is a breach of the peace [and therefore grounds for arrest] *whenever harm is actually done or is likely to be done* to a person or in his presence to his property or a person is in *fear of being so harmed* through an assault, an affray, a riot, unlawful assembly or other disturbance."[191]

As with Scots law, behaviour which provokes others to breach the

---

[183] [2006] 1 AC 459 at 479, para [30].
[184] Although the prosecutor in Scotland is "master of the instance", a court may dismiss a complaint or indictment on the ground that prosecution would be "oppressive". See Chap 19 of J Chalmers and F Leverick, *Criminal Defences and Pleas in Bar of Trial* (2006) for a discussion of "oppression", more generally.
[185] See section 5.1 above.
[186] It is, however, regarded as "an offence" for the purposes of Arts 6(3) and 5(1)(c) of the ECHR: *Steel v United Kingdom* (1998) 28 EHRR 603; [1998] Crim LR 893.
[187] The power is, however, a controversial one – see R Glover, "The Uncertain Blue Line: Police Cordons and the Common Law" [2012] 4 *Crim LR* 245.
[188] [1981] 3 WLR 501; [1982] QB 416; [1981] 3 All ER 383; (1981) 73 Cr App R 31; [1981] Crim LR 697; (1981) 125 SJ 462.
[189] [1982] QB 416 at 427.
[190] See sections 5.6–5.8 above.
[191] [1982] QB 416 at 427, per Watkins LJ (emphases added).

peace is itself a breach of the peace, but in English law it is violence which must be provoked in others. An English breach of the peace may be committed even if the only persons likely to be affected by it are in private premises and no one outside the premises is involved. Thus in *Demetriou* v *DPP*[192] (2012) in which the behaviour took place in a domestic setting, Moses LJ held that:

> "Cases [which] distinguish between situations of violence and breach of the peace in a domestic context and elsewhere are, in my view, not to be relied upon and hopelessly out of date."[193]

This is in marked contrast to the Scottish situation; as will be recalled, in *Hatcher* v *Harrower*[194] (2010) although the appellant had shouted and sworn at his wife in the family home, placing her in a state of fear and alarm, the appeal court quashed his conviction on the basis that this conduct had not threatened serious disturbance "to the community".

6.26   *Howell* was followed in *Percy* v *DPP*[195] (1995) involving a protest at a naval base. An order that the appellant be bound over to keep the peace for 12 months was quashed on appeal; there was no evidence that she had intended violence or that her behaviour had been likely to cause others to behave violently, and the court stressed that "breach of the peace is limited to violence or threats of violence".[196] This case is in marked contrast to similar Scottish cases involving peaceful protests such as *Smith* v *Donnelly* and *Jones* v *Carnegie*.[197] Since political protests are an essential part of a functioning democracy, the courts should be slow to hold that non-violent demonstrations of political expression constitute a breach of the peace.

6.27   Many breach of the peace statutes in the United States have been declared unconstitutional. As the US Supreme Court put it in a leading breach of the peace case in 1949:

---

[192] [2012] EWHC 2443; (2012) 156(18) SJLB 31.

[193] [2012] EWHC 2443 at para [8].

[194] [2010] HCJAC 92; 2011 JC 90; 2011 SCL 114; 2010 SCCR 903. See section 3.15 above.

[195] [1995] 1 WLR 1382; [1995] 3 All ER 124; (1995) 159 JP 337; [1995] Crim LR 714. Both *Howell* and *Percy* were considered by the ECtHR to have defined breach of the peace in English law with sufficient precision to meet the criterion of foreseeability: *McLeod* v *United Kingdom* (1999) 27 EHRR 493; [1998] 2 FLR 1048; [1999] 1 FCR 193; [1999] Crim LR 155. See also *Steel* v *United Kingdom* (1998) 28 EHRR 603; [1998] Crim LR 893.

[196] [1995] 1 WLR 1382 at 1394, per Collins J. For a summary of the English position, see K Kerrigan, "Breach of the Peace and the European Convention" (1999) 63(3) *JCL* 246.

[197] Discussed at sections 3.2 and 3.5 above.

"a function of free speech ... is to invite dispute. It may indeed best serve its high purpose when it induces a condition of unrest, creates dissatisfaction with conditions as they are, or even stirs people to anger".[198]

Similar sentiments were expressed by the English Court of Appeal, albeit 50 years later, in allowing an appeal against conviction for breach of the peace:

"Free speech includes not only the inoffensive but the irritating, the contentious, the eccentric, the heretical, the unwelcome and the provocative provided it does not tend to provoke violence. Freedom only to speak inoffensively is not worth having."[199]

We noted previously that breach of the peace is not an offence, as such, in Canada.[200] As with English law, it merely provides grounds for arrest, but does not lead to a conviction. In a leading case on police powers of arrest for breach of the peace, the Court of Appeal for Ontario stated:

"The balance struck between common law police powers and individual liberties puts a premium on individual freedom and makes crime prevention and peacekeeping more difficult for the police. In some situations, the requirement that there must be a real risk of imminent harm before the police can interfere with individual rights will leave the police powerless to prevent crime. The efficacy of laws controlling the relationship between the police and the individual is not, however, measured only from the perspective of crime control and public safety. We want to be safe, but we need to be free."[201]

As noted above,[202] s 92 of the *Draft Criminal Code for Scotland* offers a redefinition of breach of the peace:

"A person who intentionally or recklessly causes a disturbance by acting in a way which a reasonable observer would regard as violent, aggressive, or disorderly is guilty of the offence of breach of the peace."

It is submitted that Scots law would strike a better balance in the relationship between freedom of expression and of assembly, on the one hand, and the need to preserve good order, on the other, if breach of the peace were to be redefined in this way, such that the accused's behaviour must actually cause a disturbance. If no disturbance is caused, but the accused did intend such a disturbance, or was reckless about this, then the charge could be one of attempted

---

[198] *Terminiello* v *Chicago* 377 US 1 (1949) at 4.
[199] *Redmond-Bate* v *DPP* [2000] HRLR 249 at 251, para [20], per Sedley LJ.
[200] See section 5.1 above.
[201] *Brown* v *Durham Regional Police Force* (1998) 43 OR (3d) 223 at 251.
[202] At section 6.2.

breach of the peace. Enactment of alternative offences such as that in s 49 ("violent and alarming behaviour") and s 50 ("intrusive and alarming behaviour") of the *Draft Code* would ensure that the public is adequately protected from a range of wrongful behaviours, currently subsumed into breach of the peace.

DECRIMINALISATION

6.28 Our next critique brings us back to the criminalisation issues discussed in Chapter 5. Before enacting new legislation, instigating a prosecution or convicting an accused person, the Scottish Parliament, the Crown and the courts, respectively, need to consider whether it is appropriate to criminalise certain forms of conduct *at all*. It is submitted that some forms of behaviour which are treated as breaches of the peace ought not to be within the scope of the criminal law. One example is *Robert Stewart* (2007).[203] It will be recalled that he pled guilty to a "sexually aggravated breach of the peace" for simulating sex with a bicycle in a locked room in a hostel. However odd or distasteful we may find his behaviour, it is submitted that it is difficult to find an adequate justification for criminalising it. Another example is the so-called "Naked Rambler". As noted earlier, Stephen Gough has been attempting for the past 10 years to walk naked (save for a sun hat and some hiking boots) from one end of the British mainland to the other. During the Scottish part of his journey he was repeatedly prosecuted, though not always successfully, for breach of the peace.[204] He has been imprisoned for this for almost 6 years, at a cost to the taxpayer of £40,000 per year. As human rights lawyer John Scott, QC has pointed out, Gough "has accrued the kind of prison sentence which people usually get for doing real harm and crimes of violence".[205] As previously discussed, in *Kara v United Kingdom*[206] the European Human Rights Commission held that constraints imposed on a person's mode of dress constitute an interference with private life under Art 8 of the ECHR. Any inter-

---

[203] See "Bike sex man is placed on probation", *BBC News*, 14 November 2007, available at: http://news.bbc.co.uk/1/hi/scotland/glasgow_and_west/7095134.stm, discussed at section 6.16 above.

[204] For similar breaches of the peace, see: "Scientist walked semi-naked past bingo hall for 'cheap thrill'", *STV News*, 4 November 2011, available at: http://news.stv.tv/tayside/277702-semi-naked-scientist-walked-through-bingo-hall-car-park-for-cheap-thrill/; "Two men accused of walking naked across Tay Road Bridge", *STV News*, 24 July 2012, available at: http://news.stv.tv/tayside/112225-two-men-charged-with-breach-of-the-peace-after-walking-naked-across-bridge/.

[205] See S Brocklehurst, "Naked Rambler: the UK's oddest legal stand-off", *BBC News*, 5 October 2012, available at http://www.bbc.co.uk/news/magazine-19625542.

[206] (1998) 27 EHRR CD 272, disussed at section 6.13 above.

ference with this could also be challenged as a breach of freedom of expression. However, an attempt by the Rambler to argue that nudity is a "mode of dress" thus he has a "right" to behave as he does is likely to founder by virtue of Art 8(2). This permits state interference with the right where this is necessary "for the prevention of disorder or crime". At the time of writing, Gough is facing prosecution in Oxford.[207] Should he return to Scotland and continue to disrobe in public, further convictions for breach of the peace seem likely.

Nudity in public is a criminal offence under the Canadian Criminal Code,[208] but there is no equivalent statutory provision in Scotland, hence the prosecution's reliance on breach of the peace.[209] If public nudity is to be criminalised, then the Scottish Parliament ought to enact a specific offence. However, it is questionable whether such behaviour ought to be proscribed at all. It must be borne in mind that society can make emphatic its disapproval of conduct which it dislikes or finds "offensive" without resorting to criminalising (and punishing) those who persist in that conduct. We could, for example, make clear that the Naked Rambler is free to walk from coast-to-coast in the nude – that is his right – but forcefully remind him that he has moral responsibilities to those who would prefer not to be exposed to his nudity. We could make clear that we disapprove of his failure to take into account his responsibilities to others, but if these entreaties fall on deaf ears, it may be that we should simply ignore his behaviour. Where no harm results from behaviour, the law's stance should generally be one of tolerance.[210] At present, however, this debate, if articulated at all, is couched in claims by accused persons of their rights under the ECHR, countered by the appeal court's tendency to interpret crimes such as breach of the peace in a broad fashion, in the name of the "public interest". **6.29**

Another potential example of unjustifiable criminalisation is **6.30**

---

[207] "Rambler Stephen Gough wants to stand trial naked", *BBC News*, 13 December 2012, available at: http://www.bbc.co.uk/news/uk-england-20714088.

[208] Canadian Criminal Code 1985, s 174(1) provides: "Every one who, without lawful excuse ... is nude in a public place ... is guilty of an offence." "Nudity" is defined as being "so clad as to offend against public decency or order" (s 174(2)).

[209] See now the offence of "sexual exposure": Sexual Offences (Scotland) Act 2009, s 8. This is discussed at section 4.6 above. It is an offence to expose one's genitals to another person (in public or in a private place) without that person's consent, or a reasonable belief in consent, but there must be an intention that the complainer will see them and the exposure must be for sexual gratification or to cause humiliation, distress or alarm. For a discussion of similar English provisions (Sexual Offences Act 2003, s 66), see A Samuels, "Naked in Public" (2008) 172(28) *JPN* 451.

[210] For a discussion of public nudity as an aspect of free speech, see: L J Michaud, "Decent Exposure: An Inquiry into the Constitutionality of State Statutes Proscribing Expressive Public Nudity" (1975–76) 22 *Loy L Rev* 1018.

Paterson v *HM Advocate*.[211] It will be recalled that the second breach of the peace libelled:

> "[Y]ou ... did place your hands around [the complainer's] ... waist, did squeeze her tightly, pull her towards you and did conduct yourself in a disorderly manner and did commit a breach of the peace."

This occurred while the complainer was making coffee in the kitchen. We are told that the accused followed her, stood very close and asked her for a cuddle. The court seems to have laid some store by the fact that this was "behaviour towards a 17-year-old girl by a man 20 years her senior".[212] While this behaviour may have been reprehensible, it does not seem right to criminalise it on the basis that a 37-year-old man making a pass at a much younger woman might provoke an adverse response from, and disturbance by, other people. If Paterson's behaviour was sufficiently wrongful to merit criminalisation then we ought to be clearer about *what* it was that he did that was so unacceptable. His behaviour is more accurately characterised as a form of harassment, or indeed as an assault, and he ought instead to have been charged with either of those crimes.

6.31   In an unreported case in 2008, a man who took a photograph of a woman who was suffering from the ill effects of alcohol consumption was fined £100 for breaching the peace.[213] The sheriff who imposed the sentence is reported as saying: "The lady concerned was entitled to her privacy and not to have a passing stranger take a photograph." He justified the fine on the basis that it would "remind [the accused that] chivalry is not dead and when somebody is in distress you leave them to it".[214] It could equally be argued, however, that one should be free to take photographs in public places, unless the taking of such photographs involves a *serious* breach of privacy. "Chivalry" may be taken here to mean courtesy or kindness, and it is not the role of the criminal law to enforce such moral qualities. The statutory offence of voyeurism[215] ought to be used in appropriate cases, and less serious invasions of privacy such as this ought not to be categorised as breaches of the peace, or indeed any crime.

---

[211] [2008] HCJAC 18; 2008 JC 327; 2008 SLT 465; 2008 SCL 691; 2008 SCCR 605. See section 3.9 above.

[212] 2008 JC 327 at 336, para [22], per LJ-G Hamilton.

[213] "Man fined for taking photograph", *BBC News*, 3 October 2008, available at: http://news.bbc.co.uk/1/hi/scotland/edinburgh_and_east/7651107.stm.

[214] *Ibid*. Compare *Borwick* v *Urquhart* 2003 SCCR 243, in which the accused was acquitted of breach of the peace, despite having used a video camera to film an intoxicated 13-year-old while she vomited and urinated on herself. The case is discussed at section 3.21 above.

[215] Sexual Offences (Scotland) Act 2009, s 9. See section 4.7 above.

FAIR LABELLING

In contrast to the cases of Robert Stewart and Stephen Gough, in **6.32** which the moral wrongfulness of their behaviours is at issue, in the vast majority of breaches of the peace the appropriateness of criminalising the conduct in question does not arise: the accused have caused harm, or posed a serious risk of harm, or have behaved in a highly offensive manner, and it is reasonable that they ought to be convicted of something. As previously noted,[216] the principle of "fair labelling" requires a distinction to be made between differing types and degrees of wrongdoing, not only in imposing different sentences, but also by naming offences in a way which reflects these distinctions.[217] Having separate offences to cover different types of conduct is fairer to the accused, and to the public, than having offence labels which are over-inclusive. It is arguable that "breach of the peace" fails the fair labelling principle. Informed that someone has a conviction for breach of the peace, a sentencing judge, a prospective employer, or indeed a member of the public, is unable to form an accurate picture of the nature of the conduct, beyond knowing that the accused's behaviour caused, risked causing, or made it reasonably likely that others might cause, some sort of disturbance. The scope of the offence is excessively wide and the "harm" that the law is denouncing in, for example, criminalising inciting a riot is far removed from that occasioned by playing football in the street,[218] and different again from the making of indecent remarks or the taking of intrusive photographs. As described in Chapter 4, the Scottish Parliament has enacted a number of new offences for behaviours which would hitherto have been prosecuted as breach of the peace. These include the statutory offences of voyeurism;[219] communicating indecently;[220] threatening or abusive behaviour;[221] stalking/harassment;[222] behaving in a way which is likely to incite public disorder at a football match;[223] and making threats of serious violence.[224] The extent to which some of these will be employed in place of breach of the peace remains to be seen, although

---

[216] At sections 1.8 and 5.13 above.
[217] See also the seminal paper by J Chalmers and F Leverick, "Fair labelling in Criminal Law" (2008) 71 *MLR* 217 at p 222.
[218] *Cameron* v *Normand* 1992 SCCR 866.
[219] Sexual Offences (Scotland) Act 2009, s 9.
[220] *Ibid*, s 7.
[221] Criminal Justice and Licensing (Scotland) Act 2010, s 38.
[222] *Ibid*, s 39.
[223] Offensive Behaviour at Football and Threatening Communications (Scotland) Act 2012, s 1.
[224] *Ibid*, s 6.

anecdotal evidence does suggest that s 38 of the Criminal Justice and Licensing (Scotland) Act 2010 ("threatening or abusive behaviour") is becoming more commonly prosecuted than breach of the peace. The Crown ought more fully to employ this range of offences, rather than relying on breach of the peace to deal with such a variety of behaviours.

LACUNAE

6.33   There continue to be some gaps in the law. As previously mentioned, in *HM Advocate* v *Forbes*[225] (1994) the appeal court held that there is no crime in Scots law of "housebreaking with intent to rape". This is in contrast to the situation in England where the crime of "burglary" involves entering a building as a trespasser and encompasses not only intent to steal but (*inter alia*) intent to inflict grievous bodily harm on any person in the building.[226] There is also a separate statutory offence of trespass with intent to commit a sexual offence.[227] It is most unsatisfactory that the Crown in *Forbes* had to revert to a charge of breach of the peace; this does not adequately capture the nature of the wrong which is alleged to have been committed in the circumstances of that case. As noted previously,[228] s 39 of the Criminal Justice and Licensing (Scotland) Act 2010 defines the "conduct" which can constitute "stalking" to include "entering any premises",[229] "interfering with any property in the possession of [the victim]",[230] as well as "acting in any other way that a reasonable person would expect would cause [the victim] to suffer fear or alarm",[231] and which does cause the victim "to suffer fear or alarm"[232] – all of which matches some of the behaviours in the *Forbes* case. However, the accused must have engaged in a "course of conduct",[233] defined as "conduct on at least two occasions",[234] hence s 39 would not apply to the circumstances of *Forbes*. The situation has improved somewhat since that case was decided, in that such behaviour could now be treated as a breach of the peace with a "significant sexual aspect" for the purposes of the

---

[225] 1994 JC 71; 1994 SCCR 163, discussed at section 2.9 above.
[226] Theft Act 1968, s 9(1) and (2).
[227] Sexual Offences Act 2003, s 63.
[228] See section 4.9 above.
[229] Criminal Justice and Licensing (Scotland) Act 2010, s 39(6)(e).
[230] *Ibid*, s 39(6)(g).
[231] *Ibid*, s 39(6)(j).
[232] *Ibid*, s 39(2)(c).
[233] *Ibid*, s 39(2)(a).
[234] *Ibid*, s 39(6).

Sexual Offences Act 2003,[235] meaning that conviction would lead not only to registration as a sex offender, but to a more accurate labelling of this conduct in any list of convictions.[236] Nevertheless, it is submitted that Scots law needs a more appropriate offence than breach of the peace to cover the conduct alleged in that case. Section 78 of the *Draft Criminal Code*[237] offers a redefinition of the crime of housebreaking to close the *lacuna* in *Forbes*. Rather than being an aggravated form of theft, "breaking into a building" would become a crime in its own right where the accused has overcome the security of any building.[238] While there is no requirement of any ulterior intent or purpose under this section, an offence may be aggravated by any ultimate intention(s) of the perpetrator. Thus in the circumstances of the *Forbes* case, the accused could be charged with breaking into a building under s 78, with an aggravation that this was with intent to rape.[239]

As noted above, the requirement for a course of conduct under **6.34** s 39 of the 2010 Act would prevent cases like *Forbes* (above) from being prosecuted using this provision, in future.[240] Other breach of the peace cases whose circumstances fall foul of the need for repeated conduct include *Thomson* v *HM Advocate*[241] (2009) and *Hay* v *HM Advocate*[242] (2012). The *Draft Code's* offence of "intrusive and alarming behaviour" is committed where one person causes another person fear, alarm or significant distress. Intrusive behaviour is defined to include stalking, following, watching and spying upon a person. Crucially, the section proscribes such behaviour whether it forms a course of conduct or is an isolated act. Thus while the introduction of the crime of stalking has contributed to a reduction in the number of cases of breach of the peace,[243] this number would

---

[235] Section 80 of and Sch 3, para 60 to the 2003 Act, as amended by the Sexual Offences (Scotland) Act 2009, Sch 5, para 5(d). This aggravated form of breach of the peace is discussed at section 3.31 above.

[236] For the importance of "fair labelling", see section 5.13 above.

[237] See section 6.2 above.

[238] Section 78(1) of the *Draft Code*: "A person who, not having any right of entry, breaks into a building without the consent of a lawful occupier is guilty of the offence of breaking into a building."

[239] See s 7(2)(a) of the *Draft Code*, regarding ultimate intentions as aggravations.

[240] See also the Protection from Harassment Act 1997, s 8(1) which provides civil law remedies, including the granting of an interdict or a "non-harassment order", where a person pursues a course of conduct which amounts to harassment. Breach of a non-harassment order is an offence by virtue of s 9(1).

[241] [2009] HCJAC 1; 2009 SLT 300; 2009 SCL 376; 2009 SCCR 415; 2009 GWD 2-34. See section 4.11 above.

[242] [2012] HCJAC 28; 2012 SLT 569; 2012 SCCR 281; 2012 GWD 8-142. See section 4.11 above.

[243] See section 4.15 above.

be likely to fall even further if s 39 were amended in line with the Code.

BREACH OF THE PEACE AS A SUBSTITUTE FOR ATTEMPTS

6.35 A further criticism that can be levied at the Crown's use of breach of the peace is that it has been prosecuted in cases in which the accused had engaged in conduct which could be described as potentially harmful, but had not reached the stage of attempting to commit a crime against the person, such as assault or rape. The law distinguishes between acts which constitute attempts to commit a crime, and acts which are regarded as merely preparatory to such an attempt, and generally only the former attract criminal liability.[244] In order to constitute a criminal attempt, the accused must actually have commenced perpetration of the crime.[245] "Preparation" and "perpetration" may be "the classic terms used in identifying the offence of attempt",[246] but the distinction between them has been criticised as being "vague", "unsatisfactory" and even "meaningless",[247] and the Crown has at times opted to charge breach of the peace, instead. Thus in *Kearney* v *Ramage*[248] (2007) the complaint libelled:

> "... you ... did conduct yourself in a disorderly manner approach [two girls who suffered from learning difficulties and attended a special school] seize [one of them] by the hand, refuse to release her hand, utter sexually explicit comments, invite [them] to attend at a house with you, place them in a state of fear and alarm and commit a breach of the peace".

Likewise, we previously noted that in *LBM* v *HM Advocate*[249] the appellant was a self-confessed paedophile who pled guilty to a breach of the peace by engaging two young schoolgirls in conversation, asking them if he could tickle their legs, and attempting to entice them into his car.[250] In neither of these cases had the accused progressed from preparing to commit sexual assault to actually perpetrating that assault, but one charge which could be prosecuted was breach of the peace.

---

[244] An exception is the crime of conspiracy which is committed as soon as the protagonists agree to commit a crime. (See Gordon, para 6.67.)

[245] See *HM Advocate* v *Camerons* (1911) 6 Adam 456; 1911 SC (J) 110; *Docherty* v *Brown* 1996 JC 48; *Ford* v *HM Advocate* (2001) Scot (D) 31/10.

[246] *Hamilton* v *Vannet* 1999 GWD 8-406.

[247] Gordon, para 6.26.

[248] 2007 SCCR 35.

[249] [2011] HCJAC 96. See section 3.27 above.

[250] See also *Jude* v *HM Advocate* [2012] HCJAC 65, discussed at section 4.7 above.

We have also seen, however, that the Crown has not always **6.36**
succeeded in its endeavours to prosecute as a breach of the
peace behaviour which might best be described as preparatory to
attempting to commit another crime. It will be recalled that in *HM
Advocate* v *Greig*[251] (2005) the charge libelled that the accused, who
had previous convictions for lewd and libidinous practices involving
children, had dressed as a first aid officer at a firework display. The
sheriff upheld a plea to the relevancy of the charge on the basis
that this conduct was not alarming and disturbing *per se*, since the
"reasonable person" would be unaware of the accused's intentions,
or his previous history. The outcome was similar in *HM Advocate*
v *Murray*[252] in which the accused confided in social workers that he
planned to sexually assault and murder a young boy. It is apparent,
therefore, that there are limits on the extent to which breach of the
peace can be charged as an alternative. Nevertheless, it has proven
to be a useful crime for the Crown in cases in which the accused is
still at the stage of preparing to commit sexual assault but has not
taken sufficient steps to be said to have been perpetrating such an
assault. Some might argue in favour of such flexible applications of
breach of the peace; it allows the law to respond to the behaviour
of the accused in cases such as *Kearney* v *Ramage* and *LBM* v *HM
Advocate* before they assault their chosen victims. However, this
fails to identify correctly what it is that the accused has done which
is reprehensible. The wrongful behaviour in these cases – and also in
Greig and *Murray* – is not primarily that they caused or were likely
to cause "public disorder" or "disturbance to the community".

The American Model Penal Code defines the *actus reus* of **6.37**
attempts as anything that constitutes a "substantial step in a course
of conduct planned to culminate in commission of the crime"[253] and
specifies a list of behaviour which, if it "strongly corroborates" the
actor's criminal purpose, could be held to be sufficient to constitute
an attempt. This includes lying in wait; searching for or following the
intended victim of the crime; enticing or seeking to entice the victim
to go to the place contemplated for the crime's commission; recon-
noitering or unlawfully entering a structure, vehicle or enclosure in
which the crime is to be committed; and possession of materials to be
used in the crime.[254] Adoption of a "substantial step" test in respect
of attempted crimes in Scots law would allow for the prosecution of
attempted crimes at an earlier stage in the accused's endeavours than
at present. In *Kearney* v *Ramage* and *LBM* it is what the accused

---

[251] 2005 SCCR 465, discussed at section 3.3 above.
[252] 2007 SCCR 271, also discussed at section 3.3 above.
[253] American Model Penal Code (1985), s 501(1).
[254] *Ibid*, s 501(2).

intended to do had they succeeded in persuading the schoolgirls to accompany them which constitutes the wrongful behaviour meriting condemnation. The indictment in *Greig* makes chilling reading, but not because it was averred that the accused pretended to be a first aider, but because he was a convicted paedophile and his deception was alleged to have been a key step in his plan to sexually assault a child. The allegation in *Murray* that the accused caused alarm and upset to his social workers is disturbing, but we are rather more disturbed that someone who had seriously injured a child in the past was, by his own admission, planning a similar offence in the near future. It is beyond the scope of this book to embark on a detailed critique of the law relating to attempted crime, however, amendment of Scots law to redefine attempts in a manner similar to the American Model Penal Code is worthy of consideration; this would obviate the need for the prosecution to expand breach of the peace beyond its legitimate boundaries as an essentially public order crime.[255]

CONCLUDING THOUGHTS

6.38   This chapter has criticised the current definition of breach of the peace from a number of bases. The first criticism related to the crime's definition: its *mens rea* remains uncertain[256] and there are several problematic aspects to its *actus reus*.[257] It was argued that the crime should be redefined by statute to require that the accused intend to cause alarm or disturbance, or be reckless as to this result.[258] The current *actus reus* of breach of the peace includes unclear, unhelpful, ill-defined and/or redundant expressions: are "ordinary" and "reasonable" people synonymous?[259] What does it mean for conduct to be "severe"?[260] What is required to satisfy the requirement that there be potential for "serious disturbance to the community"?[261] Some other expressions employed by the courts in applying the definition are themselves less than helpful: is "flagrant" a term which is comprehensible to the average juror?[262] The public/private/discoverability debate following the first *Harris* case has obfuscated the *actus reus* yet further. It has been argued that breach of the peace should require that disturbance or alarm *actually be*

---

[255] For a similar argument in respect of English law, see G Williams, "Wrong Turnings on the Law of Attempt" (1991) *Crim LR* 416 at p 418.
[256] See section 6.2 above.
[257] See from section 6.3 above.
[258] See section 6.2 above.
[259] See section 6.5 above.
[260] See section 6.8 above.
[261] See section 6.9 above.
[262] See section 6.7 above.

caused by the accused, rather than criminalising conduct on the basis that *other people* might cause a disturbance,[263] and that a disjunctive test would be preferable to a conjunctive one: *either* the accused's conduct caused serious disturbance to the community *or* it caused actual alarm to the complainer(s).[264] In the latter case, the public/private nature of the locus ought to be irrelevant; if the accused intended to disturb or alarm, or was reckless about this, and did in fact cause disturbance or alarm, it ought not to matter that only the complainer was present. Additional criticisms focussed on the application of the crime, with the Crown having opted to prosecute a range of behaviours as breach of the peace when there are other more apposite alternatives,[265] raising issues of fair labelling,[266] as well as employing this crime to prosecute some behaviours which arguably ought not to be criminalised at all.[267] Thus conduct which does not cause offence and which harms or risks harm to no one (or to no one other than the accused) ought not to be prosecuted as a breach of the peace, and in some instances ought not to be prosecuted at all.[268]

A final and serious criticism of the crime's application lies in the diverse range of wrongdoing which has been subsumed in this one crime. By the end of the 1980s when Christie was writing, an enormous variety of behaviours had been prosecuted as breach of the peace. In addition to well-recognised forms such as fighting,[269] and shouting and swearing,[270] breach of the peace charges have included: abusing solvents;[271] dangerous or inconsiderate driving;[272] discharging

6.39

---

[263] See sections 6.12 and 6.27 above.

[264] See section 6.6 above.

[265] See sections 6.21–6.23 above.

[266] See sections 1.8, 5.13 and 6.32 above.

[267] See sections 6.28–6.31 above.

[268] See section 6.14 above.

[269] *Rogers v Henderson* (1892) 3 White 151; *Wright v Dewar* (1874) 2 Coup 504; (1874) 1 R (J) 1. See now *Derrett v Lockhart* 1991 SCCR 109 (discussed at section 3.37 above); and *Donnelly v HM Advocate* [2007] HCJAC 59; 2007 SCCR 577.

[270] *Boyle v Wilson* 1988 SCCR 485 (disussed at section 3.8 above); *Stewart v Jessop* 1988 SCCR 492; *MacGivern v Jessop* 1988 SCCR 511; (1988) 133 Sol Jo 211 (discussed at section 1.3 above). More recent case include: *Craig v Normand* 1997 SLT 919; 1996 SCCR 823; *Keegan v Friel* 1999 JC 185; 1999 SLT 1111; 1999 SCCR 378; 1999 GWD 15-698; *Smith v Patrick* 2005 SCCR 704; 2005 GWD 33-630; *McIntyre v Nisbet* [2009] HCJAC 28; 2009 SCL 829; 2009 SCCR 506 (discussed at section 3.10 above); *Hatcher v Harrower* [2010] HCJAC 92; 2011 JC 90; 2011 SCL 114; 2010 SCCR 903 (discussed at section 3.15 above); *Hunter v Cottam* 2011 SCCR 130.

[271] *Taylor v Hamilton* 1984 SCCR 393.

[272] *Craig v Herron* 1976 SCCR Supp 152 (discussed at section 2.8 above). See now: *Smillie v Wilson* 1990 SLT 582; 1990 SCCR 133; *Horsburgh v Russell* 1994 JC 117; 1994 SLT 942; 1994 SCCR 237; *Austin v Fraser* 1998 SLT 106; 1997 SCCR 775;

a firearm;[273] industrial action/picketing;[274] kerb crawling;[275] making indecent suggestions or remarks;[276] participation in a peaceful protest;[277] refusing to leave a car park when asked to do so by police;[278] threatening or attempting to commit suicide;[279] throwing a lit firework in a bus;[280] and wearing "inappropriate clothes".[281] If a similar list had been made in the 10 years between the publication of Christie's book and the end of the 20th century, it would have had to include: aggressively begging for money;[282] indecent exposure;[283] killing a fox by kicking it;[284] making threatening

---

1997 GWD 38-1929. The prosecution of breach of the peace in lieu of road traffic offences was critiqued at section 6.23 above.

[273] *Palazzo* v *Copeland* 1976 JC 52 (discussed at section 3.25 above). For a more recent case, see *HM Advocate* v *McGovern* [2007] HCJAC 21; 2007 JC 145; 2007 SLT 331; 2007 SCCR 173; 2007 GWD 10-180.

[274] *Tait* v *Allan* 1984 SCCR 385; *Bradford* v *McLeod* 1985 SCCR 379; *Winnik* v *Allan* 1986 SCCR 35.

[275] *Lauder* v *Heatly* 1962 (unreported, but see Christie, para 3.29; Gane, Stoddart and Chalmers, para 16-02).

[276] *Anderson* v *HM Advocate* 1974 SLT 239 (see Christie, para 3.29); *Benson* v *Tudhope* 1986 JC 107; 1987 SLT 312; 1986 SCCR 422; *Hay* v *Wither* 1988 SCCR 334. See now: *Farrell* v *Normand* 1993 SLT 793; 1992 SCCR 859; *Gibson* v *Heywood* 1997 SLT 101 (see section 4.5 above).

[277] *Docherty* v *Thaw*, January 1962 (unreported, but see Gordon, para 41-01); *Donaghy* v *Tudhope* 1985 SCCR 118. See more recently *Colhoun* v *Friel* 1996 SLT 1252; 1996 SCCR 497; *Smith* v *Donnelly* 2002 JC 65; 2001 SLT 1007; 2001 SCCR 800; *Jones* v *Carnegie* 2004 JC 136; 2004 SLT 609; 2004 SCCR 361.

[278] *Montgomery* v *McLeod* 1977 SLT (Notes) 77; (1977) SCCR Supp 164 (discussed at section 3.33 above).

[279] *John MacLean* (*The Scotsman*, 30 October 1979, cited in Gane, Stoddart and Chalmers, para 16.02). See also the cases referred to in Christie, para 3.33. More recent cases include *Blane* v *HM Advocate* 1991 SCCR 576; *Baker* v *MacLeod* 1998 GWD 11-540; and *Torbet* v *HM Advocate* 1998 SCCR 546.

[280] *McLean* v *McNaughton* 1984 SCCR 319.

[281] *Robert Fraser* (*The Scotsman*, 23 March 1978, mentioned by Gane, Stoddart and Chalmers, para 16.02 and Christie, para 3.36). More recent cases include *Stewart* v *Lockhart* 1991 SLT 835; 1990 SCCR 390 (discussed at sections 2.5, 3.25 and 6.13 above), and "Clothes claim head avoids court", *BBC News*, 10 July 2009, available at: http://news.bbc.co.uk/1/hi/scotland/north_east/8140198.stm.

[282] *Wyness* v *Lockhart* 1992 SCCR 808. Note that this requires to be done in a fashion which is liable to cause alarm; begging is not a breach of the peace, as such: *Donaldson* v *Vannet* 1998 SLT 957; 1998 SCCR 422; 1998 GWD 20-1006. See "Begging: Breach of the Peace?" (1998) 33 (Jun) *Crim LB* 4.

[283] *Hutchison* v *HM Advocate* 1998 SLT 679; 1997 SCCR 726; 1998 GWD 1-12. For more recent cases, see: *Beattie* v *HM Advocate* [2008] HCJAC 73; 2009 JC 88; 2009 SLT 151; 2009 SCL 266; 2009 SCCR 106; 2009 GWD 5-76 (see section 6.20 above); *Heatherall* v *McGowan* [2012] HCJAC 25; 2012 SLT 583; 2012 SCL 492; 2012 GWD 8-141 (discussed at sections 1.6 and 3.39 above). See now the offence of "sexual exposure": Sexual Offences (Scotland) Act 2009, s 8, discussed further at section 4.6 above.

[284] *Dempster* v *Ruxton* 1991 GWD 1–24.

phone calls;[285] painting a swastika on someone else's property;[286] playing football in the street;[287] playing loud music in one's flat;[288] masturbating;[289] pretending to be a professional hairdresser and offering to cut women's hair;[290] spectators running onto the pitch at a football match;[291] and urinating in a public fountain.[292] In one case, it was suggested by the appeal court, albeit *obiter*, that running the wrong way down a crowded escalator, barging into people, "would obviously be charged as a breach of the peace",[293] as would "manhandling the lieges in such a way as to put them in danger".[294] It is apparent, then, that the crime had been very broadly applied: one commentator referred to the latter half of the 20th century as "a period of cancerous growth",[295] a second described breach of the peace as functioning "more or less as a catch-all for every kind of disreputable conduct not covered by some other discrete offence",[296] and a third complained of "the perceived need [on the part of the courts] to endlessly adapt breach of the peace well beyond its natural or rational limits".[297] Despite the narrowing of the definition in *Smith* v *Donnelly* and *Harris (No 1)*, however, the range of behaviour remains too broad. We continue to see "classic" forms of

---

[285] *Robertson* v *Vannet* 1999 SLT 1081; 1998 SCCR 668.

[286] Unreported, but see *The Herald*, 7 January 1999.

[287] *Cameron* v *Normand* 1992 SCCR 866. See also *John Meekison and Tutor* v *Mackay* (1848) Ark 503 (playing marbles on a Sunday).

[288] *Hughes* v *Crowe* 1993 SCCR 320. See section 3.24 above.

[289] *Hutchison* v *HM Advocate* 1998 SLT 679; 1997 SCCR 726; 1998 GWD 1-12. More recent cases include: *Kelly* v *HM Advocate* 2001 JC 12; *Beattie* v *HM Advocate* [2008] HCJAC 73; 2009 JC 88; 2009 SLT 151; 2009 SCL 266; 2009 SCCR 106; 2009 GWD 5-76 (note that this case shows that breach of the peace may be committed even where the masturbation does not occur in a public place: see section 6.20 above); *Halcrow* v *Shanks* [2012] HCJAC 23; 2012 SLT 579; 2012 SCL 517; 2012 GWD 8-144 (discussed at section 1.3 above); *McGuire* v *Dunn* [2012] HCJAC 86; 2012 GWD 23-473.

[290] Unreported, but see *The Scotsman*, 7 December 1999.

[291] *Huston* v *Buchanan* 1994 SCCR 512; *Hannah* v *Vannet* 1999 GWD 29-1380. For more recent cases, see: *Allison* v *Higson* 2004 SCCR 720 (discussed at section 6.8 above); and "Pitch invasion fans plead guilty", *BBC News*, 8 May 2009, available at: http://news.bbc.co.uk/1/hi/scotland/edinburgh_and_east/8039297.stm.

[292] *Hepburn* v *Howdle* 1998 JC 204; 1998 SLT 808; 1998 SCCR 363; 1998 GWD 8-141.

[293] *Harris* v *HM Advocate* 1993 SCCR 559 at 570.

[294] *Ibid.*

[295] See the commentary by Gerald Gordon to *Jones* v *Carnegie* 2004 SCCR 361 at 383.

[296] M Plaxton, "*Macdonald* v *HM Advocate*: Privately Breaching the Peace" (2008) 12 *Edin LR* 476 at p 481. See also F Stark, "Breach of the Peace Revisited (Again)" (2010) 14 *Edin LR* 134 at p 137, referring to the fact that "breach of the peace is no longer a 'catchall' offence".

[297] Comment on *Hatcher* v *Harrower* (2011) *SCL* 114 at p 120.

breach of the peace by fighting, shouting and swearing, and threatening violence,[298] as well as further examples of behaviours well recognised prior to *Smith v Donnelly* such as "Peeping Toms";[299] making hoax phone calls;[300] and threatening to commit suicide.[301] Other forms of conduct prosecuted as breaches of the peace in recent years include: inciting a riot using Facebook;[302] playing the bagpipes in public;[303] posting a threatening Twitter comment;[304] showing images of suicide bombers and threatening to carry out acts of terrorism;[305] walking across an airport runway;[306] lying on a railway line;[307] and setting off a smoke bomb in a pub.[308] Some of these may be examples of an "old crime [being] committed in a new way":[309]

---

[298] *WM v HM Advocate* [2010] HCJAC 75; 2011 JC 49; 2010 GWD 26-488; *Clark v HM Advocate* [2010] HCJAC 88; 2010 GWD 31-643. For a breach of the peace by posting threats on Twitter, see: "Football ban order for Celtic Twitter comment overturned", *BBC News*, 26 October 2012, available at: http://www.bbc.co.uk/news/uk-scotland-north-east-orkney-shetland-20094243.

[299] See "Cornelius O'Brien jailed for looking in windows in Glasgow", *BBC News*, 25 April 2012, available at: http://www.bbc.co.uk/news/uk-scotland-glasgow-west-17840172. This was the accused's second offence for this. He was sentenced to 6 months' imprisonment and placed on the sex offenders' register.

[300] "Man jailed over Pope visit Edinburgh Airport bomb hoax", *BBC News*, 31 March 2011, available at: http://www.bbc.co.uk/news/uk-scotland-edinburgh-east-fife-12923630. For a breach of the peace charge based on a hoax "help" sign stamped in snow on a mountainside, see "Rescuers refuse hoaxer's donation", *BBC News*, 17 July 2009, available at: http://news.bbc.co.uk/1/hi/scotland/highlands_and_islands/8155398.stm.

[301] "Man sentenced over petrol fire threat", *BBC News*, 9 September 2010, available at: http://www.bbc.co.uk/news/uk-scotland-tayside-central-11244209.

[302] *Divin v HM Advocate* [2012] HCJAC 81; 2012 SCL 837; 2012 GWD 19-395 (see sections 1.3 and 3.32 above).

[303] "Edinburgh buskers 'to pipe down'", *BBC News*, 12 June 2008, available at: http://news.bbc.co.uk/1/hi/scotland/edinburgh_and_east/7451328.stm.

[304] "Man avoided jail for Celtic Twitter comment about Peter Lawwell", *BBC News*, 24 May 2012, available at: http://www.bbc.co.uk/news/uk-scotland-north-east-orkney-shetland-18195970.

[305] *Siddique v HM Advocate* [2010] HCJAC 7; 2010 JC 110; 2010 SLT 289; 2010 SCL 380, 2010 SCCR 236; 2010 GWD 5-80, discussed at section 1.4 above.

[306] See *Bowes v Frame* [2010] HCJAC 55; 2010 JC 297; 2010 SLT 683; 2010 SCL 761; 2010 SCCR 657, discussed at section 3.12 and critiqued at section 6.10 above.

[307] "Man jailed for lying on rail line", *BBC News*, 18 January 2007, available at http://news.bbc.co.uk/1/hi/scotland/edinburgh_and_east/6276323.stm. This may, however, have been a prelude to a suicide attempt, which is a well-recognised form of breach of the peace.

[308] See "Man fined over stag night smoke bomb in Aberdeen bar", *BBC News*, 3 May 2011, available at: http://www.bbc.co.uk/news/uk-scotland-north-east-orkney-shetland-13271185.

[309] This expression was used by Lord Cockburn in describing the High Court's powers to expand the criminal law without recourse to its declaratory power, in his dissenting speech in the case of *Bernard Greenhuff* (1838) 2 Swin 236 at 277.

there is little new in inciting a riot being treated as a breach of the peace – it is merely the medium of a social networking site which makes this appear novel.[310] Making loud noises or threats of violence are well-recognised examples of breaching the peace, even if threatening to become a suicide bomber is a 21st-century phenomenon so far as breach of the peace is concerned. Disrupting traffic, whether on a road, railway or runway, has long been considered a breach of the peace, and setting off a smoke bomb in a pub is reminiscent of igniting a firework in a bus.[311] However, other cases do seem to involve novel ways of breaching the peace. Examples include: taking photographs of a drunk woman;[312] or up women's skirts[313] (though perhaps these differ little from the behaviour of a "Peeping Tom"?); tombstoning;[314] and even "yawning in a court room".[315] The various behaviours on this lengthy list have little in common, other than that they caused, or were judged to have had the potential to cause, public alarm or disturbance, either by the accused, or by others who witnessed, or within a short time came to hear of,[316] the accused's behaviour. Despite the narrower definitions being currently employed, the range of conduct which continues to be prosecuted as breach of the peace is too great to be subsumed in this one crime. Lord Bonomy noted that in the decade following *Smith v Donnelly* there had been "a series of cases ... in which the court has been invited to clarify the definition of the crime of breach of the peace".[317] Despite these many cases, clarity remains elusive. It is time for this common law crime to become a more clearly defined statutory offence.

---

[310] See *Kelly* v *Tudhope* 1987 SCCR 445, in which the breach of the peace charge libelled that the accused did "distribute leaflets which incited the lieges to violence".
[311] See *McLean* v *McNaughton* 1984 SCCR 319.
[312] "Man fined for taking photograph", *BBC News*, 3 October 2008, available at: http://news.bbc.co.uk/1/hi/scotland/edinburgh_and_east/7651107.stm.
[313] "Probation over skirt photographs", *BBC News*, 15 October 2009, available at: http://news.bbc.co.uk/1/hi/scotland/glasgow_and_west/8308945.stm.
[314] "Youth charged over 'tombstoning'", *BBC News*, 1 June 2009, available at: http://news.bbc.co.uk/1/hi/scotland/tayside_and_central/8077061.stm.
[315] Unreported, but see *Metro*, 10 May 2012.
[316] "Probation over skirt photographs", *BBC News*, 15 October 2009, available at: http://news.bbc.co.uk/1/hi/scotland/glasgow_and_west/8308945.stm.
[317] *Hatcher* v *Harrower* [2010] HCJAC 92; 2011 SC (JC) 90; 2011 SCL 114; 2010 SCCR 903; at para [1].

APPENDIX A

THE LOCUS

A.1 Accused's home

Ferguson v *Carnochan* (1889)
Avery v *Hilson* (1906)
M'Arthur v *Grosset* (1952)
McPherson v *HM Advocate* (1986)
Friend v *Normand* (1988)
McMillan v *Normand* (1989)
Hughes v *Crowe* (1993)
Cavanagh v *Wilson* (1995)
Grogan v *Heywood* (1999)
Borwick v *Urquhart* (2003)
Beattie v *HM Advocate* (2008)
Hatcher v *Harrower* (2010)

A.2 Airport

Gifford v *HM Advocate* (2011)

A.3 Bingo hall

Norris v *McLeod* (1988)

A.4 Bus

McLean v *McNaughton* (1984)

A.5 Bus station

Burns v *Lees* (1992)

A.6   Car

Bott v *Anderson* (1995)
Mellors v *Normand* (1995)
Peralta v *Carnegie* (1999)
Monson v *Higson* (2000)
Paterson v *HM Advocate* (2008) (first charge)

A.7   Car park

Montgomery v *McLeod* (1977)
Horsburgh v *Russell* (1994)

A.8   Church

Hugh Fraser (1839)
Dougall v *Dykes* (1861)

A.9   College

Siddique v *HM Advocate* (2010)

A.10 Colliery

Gallocher v *Weir and Patrick* (1902)

A.11 Court

Dyce v *Aitchison* (1985)

A.12 Domestic premises (*see also* **Accused's home** above)

Carmichael v *Boyle* (1985)
Cavanagh v *Wilson* (1995)
Gibson v *Heywood* (1997) (complainer's house)
McIntyre v *Nisbet* (2009)
Jude v *HM Advocate* (2012) (complainer's bathroom)

A.13 Field

Rogers v *Henderson* (1892)

A.14 Football stadia (at or near)

Duffield v *Skeen* (1981)

Wilson v *Brown* (1982)
Alexander v *Smith* (1984)
MacGivern v *Jessop* (1988)
Butcher v *Jessop* (1989)
Huston v *Buchanan* (1994)
Hannah v *Vannet* (1999)
Wright v *HM Advocate* (2000)
Allison v *Higson* (2004)
Anderson v *Griffiths* (2005)
Dyer v *Hutchison* (2006)
Walls v *Brown* (2009)

A.15 Hospital

McLachlan, Petitioner (1987) (hospital grounds)
Hewitt v *Vannet* (1997)
McDonald v *Heywood* (2002)
Clark v *HM Advocate* (2010)

A.16 Hostel

Blane v *HM Advocate* (1991)
Robert Stewart (unreported, 2007)

A.17 Hotel

Steele v *MacKinnon* (1982)
Edmond v *Reith* (1999)

A.18 Park

Hay v *Wither* (1988)
MacNeill v *McTaggart* (1976)
Brodie v *HM Advocate* (1993)
Carpenter v *Hamilton* (1994)

A.19 Petrol station

Murray v *HM Advocate* (2000)

A.20 Police car

MacLeod v *Teale* (2009)
Clark v *HM Advocate* (2010)
Boyle v *Wilson* (1988)

A.21 Police station/office

Carmichael v *Monaghan* (1986)
Ross v *McLeod* (1987)
Hawthorne v *Jessop* (1991)
Stocks v *Hamilton* (1991)
Craig v *Normand* (1996)
Campbell v *Munro* (1997)
Harris v *HM Advocate* (2009)
Boyle v *Wilson* (1988)

A.22 Prison

Ralston v *HM Advocate* (1989)
Macdonald v *HM Advocate* (2008)

A.23 Private office

Young v *Heatly* (1959) (over-ruled)

A.24 Private road

Saltman v *Allan* (1989)

A.25 Public house

Steele v *MacKinnon* (1982)
Brown v *Carmichael* (1987)
Kilbane v *HM Advocate* (1990)
Ely v *Donnelly* (1996)
Stephen v *McKay* (1997)
Donnelly v *HM Advocate* (2007)

A.26 Public meeting

Hendry v *Ferguson* (1883)
Armour v *Macrae* (1886): "interrupt, obstruct, and disturb the proceeding"

A.27 Public road or street

Whitchurch v *Millar* (1895)
Smith v *Paterson* (1982)
Tudhope v *Donaldson* (1983)
McDonald v *HM Advocate* (1995)

Smith v *Donnelly* (2002)
Lucas v *United Kingdom* (2003)
McMillan v *Higson* (2003)
Paterson v *HM Advocate* (2008) (first charge: in a car on a public road)
Angus v *Nisbet* (2010)
LBM v *HM Advocate* (2011)
Halcrow v *Shanks* (2012)

A.28 Public swimming pool

Deasley v *Hogg* (1976)
MacDougall v *Dochree* (1992)

A.29 Public toilet

Hay v *Wither* (1988)
Thompson v *MacPhail* (1989) (restaurant toilet)

A.30 Restaurant

Brown v *HM Advocate* (2000)
Thompson v *MacPhail* (1989) (see above under **Public toilet**)

A.31 School/school playground

Nelson v *Lockhart* (1986)
HM Advocate v *Carson* (1997)
Russell v *Thomson* (2010)
George v *HM Advocate* (2011)

A.32 Scottish Parliament chambers

Tallents v *Gallacher* (2004)

A.33 Shop

McKenzie v *Normand* (1992)
Cochrane v *Heywood* (1998)
Elliott v *Vannet* (1999)
Clark v *HM Advocate* (2000)
Czajkowski v *Vannet* (2000)
Watson v *Robertson* (2009)
Akdeniz v *Cameron* (2012)

A.34 Shopping centre

Farrell v *Normand* (1992)

A.35 Smithy

James Ainslie (1842)

A.36 Supermarket

James Jardine (2009): taking photographs up women's skirts
Hunter v *Cottam* (2011)

A.37 Taxi

Bowes v *Frame* (2010)

A.38 Train

Hackston v *Millar* (1906)
Cottam v *AB* (2010)

A.39 Waste ground

Allan v *Lockhart* (1986)

A.40 Woods

Colhoun v *Friel* (1996)

A.41 Yacht/boat

McNaughton v *McPherson* (1980)
McDevitt v *McLeod* (1982)

APPENDIX B

THE CONDUCT

B.1   Begging for money

Wyness v *Lockhart* (1992) (but see also *Donaldson* v *Vannet* (1998))
Daly v *Vannet* (1999)

B.2   Brandishing items

MacNeill v *Robertson* (1982) (sticks, bars and broken bottles)
HM Advocate v *Ferrie* (1983)
Tudhope v *Donaldson* (1983) (sticks, a golf club, umbrella shafts, plastic tubing)
HM Advocate v *Maitland* (1985) (knives)
Keane v *HM Advocate* (1986) (sticks and poles)
McPherson v *HM Advocate* (1986) (a bandolier belt and a bottle)
Barr v *MacKinnon* (1988) (a clothes pole)
Ralston v *HM Advocate (*1989) (a metal bar)
Kilbane v *HM Advocate* (1990) (a machete, a knife, a wooden block, two metal bars, a piece of wood, part of a snooker cue, a toby bar, a chisel and a hammer)
Grugen v *HM Advocate* (1991) (a sword, knives and a hammer)
Brown v *HM Advocate* (1992) (baseball bats)
Hamilton v *Wilson* (1993) (a knife)
Boyle v *HM Advocate* (1993) (sticks, baseball bats, metal bars, bottles, knives)
Reid v *Normand* (1994) (a baseball bat)
Kheda v *Lees* (1995)(a knife)
Robertson v *HM Advocate* (1996) (sticks, metal bars and air rifles)
Chittick v *Fraser* (1997) (a hockey stick)

Leys v *Higson* (1999) (a knife)
McDonald v *McFadyen* (1999) (knives)
Brown v *HM Advocate* (2000)(baseball bat)
Paterson v *Webster* (2002) (knives)
Goldie v *HM Advocate* (2002)
McGraw v *HM Advocate* (2004) (a set of keys)
Watson v *Robertson* (2009) (a knife and a piece of wood)
Kidd and Tiffoney v *HM Advocate* (2010) (a Samurai sword)

B.3 Cruelty to animals

Dempster v *Ruxton* (1991) (beating, kicking, ill-treating and killing a fox)

B.4 Discharging firearms

Palazzo v *Copeland* (1976)
Robertson v *HM Advocate* (1996)
Buttercase v *Russell* (1999)
HM Advocate v *McGovern* (2007)

B.5 Fighting/assault

Jas Bower Burn (1842): a duel
Wright v *Dewar* (1874)
Rogers v *Henderson* (1892)
Dobbs v *Neilson* (1899): engaging in a prize fight, and striking each other with their fists on the head, face, and body, to the injury of their persons
Gallocher v *Weir and Patrick* (1902): "quarrel and fight"
Skilling v *McLeod* (1987): "challenge ... to fight"
Slater v *HM Advocate* (1987): "challenge ... to fight"
Milligan v *Jessop* (1988): "challenge ... to fight"
Barr v *MacKinnon* (1988)
Butcher v *Jessop* (1989)
Derrett v *Lockhart* (1991)
Stocks v *Hamilton* (1991): "challenge police officers to fight"
Reid v *Normand* (1994): "challenge the lieges to fight"
Sloan v *Crowe* (1996): "take hold of ... and pull her, and struggle with her ..."
Connal v *Crowe* (1996): challenging to fight, accompanied by rude gestures and threats
Robb v *HM Advocate* (1999)
Lindsay v *McLeod* (1999): challenging to fight
Stephen v *Dickson* (1999)

McLay v *HM Advocate* (2000): challenging to fight
Kidd v *HM Advocate* (2000)
Buglass v *Stott* (2001): "argue and fight with ..."
HM Advocate v *Hegarty* (2002): "kick [the complainer] on the body and knock her to the ground, all to her injury, and commit a breach of the peace"
Donnelly v *HM Advocate* (2007)
Pickett v *HM Advocate* (2007)
Hunter v *Cottam* (2011): challenging to fight
MacNeill v *McTaggart* (1976)
Connorton v *Annan* (1981): "challenge ... to fight"
Campbell v *Munro* (1997): struggling with a police officer
Sproull v *McGlennan* (1999)

B.6 Incitement to riot

Divin v *HM Advocate* (2012): "did create or contribute to an event listing on the social networking site namely Facebook ... and did ... incite others to riot within the City of Dundee"

B.7 Indecent exposure

Hutchison v *HM Advocate* (1997)
Usai v *Russell* (2000): "within [your] dwellinghouse ... and whilst naked stand at a living-room window and stare at [the complainer] at her house"
Beattie v *HM Advocate* (2009)
George v *HM Advocate* (2011)
Heatherall v *McGowan* (2012)
Halcrow v *Shanks* (2012)
McGuire v *Dunn* (2012)

B.8 Indecent/obscene/sexual remarks or suggestions

Young v *Heatly* (1959) (overruled)
MacNab v *McDonald* (1972): "use obscene language"
Sinclair v *Annan* (1980)
Benson v *Tudhope* (1986)
McLachlan, Petitioner (1987)
Farrell v *Normand* (1992)
Gibson v *Heywood* (1997)
Bowes v *Frame* (2010)
Anoliefo v *HM Advocate* (2012)

B.9 Industrial dispute

Tait v *Allan* (1984)
Bradford v *McLeod* (1985)
Winnik v *Allan* (1986): "form part of a crowd of noisy and disorderly persons who shouted and swore and tore down a stone boundary wall and threw missiles"

B.10 Interrupting a football match/pitch invasion

Huston v *Buchanan* (1994)
Hannah v *Vannet* (1999)
Allison v *Higson* (2004)

B.11 Loud noises

Deakin v *Milne* (1882): "Marched in procession ... singing and shouting aloud at the top of their voices"
Whitchurch v *Millar* (1895): in the street "did march along the said street playing on a concertina or other similar instrument, and refuse to desist"
Hughes v *Crowe* (1993): in the accused's home

B.12 Masturbation

Hutchison v *HM Advocate* (1998)
Kelly v *HM Advocate* (2001)
Beattie v *HM Advocate* (2009)
Halcrow v *Shanks* (2012)
McGuire v *Dunn* (2012)

B.13 Miscellaneous

John Meekison and Tutor v *Mackay* (1848): playing marbles on a Sunday
Sleigh and Russell v *Moxey* (1850): interrupting a public meeting
Montgomery v *Herron* (1976): "deliberately obstruct the footway whereby the public were prevented free access"
Montgomery v *McLeod* (1977): refusing to leave a car park
Smith v *M* (1983): "shout and swear, kneel in the roadway, wrench the exhaust pipe from a motor taxi ... and strike said motor taxi therewith, run about the roadway causing motor vehicles to swerve to avoid striking you, remove your clothing, lie in the roadway ..."

McLean v *McNaughton* (1984): throwing a lit firework on a bus

Brown v *Carmichael* (1987): "refuse to leave" (accused had been barred from a public house)

Kelly v *Tudhope* (1987): "distribute leaflets which incited the lieges to violence"

MacGivern v *Jessop* (1988): "taunt rival football supporters"

McAvoy v *Jessop* (1989): Orange Order band playing near Catholic church

Carrick v *HM Advocate* (1990): "remove the nameplate from the door of [a] house"

Stocks v *Hamilton* (1991): "in the detention room and thereafter within cell no 13, Police Office, ... you did ... persistently attempt to leave the detention room and prevent the door of said room from being closed, ... remove your shirt, tear it into pieces, urinate on same, wave the shirt in the air in an attempt to contaminate police officers with urine, place a length of said shirt around your neck and exert pressure in an attempt to injure yourself ..."

Burns v *Lees* (1992): "board a public service vehicle when told by the driver thereof not to do so, refuse to get off said public service vehicle when told by said driver to do so"

Cameron v *Normand* (1992): "kick a ball in the street, hinder passing vehicles and pedestrians"

Lees v *Greer* (1996): following his wife by driving behind her while she was on a bus

Scott v *McFadyen* (1999): pointing a garden hose directly at the window of the complainers' flat, causing water to enter the flat

Petro v *Heywood* (1999): attempting to force entry into a private house, having been recruited for that purpose

McCrae v *Henderson* (1999): kicking over two motorbikes

HM Advocate v *Murray* (2007): "state to [a social worker] ... that you [planned to] sexually assault and murder a child"

Angus v *Nisbet* (2010): giving his phone number to the 14-year-old girl who delivered his newspapers

Harvie v *Harman* (2010): sending a letter to an art gallery, informing them that the accused had selected the gallery for a project which involved him throwing something through the gallery window, throwing a pole through the gallery window, showing a recording of this incident at another gallery

O'Neill v *HM Advocate* (2010): "remove [a 6-year-old boy] from the care of his mother"

B.14 Nudity

"Scientist walked semi-naked past bingo hall for 'cheap thrill'", *STV News*, 4 November 2011, available at: http://news.stv.tv/tayside/277702-semi-naked-scientist-walked-through-bingo-hall-car-park-for-cheap-thrill/

"Drunk man walked out of his house naked and taunted group of youths", *STV News*, 21 December 2011, available at: http://local.stv.tv/edinburgh/289713-drunk-man-walked-out-of-his-house-naked/

"Naked rambler Stephen Gough denies park nudity charge", *BBC News*, 23 July 2012, available at: http://www.bbc.co.uk/news/uk-scotland-edinburgh-east-fife-18956350

"Two men accused of walking naked across Tay Road Bridge", *STV News*, 24 July 2012, available at: http://news.stv.tv/tayside/112225-two-men-charged-with-breach-of-the-peace-after-walking-naked-across-bridge/

B.15 Offensive gestures

Wilson v *Brown* (1982): gesturing in an offensive manner
Worsfold v *Walkingshaw* (1987): "perform a Nazi-style salute"
MacLeod v *Tiffney* (1994): gesticulating at police officers
Bott v *Anderson* (1995): "gesticulate in an offensive manner"
Connal v *Crowe* (1996): "gesticulate rudely"
Chittick v *Fraser* (1997): "gesticulate in a threatening manner, brandish a hockey stick"

B.16 Persistent following

Shannon v *Skeen* (1977)
McLachlan, Petitioner (1987)
Grugen v *Jessop* (1988): "persistently follow [the complainers] ... demand that [the first complainer] hand over to you Temgesic tablets ..."
Milligan v *Jessop* (1988)
Egan v *Normand* (1997)
Flanigan v *Napier* (1999)
Thomson v *HM Advocate* (2009): "follow [a 10-year-old girl] in your motor car"
Hay v *HM Advocate* (2012): "unaccompanied females"

B.17 Political protests

Duffield v *Skeen* (1981): shouting pro-IRA slogans outside a football stadium

Alexander v *Smith* (1984): selling National Front literature outside a football stadium

Smith v *Donnelly* (2002): protesting outside Faslane Naval Base

Lucas v *United Kingdom* (2003): protesting outside Faslane Naval Base

Barrett v *Carnegie* (2004): sitting on a road

Carberry v *Currie* (2004)

Jones v *Carnegie* (2004): sitting on a roadway

Park v *Frame* (2004)

Tallents v *Gallacher* (2004): tying herself to a railing

Quinan v *Carnegie* (2005): MSP engaging in anti-nuclear protest

B.18 Prison disturbances

Ralston v *HM Advocate* (1989)

B.19 Public protest

Donaghy v *Tudhope* (1985): climbing to the top of cranes on a building site and there displaying banners

Colhoun v *Friel* (1996): "sit on a felled tree then being cut, refuse to move when requested to do so"

Dyer v *Brady* (2006)

Gifford v *HM Advocate* (2011)

B.20 Racial aggravation

Brown v *HM Advocate* (2000)

Clark v *HM Advocate* (2000)

McLean v *Buchanan* (2001)

Cowan v *PF Falkirk* (2003)

Waugh v *HM Advocate* (2005)

Anderson v *Griffiths* (2005)

Dyer v *Hutchison* (2006)

Martin v *Howdle* (2006)

HM Advocate v *Kelly* (2010)

B.21 Religious aggravation/sectarianism

Marr v *M'Arthur* (1878)

Walls v *Brown* (2009)

"Trio accused of sectarianism banned from football games", *STV News*, 26 September 2011, available at: http://local.stv. tv/edinburgh/271989-trio-accused-of-sectarianism-banned-from-football-games/

"Rangers player Grant Adam in court for sectarian breach of the peace", *STV News*, 10 February 2012, available at: http://local.stv.tv/glasgow/297030-rangers-player-faces-sectarian-breach-of-the-peace-trial/

"Strathclyde Police officer charged with sectarian breach of the peace", *STV News*, 19 May 2012, available at: http://local. stv.tv/glasgow/102292-strathclyde-police-officer-charged-with-sectarian-breach-of-the-preace/ [*sic*]

B.22 Road traffic incidents/poor driving

Craig v *Herron* (1976)
Smillie v *Wilson* (1990)
Horsburgh v *Russell* (1994)
Austin v *Fraser* (1997)
McMillan v *Higson* (2003) (blocking the roadway with a car)

B.23 Running on the roadway

Muldoon v *Herron* (1970)
Tudhope v *Donaldson* (1983): "run about the roadway, cause vehicles to brake and take evasive action"
Smith v *M* (1983): "run about the roadway causing motor vehicles to swerve to avoid striking you, lie in the roadway ..."

B.24 Sexual misconduct (see also **Indecent exposure** above)

Raffaelli v *Heatly* (1949): Peeping Tom: pedestrian staring through a gap in the curtains into a lit room of a house
Lauder v *Heatly* (1962): kerb crawling
Turner v *Kennedy* (1972): distributing to schoolgirls leaflets advocating greater sexual freedom for children
Hay v *Wither* (1988): embracing a 14-year-old boy from behind, in a public toilet (charge 1); "accost [the 16-year-old complainer] ... for the purpose of sex" (charge 2)
MacDougall v *Dochree* (1992): spying on women using sunbeds
Carpenter v *Hamilton* (1994): jumping out in front of a female while making a "suggestive noise" (of a sexual nature)

Faroux v *Brown* (1996): repeatedly driving past and staring at groups of young women

Bryce v *Normand* (1997): clandestine filming of a 15-year-old girl undressing

HM Advocate v *Carson* (1997): taking clandestine photographs of schoolchildren

HM Advocate v *Campbell* (1997): "you did remove your clothing, enter a bed occupied by [the complainer] ... place your penis against her vagina and place her in a state of fear and alarm and did thus commit a breach of the peace"

Hutchison v *HM Advocate* (1997): indecent exposure and masturbation

Biggins v *Stott* (1999): "repeatedly invite [the complainer] aged thirteen years ... to accompany you into [your] flat ... attempt to induce her to accompany you to said flat by offering her money, place her in a state of fear and alarm ..."

Webster v *Dominick* (2003): inducing children to view material showing naked people

Dudley v *HM Advocate* (2004): 24 charges involving telephoning various women, claiming to be a police officer and advising them that they were in danger from men about to break into their homes; directing them to go upstairs to a bedroom, asking for personal details and threatening them or their children with injury; in some cases asking about clothing, particularly underwear, and directing them to retrieve items of clothing or to undress

Kearney v *Ramage* (2007): "approach [the two complainers], seize [one of them] by the hand, refuse to release her hand, utter sexually explicit comments, invite said [complainers] to attend at a house with you, place them in a state of fear and alarm ..."

Robert Stewart (2007): simulating sex with a bicycle

Paterson v *HM Advocate* (2008): induce [the 17-year-old complainer] ... to sit on your knee causing your private member to become erect" (charge 1); "place your hands around [the same complainer's] ... waist, did squeeze her tightly, pull her towards you" (charge 2)

Christopher Walker (2009): sending a phone video message containing footage of his genitals to a stranger, having incorrectly dialled his girlfriend's phone number

Burns v *HM Advocate* (2009): "by means of communications over the internet, encourage others to commit indecent acts with children and distribute images depicting said indecent acts by means of the internet ..."

Jardine (James) (2009): taking photographs up women's skirts

Cottam v *AB* (2010): rubbing the legs of a sleeping woman, during a train journey

LBM v *HM Advocate* (2011): engaging two schoolgirls aged 10 and 11 in conversation; asking if he could tickle their legs; and trying to entice them into a car

Akdeniz v *Cameron* (2012): repeatedly cuddling two teenage female employees, pulling their heads to his chest, and touching their bodies

Halcrow v *Shanks* (2012): the complaint narrated that the accused had "on various occasions" handled and repeatedly rubbed his private parts over his clothing, on a public street. No members of the public seemed to have been aware of what he was doing, but his behaviour was captured on CCTV

Jude v *HM Advocate* (2012): secreting a camera with a view to taking indecent photographs

Anoliefo v *HM Advocate* (2012): "repeatedly demand that [the complainer] enter your car"

B.25 Shouting

Duffield v *Skeen* (1981): "shout inflammatory slogans"
Dower v *Donnelly* (1982): "bawl, shout"
Nelson v *Lockhart* (1986): "bawl and shout"
Keane v *HM Advocate* (1986): "shout gang slogans"
Hawkins v *Carmichael* (1992)
McMillan v *Walkingshaw* (1997)
McGlennan v *McKinnon* (1998)
Anderson v *Griffiths* (2005): shouting racially abusive remarks

B.26 Shouting and swearing

Hendry v *Ferguson* (1883): "shouting and screaming at the top of his voice"
Ferguson v *Carnochan* (1889)
Johnstone v *Lindsay* (1907): "curse and swear, use foul and obscene language"
Liszewski v *Thomson* (1942): "loudly shout, curse and swear"
O'Hara v *HM Advocate* (1948): "use abusive and insulting language in a loud voice"
Stirling v *Henon* (1976): "bawl, shout and swear"
Smith v *Paterson* (1982)
Tudhope v *O'Neill* (1982)
Tudhope v *Donaldson* (1983): "bawl, shout, curse and swear"
HM Advocate v *Ferrie* (1983): "shout, swear, shout gang slogans"

Capuano v *HM Advocate* (1984)

Carmichael v *Boyle* (1985): "shout, swear, use obscene and abusive language"

Bradford v *McLeod* (1985)

Marshall v *MacDougall* (1986): "bawl and shout, curse and swear"

Ross v *McLeod* (1987)

McGuigan v *Wilson* (1988)

Boyle v *Wilson* (1988): "shout, swear and sing"

Norris v *McLeod* (1988)

Saltman v *Allan* (1988)

MacGivern v *Jessop* (1988)

Stewart v *Jessop* (1988): "taunt rival football supporters, shout and swear"

Jacobs v *Wilson* (1989)

McMillan v *Normand* (1989)

Quinn v *Lowe* (1991)

McLeod v *Lowe* (1991)

Woods v *Normand* (1992)

Harrower v *Scott* (1993)

Prior v *Normand* (1993)

McMahon v *Lees* (1993): shouting, swearing, chanting gang slogans

Kheda v *Lees* (1995)

McDonald v *HM Advocate* (1995): "shout, swear, follow ... your wife"

Craig v *Normand* (1996)

Hewitt v *Vannet* (1997)

Boyes v *McLeod* (1998)

Mackay v *Heywood* (1998)

Edmond v *Reith* (1999)

McGuire v *Watt* (2000): shouting undirected abuse

Adams v *Heywood* (2000)

Brown v *HM Advocate* (2000): "shout racial abuse ... swear"

Fraser v *HM Advocate* (2000)

Wright v *HM Advocate* (2000): shouting, swearing, singing sectarian songs

Smith v *Patrick* (2005)

MacLeod v *Teale* (2009)

McIntyre v *Nisbet* (2009)

Hatcher v *Harrower* (2010)

Hunter v *Cottam* (2011): challenging to fight, and shouting and swearing

B.27 Spitting

Thomson v *Allan* (1987): at rival football supporters
Smitheman v *Lees* (1998): at a police car

B.28 Stalking/harassing

McAlpine v *Friel* (1997)
Egan v *Normand* (1997)
Morris v *HM Advocate* (2000)
Johnstone v *HM Advocate* (2011)

B.29 Substance abuse

Taylor v *Hamilton* (1984): "sniff glue"
Allan v *Lockhart* (1986): "inhale from a bag containing petrol
  or other similar intoxicating liquid ... stagger about"

B.30 Swearing (without also "shouting")

Gallocher v *Weir and Patrick* (1902): "curse and swear"
Elliot v *Tudhope* (1987)

B.31 Threatening gestures

Dyce v *Aitchison* (1985): "strike your fist hard on the dock [of
  a court room]"
Monson v *Higson* (2000): producing a knife and drawing it
  across his face and neck in a slashing manner

B.32 Threatening to commit suicide

John MacLean (1979)
Blane v *HM Advocate* (1991)
Baker v *MacLeod* (1998)
Torbet v *HM Advocate* (1998)
Siddique v *HM Advocate* (2010): threatening to become a
  "suicide bomber"

B.33 Threats of violence

Avery v *Hilson* (1906): threatening to shoot his wife "with a
  gun which he had in his hand at the time"
Carey v *Tudhope* (1984): by a police officer
HM Advocate v *Maitland* (1985)

Dyce v *Aitchison* (1985): "threaten violence towards Sheriff Booker-Milburn who was then on the bench"

Grugen v *HM Advocate* (1991): "threaten the lieges with violence"

Hawthorne v *Jessop* (1991): "threaten the police with violence"

Mellors v *Normand* (1995): utter threats and threaten to kill

MacDonald v *Munro* (1996)

McGowan v *Ritchie* (1997): "threaten [the complainers] with violence because they had had given evidence" at a trial

Cochrane v *Heywood* (1998)

Robertson v *Vannet* (1998): annoying or threatening telephone calls

Friel v *Carnegie* (1999)

Shepherd v *HM Advocate* (1999): offensive and threatening letters and phone calls

Peralta v *Carnegie* (1999): "threaten to shoot"

McKendrick v *HM Advocate* (1999): "threaten violence towards the occupants of said house"

McDonald v *Hutchison* (1999): threatening a police officer that the accused would set fire to his house

Harper v *Higson* (2000): threatening to "smash his wife's face in" and kill her

Youngson v *Higson* (2000): "threaten to assault"

McDonald v *Heywood* (2002): "threaten police officers with violence"

Goldie v *HM Advocate* (2002): threatening to stab

Blyth v *HM Advocate* (2005)

MacLeod v *Griffiths* (2005)

Lindsay v *HM Advocate* (2005)

Bennett v *HM Advocate* (2006)

Arshad v *HM Advocate* (2006)

Price v *HM Advocate* (2007): "threaten to shoot" six complainers

Rooney v *HM Advocate* (2007)

WM v *HM Advocate* (2010): "threaten to harm ... your son ... his family and others if he gave information to any person in respect of the [sexual assaults] libelled ..."

HM Advocate v *Kelly* (2010)

Clark v *HM Advocate* (2010)

Siddique v *HM Advocate* (2010): threatening to become a "suicide bomber"

Connorton v *Annan* (1981)

B.34 Throwing things

M'Arthur v *Grosset* (1952): "throw articles of furniture about [your] living room"
Muldoon v *Herron* (1970): "throw stones"
Skilling v *McLeod* (1987): "throw lumps of concrete"
Spink v *HM Advocate* (1989): "throw stones at the lieges"
Elliot v *HM Advocate* (1999): throwing sticks, stones and pieces of wood

B.35 Unwanted gifts (*inter alia*)

Elliott v *Vannet* (1999)
Johnstone v *HM Advocate* (2012)

B.36 Urinating

Hawthorne v *Jessop* (1991): in a police station
Hepburn v *Howdle* (1998)

B.37 Vandalism/malicious mischief

McKendrick v *HM Advocate* (1999): "… smash a window of said house"
Walsh v *Heywood* (2000): kicking a bus, striking its window with a pair of scissors, throwing a stone and breaking its windscreen
Black and Sneddon v *HM Advocate* (2006): breaking the windscreens, and scratching and denting the bodywork of two cars; breaking the window and glass door panels of a house
Harvie v *Harman* (2010): throwing a pole through a window
Eccles v *HM Advocate* (2012): kicking a car (but unclear whether any damage caused)

B.38 Wearing inappropriate clothes/cross dressing

Robert Fraser (1978)
Stewart v *Lockhart* (1990)

BIBLIOGRAPHY

BOOKS AND CONTRIBUTIONS TO BOOKS

Ashworth, A, "The Elasticity of *Mens Rea*" in C F H Tapper (ed), *Crime, Proof and Punishment: Essays in Memory of Sir Rupert Cross* (Butterworths, London, 1981)

—, *Principles of Criminal Law* (Oxford University Press, Oxford, 6th edn, 2009)

Baker, D J, *The Right Not to be Criminalized: Demarcating Criminal Law's Authority* (Ashgate Applied Legal Philosophy Series, London, 2011)

Bingham, T, *The Rule of Law* (Penguin, London, 2010)

Chakraborti, N, and J Garland, *Hate Crime: Impact, Causes and Responses* (Sage, London, 2009)

Chalmers, J, *The New Law of Sexual Offences in Scotland: Supplement I to Volume II of Gordon's Criminal Law* (W Green/Scottish Universities Law Institute, Edinburgh, 2010)

Chalmers, J, and F Leverick, *Criminal Defences and Pleas in Bar of Trial* (W Green/Scottish Universities Law Institute, Edinburgh, 2006)

Charleton, P, P A McDermott and M Bolger, *Criminal Law* (Butterworths, Dublin, 1999)

Christie, M G A, *Breach of the Peace* (Butterworths, Edinburgh, 1990)

Devlin, P, *The Enforcement of Morals* (Oxford University Press, Oxford, 1965)

Duff, R A, *Answering for Crime: Responsibility and Liability in the Criminal Law* (Hart, Oxford, 2007)

Duff, R A, L Farmer, S E Marshall, M Renzo and V Tadros (eds), *The Structures of the Criminal Law* (Oxford University Press, Oxford, 2011)

Feinberg, J, *The Moral Limits of the Criminal Law Volume 1: Harm to Others* (Oxford University Press, Oxford, 1984)

—, *The Moral Limits of the Criminal Law Volume 2: Offense to Others* (Oxford University Press, New York, 1985)

—, *The Moral Limits of the Criminal Law Volume 3: Harm to Self* (Oxford University Press, New York, 1986)

Feinberg, J, *The Moral Limits of the Criminal Law Volume 4: Harmless Wrongdoing* (Oxford University Press, New York, 1988)

Feldman, D, *Civil Liberties and Human Rights in England and Wales* (Clarendon Press, Oxford, 1993)

Ferguson, P R, "Controversial Aspects of the Law of Rape: An Anglo-Scottish Comparison" in R F Hunter (ed), *Justice and Crime: Essays in Honour of the Right Honourable the Lord Emslie* (Butterworths, Edinburgh, 1993)

—, "Criminal Law and Criminal Justice: An Exercise in Ad Hocery" in E E Sutherland, K E Goodall, G F M Little and F P Davidson (eds), *Law Making and the Scottish Parliament: The Early Years* (Edinburgh University Press, Edinburgh, 2011)

Frazer, E, and N Lacey, *The Politics of Community: A Feminist Critique of the Liberal–Communitarian Debate* (Harvester Wheatsheaf, 1993)

Fuller, L L, *The Morality of Law* (Yale University Press, 1969)

Gane, C, "The Substantive Criminal Law" in R Reed (ed), *A Practical Guide to Human Rights Law in Scotland* (Butterworths, Edinburgh, 2001)

Gane, C H W, *Sexual Offences* (Butterworths, Edinburgh, 1992)

Gane, C H W, C N Stoddart and J Chalmers, *A Casebook on Scottish Criminal Law* (W Green, Edinburgh, 4th edn, 2009)

George, R P, *Making Men Moral: Civil Liberties and Public Morality* (Clarendon Press, Oxford, 1993)

Gordon, G H, *The Criminal Law of Scotland* (W Green & Son Ltd/ Scottish Universities Law Institute, Edinburgh, 1st edn, 1967; 2nd edn, 1978)

—, *The Criminal Law of Scotland* (W Green/Scottish Universities Law Institute, Edinburgh, 3rd edn (ed by M G A Christie), 2000 (vol 1); 2001 (vol 2))

Hume, D, *Commentaries on the Law of Scotland Respecting Crimes* (4th edn, 1844, ed by B R Bell)

Husak, D, *Overcriminalization: The Limits of the Criminal Law* (Oxford University Press, New York, 2008)

Jaggar, A M, *Feminist Politics & Human Nature* (Rowman & Littlefield, Lanham, 1983)

Jones, T H G, and M G A Christie, *Criminal Law* (W Green, Edinburgh, 5th edn, 2012)

Jury Manual (Judicial Studies Committee for Scotland, Feb 2012), available at: http://www.scotland-judiciary.org.uk/Upload/Documents/JURYMANUALFeb12.pdf

Kadish, S H, *Blame and Punishment: Essays in the Criminal Law* (Macmillan, New York, 1987)

Kleinig, J, *Paternalism* (Manchester University Press, Manchester, 1983)

Lacey, N, *State Punishment: Political Principles and Community Values* (Routledge, London and New York, 1998)

Macdonald, J H A, *A Practical Treatise on the Criminal Law of Scotland* (W Green, Edinburgh, 4th edn, 1929)

—, *A Practical Treatise on the Criminal Law of Scotland* (W Green, Edinburgh, 5th edn by J Walker and D J Stevenson, 1948)

MacKinnon, C A, *Women's Lives, Men's Laws* (Harvard University Press, 2007)

More, J S, *Lectures on the Law of Scotland: Volume II* (Bell & Bradfute, Edinburgh, 1864)

Munro, V E, "Dev'l-in disguise? Harm, Privacy and the Sexual Offences Act 2003" in V E Munro and C Stychin, *Sexuality and the Law* (Routledge–Cavendish, Abingdon and New York, 2007)

Murdoch, J, *Freedom of Thought, Conscience and Religion* (Human Rights Handbooks No 9, Council of Europe, 2007)

Napier, B, "Human Rights in Employment Law" in R Reed (ed), *A Practical Guide to Human Rights Law in Scotland* (Butterworths, Edinburgh, 2001)

New Collins Dictionary and Thesaurus

Oxford English Dictionary, available online at: http://oxforddictionaries.com

Packer, H, *The Limits of the Criminal Sanction* (Stanford University Press, 1969)

Robinson, P H, *Structure and Function in Criminal Law* (Clarendon Press, Oxford, 1997)

Tadros, V, *The Ends of Harm: The Moral Foundations of Criminal Law* (Oxford University Press, Oxford and New York, 2011)

Tasioulas, J, "Crimes of Offence" in A von Hirsch and A P Simester, *Incivilities: Regulating Offensive Behaviour* (Hart, Oxford, 2006)

von Hirsch, A, "Extending the Harm Principle: 'Remote' Harms and Fair Imputation" in A P Simester and A T H Smith (eds), *Harm and Culpability* (Clarendon Press, Oxford, 1996)

Wadham, J, H Mountfield and A Edmundson, *Blackstone's Guide to the Human Rights Act 1998* (Oxford University Press, Oxford, 6th edn, 2011)

ARTICLES

Baker, D J, "A Critical Evaluation of the Historical and Contemporary Justifications for Criminalising Begging" (2009) 73(3) *Journal of Criminal Law* 212

Beale, S S, "The Many Faces of Overcriminalization: From Morals and Mattress Tags to Overfederalization" (2004–5) *American University Law Review* 747

Brown, H H, "Breach of the Peace" (1895) 3 *Scots Law Times* 151

Chalmers, J, and F Leverick, "Fair Labelling in Criminal Law" (2008) 71 *Modern Law Review* 217

Christie, S, "The Offensive Behaviour at Football and Threatening Communications (Scotland) Bill – Strong on Rhetoric but Weak on Substance?" (2011) 25 *Scots Law Times* 185

Comment: "Begging: Breach of the Peace?" (1998) 33 (Jun) *Criminal Law Bulletin* 4

Comment: "Four Months for Breach of the Peace" (1999) 37 (Feb) *Criminal Law Bulletin* 2

—, "Police Powers: Arrest of Anti Nuclear Demonstrators for 'Breach of the Peace' in Scotland" (2003) 4 *European Human Rights Law Review* 464

Commentary on *Beattie v HM Advocate* (2009) *Scottish Criminal Law* (Mar) 266

Commentary on *Dyer v Brady* (2009) *Scottish Criminal Law* (April) 385

Commentary on *Hatcher v Harrower* (2010) 107 (Oct) *Criminal Law Bulletin* 5

Commentary on *McIntyre v Nisbet* (2009) *Scottish Criminal Law* (Aug) 829

Esmonde, J, "The Policing of Dissent: The Use of Breach of the Peace Arrests at Political Demonstrations" (2002) 1:2 *Journal of Law and Equity* 246

Ferguson, P R, "Breach of the Peace and the European Convention on Human Rights" (2001) 5 *Edinburgh Law Review* 145

Field, D, "Once more unto the breach: the retreat from *Logan v Jessop*" 1989 13 *Scots Law Times* 145

Finley, L, "Breaking Women's Silence in Law: the Dilemma of the Gendered Nature of Legal Reasoning" (1989) 64 *Notre Dame Law Review* 886

Force, R, "Decriminalization of Breach of the Peace Statutes: A Nonpenal Approach to Order Maintenance" (1972) 46:3 *Tulane Law Review* 367

Gillespie, A A, "'Up-skirts' and 'Down Blouses': Voyeurism and the Law" [2008] *Criminal Law Review* 370

Glover, R, "The Uncertain Blue Line: Police Cordons and the Common Law" [2012] 4 *Criminal Law Review* 245

Goodall, K, "Tackling Sectarianism through the Criminal Law" (2011) 15(3) *Edinburgh Law Review* 423

Gordon, G, "Breach of the Peace" 1959 *Scots Law Times* (News) 229

—, "Crimes without Laws?" 1966 *Juridical Review* 214

—, Commentary on *Donaldson v Vannet* 1998 SCCR 421

—, Commentary on *HM Advocate v Roose* 1999 SCCR 259

—, Commentary on *Webster v Dominick* 2003 SCCR 525

Gordon, G, Commentary on *Jones* v *Carnegie* 2004 SCCR 361

—, Commentary on *Dyer* v *Hutchison* 2006 SCCR 377

—, Commentary on *Paterson* v *HM Advocate* 2008 SCCR 605

—, Commentary on *Paterson* v *HM Advocate* (2008) *Scottish Criminal Law* 691

Hampton, J, "Correcting Harms versus Righting Wrongs: the Goal of Retribution" (1992) 39 *UCLA Law Review* 1659

Horder, J, "Re-thinking Non-fatal Offences Against the Person" (1994) 14 *Oxford Journal of Legal Studies* 335

Howie, M, "Racist escapes terror charge after threat to behead and bomb Muslims", *The Scotsman*, 14 April 2009, available at: http://www.scotsman.com/news/racist-escapes-terror-charge-after-threat-to-behead-and-bomb-muslims-1-1034288

Kerrigan, K, "Breach of the Peace and the European Convention" (1999) 63(3) *Journal of Criminal Law* 246

Leverick, F, "Breach of the Peace after *Smith* v *Donnelly*" 2011 34 *Scots Law Times* 257

Mays, R, "'Every Breath You Take … Every Move You Make': Scots Law, the Protection from Harassment Act 1997 and the Problem of Stalking" (1997) 6 *Juridical Review* 331

McArdle, D, "Too Much Heat, Not Enough Light" (2011) 56(7) *Journal of the Law Society of Scotland* 9

Meszaros, J, "Achieving Peace of Mind: The Benefits of Neurobiological Evidence for Battered Women Defendants" (2001) 23:1 *Yale Journal of Law and Feminism* 117

Michaud, L J, "Decent Exposure: An Inquiry into the Constitutionality of State Statutes Proscribing Expressive Public Nudity" (1975–76) 22 *Loyola Law Review* 1018

Middlemiss, S, and L Sharp, "A Critical Analysis of the Law of Stalking in Scotland" (2009) (73)1 *Journal of Criminal Law* 89

Oliver, S A, "Recent Trends in Breach of the Peace" 1997 36 *Scots Law Times* 293

O'Neill, A, "Common Law Offence: Breach of the Peace: *Thorpe* v *DPP*" (2007) 71(1) *Journal of Criminal Law* 21

Phillips, K, Comment (2002) 60 (Dec) *Criminal Law Bulletin* 5

—, "Breach of the Peace – Significant Sexual Aspect" (2009) 102 (Dec) *Criminal Law Bulletin* 7

Plaxton, M, "*Macdonald* v *HM Advocate*: Privately Breaching the Peace" (2008) 12 *Edinburgh Law Review* 476

Samuels, A, "Naked in Public" (2008) 172(28) *Justice of the Peace and Local Government Law* 451

Schwartz, L B, "Morals Offenses and the Model Penal Code" (1963) 63 *Columbia Law Review* 669

Shead, C, "Breach of the Peace: 'A Reconsideration'" (2009) *Scottish Criminal Law* (June) 560

Simester, A P, and A von Hirsch, "Rethinking the Offense Principle" (2002) 8 *Legal Theory* 269

Stark, F, "Bowes v McGowan: Cause for Fear and Alarm" (2010) *Scottish Criminal Law* (Aug) 721

—, "Breach of the Peace Revisited (Again)" (2010) 14 *Edinburgh Law Review* 134

Stephen, C, "Recapturing the Essence of Breach of the Peace: *Harris v HM Advocate*" (2010) 1 *Juridical Review* 15

Vannet, A D, "Disclosure of previous convictions in the charge" (2008) *Scottish Criminal Law* (March) 271

von Hirsch, A, "The Offence Principle in Criminal Law: Affront to Sensibility or Wrongdoing?" (2000) 11(1) *King's College Law Journal* 78

Williams, G, "Arrest for Breach of the Peace" [1954] *Criminal Law Review* 578

—, "Convictions and Fair Labelling" (1983) 42 *Cambridge Law Journal* 85

—, "Wrong Turnings on the Law of Attempt" (1991) *Criminal Law Review* 416

REPORTS

Clive, E, P R Ferguson, C H W Gane and A A McCall Smith, *A Draft Criminal Code for Scotland, with Commentary* (2003), available at: http://www.scotslawcom.gov.uk/downloads/cp_criminal_code.pdf

Doyle, K, *Use of Section 74 of the Criminal Justice (Scotland) Act 2003 – Religiously Aggravated Reported Crime: An 18 Month Review* (Scottish Executive Social Research, 2006), available at: http://www.scotland.gov.uk/Publications/2006/11/24133659/0

Justice Committee Official Report: 22 June 2011, available at: http://www.scottish.parliament.uk/parliamentarybusiness/28862.aspx?r=6366&mode=pdf

Scottish Parliament Official Report, 30 June 2010, available at: http://www.scottish.parliament.uk/parliamentarybusiness/28862.aspx?r=5608&mode=html

Statistical Bulletin: *Recorded Crime in Scotland, 2010–11*, available at: http://www.scotland.gov.uk/Publications/2011/09/02120241/0

WEBSITES

"Ayr United fan faces Dumfries offensive singing charge", *BBC News*, 2 April 2012, available at: http://www.bbc.co.uk/news/uk-scotland-south-scotland-17584972

"Bike case sparks legal debate", *BBC News*, 16 November 2007, available at: http://news.bbc.co.uk/1/hi/scotland/glasgow_and_west/7098116.stm

"Bike sex man is placed on probation", *BBC News*, 14 November 2007, available at: http://news.bbc.co.uk/1/hi/scotland/glasgow_and_west/7095134.stm

"Church heckler jailed for breach", *BBC News*, 23 July 2008, available at: http://news.bbc.co.uk/1/hi/scotland/tayside_and_central/7521925.stm

"Clothes claim head avoids court", *BBC News*, 10 July 2009, available at: http://news.bbc.co.uk/1/hi/scotland/north_east/8140198.stm

"Cornelius O'Brien jailed for looking in windows in Glasgow", *BBC News*, 25 April 2012, available at: http://www.bbc.co.uk/news/uk-scotlandglasgow-west-17840172

"Derek Riordan fined for homophobic abuse of Edinburgh bouncers", *BBC News*, 23 November 2012, available at: http://www.bbc.co.uk/news/uk-scotland-edinburgh-east-fife-20461818

"Drunk man walked out of his house naked and taunted group of youths", *STV News*, 21 December 2011, available at: http://local.stv.tv/edinburgh/289713-drunk-man-walked-out-ofhis-house-naked/

"Edinburgh buskers 'to pipe down'", *BBC News*, 12 June 2008, available at: http://news.bbc.co.uk/1/hi/scotland/edinburgh_and_east/7451328.stm

Explanatory Notes accompanying the Offensive Behaviour at Football and Threatening Communications (Scotland) Bill, available at: http://www.scottish.parliament.uk/S4_Bills/Offensive%20Behaviour%20at%20Football%20and%20Threatening%20Communications%20(Scotland)%20Bill/b1s4-introd-en.pdf

"Football ban order for Celtic Twitter comment overturned", *BBC News*, 26 October 2012, available at: http://www.bbc.co.uk/news/uk-scotland-north-east-orkney-shetland-20094243

"Genital video caller avoids jail", *BBC News*, 4 March 2009, available at: http://news.bbc.co.uk/1/hi/scotland/tayside_and_central/7924271.stm

"Golfer David Drysdale fined for assault in McDonalds in Edinburgh", *BBC News*, 27 November 2012, available at: http://www.bbc.co.uk/news/uk-scotland-edinburgh-east-fife-20510096

"Guitars attacked for playing away", *BBC News*, 15 May 2009, available at: http://news.bbc.co.uk/1/hi/scotland/north_east/8052371.stm

"Man avoided jail for Celtic Twitter comment about Peter Lawwell", *BBC News*, 24 May 2012, available at: http://www.bbc.co.uk/news/uk-scotland-northeast-orkney-shetland-18195970

"Man fined for taking photograph", *BBC News*, 3 October 2008, available at: http://news.bbc.co.uk/1/hi/scotland/edinburgh_and_east/7651107.stm

"Man fined £1,000 for teenage party sex video", *BBC News*, 14 April 2010, available at: http://news.bbc.co.uk/1/hi/scotland/south_of_scotland/8620284.stm

"Man fined over stag night smoke bomb in Aberdeen bar", *BBC News*, 3 May 2011, available at: http://www.bbc.co.uk/news/uk-scotland-north-eastorkney-shetland-13271185

"Man jailed for lying on rail line", *BBC News*, 18 January 2007, available at: http://news.bbc.co.uk/1/hi/scotland/edinburgh_and_east/6276323.stm

"Man jailed over Pope visit Edinburgh Airport bomb hoax", *BBC News*, 31 March 2011, available at: http://www.bbc.co.uk/news/uk-scotland-edinburgheast-fife-12923630

"Man sentenced over petrol fire threat", *BBC News*, 9 September 2010, available at: http://www.bbc.co.uk/news/uk-scotland-tayside-central-11244209

"Man spied on girl as she changed", *BBC News*, 6 January 2010, available at: http://news.bbc.co.uk/1/hi/scotland/tayside_and_central/8444008.stm

"Naked rambler Stephen Gough denies park nudity charge", *BBC News*, 23 July 2012, available at: http://www.bbc.co.uk/news/uk-scotland-edinburgh-east-fife-18956350

"Naked rambler Stephen Gough jailed for five months", *BBC News*, 13 September 2012, available at: http://www.bbc.co.uk/news/uk-scotland-edinburgh-east-fife-19585483

"Naked Rambler: the UK's oddest legal stand-off", *BBC News*, 5 October 2012, available at: http://www.bbc.co.uk/news/magazine-19625542

"Pink thong fetish flasher jailed", *BBC News*, 23 October 2009, available at: http://news.bbc.co.uk/1/hi/scotland/glasgow_and_west/8322441.stm

"Pitch invasion fans plead guilty", *BBC News*, 8 May 2009, available at: http://news.bbc.co.uk/1/hi/scotland/edinburgh_and_east/8039297.stm

"Probation over skirt photographs", *BBC News*, 15 October 2009, available at: http://news.bbc.co.uk/1/hi/scotland/glasgow_and_west/8308945.stm

"Rambler Stephen Gough wants to stand trial naked", *BBC News*, 13 December 2012, available at: http://www.bbc.co.uk/news/uk-england-20714088

"Rangers player Grant Adam in court for sectarian breach of the peace", *STV News*, 10 February 2012, available at: http://local.stv.tv/glasgow/297030-rangers-player-facessectarian-breach-of-the-peace-trial/

"Rescuers refuse hoaxer's donation", *BBC News*, 17 July 2009, available at: http://news.bbc.co.uk/1/hi/scotland/highlands_and_islands/8155398.stm

"St Andrews student sentenced for Israel flag racism", *BBC News*, 13 September 2011, available at: http://www.bbc.co.uk/news/uk-scotland-edinburgh-east-fife-14897612

"Scientist walked semi-naked past bingo hall for 'cheap thrill'",
  STV News, 4 November 2011, available at: http://news.stv.tv/
  tayside/277702-semi-naked-scientist-walkedthrough-bingo-hall-
  car-park-for-cheap-thrill/

"Six charged with breach of the peace over antisemitic website",
  16 May 2012, available at: http://local.stv.tv/glasgow/100111-
  six-charged-with-breach-of-the-peace-after-anti-semitic-website-
  discovered/3

Stone, R, "Breach of the Peace: the Case for Abolition" (2001)
  2 Web JCLI, available at: http://webjcli.ncl.ac.uk/2001/issue2/
  stone2.html

"Strathclyde Police officer charged with sectarian breach of the
  peace", *STV News*, 19 May 2012 available at: http://local.
  stv.tv/glasgow/102292-strathclyde-police-officer-chargedwith-
  sectarian-breach-of-the-preace/ [*sic*]

"Student admits splattering Nick Clegg with paint in Glasgow",
  BBC News, 20 February 2012, available at: http://www.bbc.
  co.uk/news/uk-scotland-glasgow-west-17102979

"Teacher fined for firing pistol", *BBC News*, 12 May 2009,
  available at: http://news.bbc.co.uk/1/hi/scotland/edinburgh_and_
  east/8046375.stm

"Trio accused of sectarianism banned from football games", *STV
  News*, 26 September 2011, available at: http://local.stv.tv/
  edinburgh/271989-trio-accused-of-sectarianism-bannedfrom-
  football-games/

"Two men accused of walking naked across Tay Road Bridge",
  STV News, 24 July 2012, available at: http://news.stv.tv/
  tayside/112225-two-men-charged-with-breach-of-thepeace-
  after-walking-naked-across-bridge/

"Youth charged over 'tombstoning'", *BBC News*, 1 June 2009,
  available at: http://news.bbc.co.uk/1/hi/scotland/tayside_and_
  central/8077061.stm

INDEX